"Fascinating . . . a joy to read. . . . In addition to personal history, he exposes us to his personal philosophy on marital harmony, women's liberation, economic theory, taxation, welfare, etc. The reader may not agree with his opinions, but there is a great deal of wisdom and enthusiasm in the way they are presented. Essential reading for anyone who enjoys learning the personalities of people in the public eye."

—*Library Journal*

"Getty writes as one full of ideas on all subjects. . . . He boasts about sexual conquests, political prescience and friendships with royalty . . . he dispenses wisdom about the sexes . . . he almost convinces us that he was never the lonely recluse he was so long depicted as in the envious media . . ."

—*New York Times*

"Getty lets the reader know he is not embarrassed to be wealthy. . . . He intones his fears . . . decries the politicians . . . exhibits his diversities, too. . . . Mr. Getty attempts to set the record straight on the many distortions which he contends the media have made of his life."

—*Christian Science Monitor*

AS I SEE IT

THE AUTOBIOGRAPHY OF
J. PAUL GETTY

BERKLEY BOOKS, NEW YORK

AS I SEE IT
The Autobiography of J. Paul Getty

A Berkley Book / published by arrangement with
the author's agent

PRINTING HISTORY
Prentice-Hall edition published 1976
Berkley edition / November 1986

ISBN: 0-425-09653-X

A BERKLEY BOOK ® TM 757,375
Berkley Books are published by The Berkley Publishing Group,
200 Madison Avenue, New York, NY 10016.
The name "BERKLEY" and the "B" logo
are trademarks belonging to Berkley Publishing Corporation.

PRINTED IN THE UNITED STATES OF AMERICA

10   9   8   7   6   5   4   3   2

Dedication

To the memory of my father and mother, George F. and Sarah Getty.

To the memory of my youngest and oldest sons, Timothy Getty and George F. Getty II.

To my three surviving sons: Ronald, Paul Jr. and Gordon.

And to all my grandchildren.

These are the individuals who have been nearest and dearest to me throughout my life—and will continue to be, as long as I live.

Author's Note

BORN IN 1892 and an active businessman since 1914, I have lived and worked through the most exciting and exhilarating—and most turbulent and terrible—eight decades of human history.

Numerous factors—over many of which I had no control—enabled me to observe the ever-accelerating changes and violent upheavals of these decades from widely-varied vantage points. It is not my intent to boast or impress when I say that I have brawled with oilfield roustabouts (I was once one myself), fought even fiercer battles in panelled boardrooms—and have chatted amiably with ruling monarchs in their audience chambers. I cite such random, extreme contrasts solely to suggest the broad range of experience from which my opinions and perspectives have developed. Yet, I hasten to add, they were formed and refined finally by no one save myself.

But I digress. I began by referring to the changes I have seen and still see taking place in the world around me. Some have immensely enhanced our human condition and the promise for its future. *Vide* the strides made by science and technology.

In 1900—when I was eight—the average life-span in the United States was barely more than 47 years. Now it is above the 70-year-mark and steadily rising. The largest share of the credit for this phenomenal increase in human life-expectancy belongs to medical science and its triumphs over many diseases which once claimed countless lives annually. As an illustration, the 1900 U.S. death-rate from tuberculosis was 209.9 per 100,000 population. By 1973, that rate was down to 1.8, less than one per cent of what it had been at the turn of the century.

Technological advances have been no less spectacular. In 1903—I was then ten—the Wright brothers made their first successful flight in a mechanically-propelled, heavier-than-air 'flying machine'. Wilbur Wright piloted an ungainly contraption 852 feet through the air in 59 seconds. Today, jet-engined commercial airliners regularly carry 350 and more passengers across continents and oceans at over 600 miles per hour, and the supersonic Anglo-French *Concorde* travels at considerably more than twice that speed.

The conquest of space, still nothing but a fantasy when I had reached my fifties, has been even more wondrous. Men have walked on the moon. American astronauts and Soviet cosmonauts have dined and joked together while their linked-up space craft hurtled around the earth in a 140-mile-high, 17,500-mile-an-hour orbit.

On the other hand, during these same eight decades, the world has been convulsed by an endless series of grim and ghastly events. Wars, revolutions, internecine strife and genocidal holocausts have slaughtered human beings by the tens of millions. Empires of one kind have been destroyed or dismantled—only to be replaced by others of different, if not necessarily more benign, stamp. Whole countries have been erased from the maps, their territories and populations renamed, redistributed, splintered, or absorbed. Entire long-established political systems have been demolished for one reason—or on one pretext—or another. Claims that old oppressions and injustices were thus eliminated have all too often meant that new ones, even more brutal and savage, have been substituted for them. And, since August 6, 1945—the day Hiroshima was atom-bombed—who among us has not harboured the pervasive, mind-and-nerve corroding fear of total nuclear annihilation?

Unfortunately, it may well be as someone once said: humanity demonstrates a rare and perverse propensity for losing ground even as it moves forward at a breakneck pace.

Be that as it may, certainly almost every level and sector of human existence and activity has undergone dramatic transformation during my lifetime and my still-continuing active business career. The nature of my work and my life-style have kept me very much in the mainstream of many changing patterns. My personal nature has made me a close and fascinated observer of all others.

Although this book may not be strictly an autobiography, it is based almost entirely on autobiographical material—on what I have experienced and observed. Only from such sources can I hope to provide a summation of my views, the lessons I have learned and the conclusions I have drawn, both as an individual and as a businessman. My aim is a clear and comprehensive statement of how I view myself, my life and my work—and the world: past, present and future. In short, this is how I've seen it all during my 83 years—and as I see it all now.

J. PAUL GETTY
Sutton Place
Guildford, Surrey
1976

1

You cannot bring about prosperity by discouraging thrift. You cannot help the wage-earner by pulling down the wage-payer. You cannot further the Brotherhood of Man by encouraging class hatred. You cannot help the poor by destroying the rich. You cannot keep out of trouble by spending more than you earn. You cannot build character and courage by taking away a man's initiative. You cannot help men permanently by doing for them what they could and should do for themselves.

I ACCEPT THESE tenets wholeheartedly, without reservation. Indeed, they go a very long way toward defining my basic philosophy. No, I cannot lay claim to having written them. The words are widely attributed to one of the greatest—perhaps *the* greatest—of all American Presidents, Abraham Lincoln.

And, just as these lines accurately reflect my fundamental beliefs, so do some other words of Abraham Lincoln accurately reflect my worst fears for our society and civilization.

Making his immortal 'Gettysburg Address' in 1863, at the height of the American Civil War, President Lincoln pledged the nation to the cause 'that government of the people, by the people, for the people shall not perish from the earth.'*

* *Editor's note:* President Lincoln spoke at the dedication of a military cemetery for the soldiers killed in the crucial battle fought near the Pennsylvania town of Gettysburg. The reader might be interested to know that the town was named for James Getty, a cousin of J. Paul Getty's great-great grandfather, in 1800.

The danger that such government might 'perish from the earth' has not receded. It looms large and menacing in our present day—even in those nations that consider themselves to be the most free in what we have come to call the 'Free World.'

While the writing has not—as yet—appeared indelibly on the wall, clear and unmistakable warning signals abound everywhere around us. If I add my own, will they be rejected out of hand by the reader because I am rich and the prevailing tendency is to damn or deride whatever 'the rich' have to say?

It's a good question.

2

MY WEALTH IS not a subject I relish discussing. However, I am ruefully aware that it seems to arouse near-morbid curiosity in the news media and therefore—I must assume—in a goodly segment of the general public. Since any attempt to avoid or evade the issue would inevitably draw acid comments about my 'secretiveness,' I suppose it's best to face and dispose of it now, at the start.

Actually, my wealth and I enjoyed almost total anonymity until October, 1957. It was then that *Fortune* Magazine published an article listing the wealthiest people in the United States. My name headed the list, and the authors of the article identified me as a 'billionaire' and stated that I was 'the richest American.' By extrapolation, newspapers and other media thereafter variously described me as a 'multi-billionaire,' and 'the world's richest man.'

These are eye-catching labels. People are mesmerized by superlatives, a fact that impresarios like P. T. Barnum recognized and exploited to the full. A midget is, after all, only a midget—but 'The World's Shortest Midget' is something else again. The world's largest gawking crowds will jam the sideshow tent in which *he* appears.

'Are you *really* the world's richest man?' is a question that has been put to—or hammered at me—more times than I could possibly count in the last eighteen years.

My reply has been consistent, unvarying. I don't know. I have no way of knowing—and I make no claims.

While I may be very wealthy, there are many other very wealthy individuals in the world. Although some of them are my friends or business acquaintances, I can assure you that we play no bizarre showdown games with our personal financial statements in efforts to determine who is the richest of the rich. In any event, there are heads of royal families who control hereditary fortunes that defy comprehension, much less calculation. And, for that matter, it is entirely possible that there are any numbers of totally anonymous individuals who possess vast secret hordes of cash, gold, platinum, diamonds or whatever.

I am not being coy. I am simply pursuing the argument that the question of whether I am the world's richest man—and, by extension, if I am not, then who is?—defies positive answer. All it is possible for me to say is that, as an active businessman, my *rated wealth* is probably sufficiently great to rank me among the dozen or so richest *private individuals* in the Western World.

Please note the words on which I have placed emphasis. They are key terms and sharply definitive (and, limiting).

'Rated wealth' is on-paper wealth. It is a theoretical figure, a reasoned estimate made in accordance with pertinent laws and the rules of standard accounting practices, but still only an estimate. A businessman's rated wealth represents his net worth based on the reasonably presumed market values of his holdings, less his debts and other liabilities. But even the most reasonably presumed market-value of any holding can be—and often is—grossly misleading, either over or under.

I have held properties which I conservatively estimated to have a market-value of, say, a million dollars. However when—for one reason or another—I sought to sell, no buyers came forward with offers of not more than half the amount.

Of course, the converse is often true in business. I have bought stocks which the market valued at two or three dollars a share even though the net underlying asset value of the shares was many times the price I paid.

In this vein, I'd like to cite one specific (and textbook) example from my own experience, but it involves an oil and gas lease rather than stocks. In 1926, C. R. Houser—a California lease-broker—purchased the oil and gas lease on the 'Cleaver Property,' a piece of land located in Alamitos Heights.

A seasoned businessman, Houser was hardly given to under-valuing his holdings when he wanted to sell them. He thought $8,000 to be the top price the market would bear for the Cleaver Lease. I bought it from him, drilled on the land and struck oil. Ultimately, my excess recovery—net profit on oil produced by the property—was nearly $800,000. Did Houser fume and berate himself for having so greatly undervalued the lease? Of course not. A business veteran, he understood that such things do sometimes happen.

So much—for the moment—about the listed values of a businessman's assets as versus the actual prices they will (or will not) fetch in the marketplace. As for emphasizing the words 'private individual,' these define a category of person apart from the possessors of vast monarchical or semi-public fortunes. Three representative examples come instantly to mind: H.R.H. the Emir of Kuwait, the Royal Family of the Netherlands and the late Nizam of Hyderabad.

'Just how rich are you?' is a standard follow-up with which my inquisitors persist.

I don't—and can't—know that, either. Not with any degree of accuracy. Being a businessman, I repeat that the over-whelming majority of my rated wealth consists of investments in companies that produce goods and services. How should I calculate the size of my fortune—by tallying the market value of my shares in the companies I own or control? It's one method—but the total, as will become apparent, would be just another on-paper figure of dubious and only transient reliability.

Equities markets fluctuate greatly, from month to month and not infrequently from day to day. For example, Getty Family interests control the Getty Oil Company. I own about four million shares of Getty Oil stock personally. Nearly eight million more shares are owned by the Sarah C. Getty Trust, of which I am sole trustee. I receive approximately eighty per cent of the income from the trust during my lifetime, but I cannot as a practical matter dispose of the shares—which are held in trust.

What are those holdings worth?

It is a good question. The table below demonstrates how widely market values may vary in the course of a single year.

It shows the High and Low market prices of Getty Oil Company stock by quarter for 1974:*

QUARTER	HIGH	LOW
First	175	125½
Second	141	97½
Third	122¾	96
Fourth	159½	105½

Control of a company does not carry with it the ability to control the price of its stock. This is especially true in the United States where such alert watchdog agencies as the Securities and Exchange Commission keep a very sharp eye on all 'insider's' stock transactions. The price of Getty Oil shares—and thus the value of my own share holdings—is determined by the other, the 'outside,' investors (private and institutional) who own Getty oil stocks. It is they who trade their shares, buying and selling, and thereby set the market.

Now, my shares can be translated into actual cash—into stacks of banknotes—O N L Y if I sell them. The amount I realized would depend, first and foremost, on *when* I sold. Need I point out that there is a giant-sized differential between a First Quarter High of $175 per share and a Third Quarter Low of $96?

Obviously, any attempt to measure one's wealth in terms of stock share values is an extremely iffy exercise. But there are alternate yardsticks. I am primarily an oilman. Suppose I began by calculating the value of such of my companies' assets as their belowground crude reserves?

Assume—for the sake of argument—that I own a company outright and it has what are said to be proven belowground reserves amounting to a billion barrels of crude oil. Assume further that crude is bringing ten dollars a barrel at the wellhead. At first glance it appears that the company—and I, as its sole owner—have $10 billion in assets in the form of belowground crude reserves.

But these of course are by no means net assets. Royalties; exploration, development and production costs; taxes and a

---

Editor's note: The Getty Oil Company is an American corporation whose shares are listed on the New York Stock Exchange. Prices shown in the table are in dollars: 175 being $175 per share; 97 1/2 being $97.50; 122 3/4 being $122.75 and so on.

myriad other costs and expenses must be deducted or allowed for in order to arrive at anything even vaguely approximating an on-paper net figure. And even that could be utterly meaningless.

Oil belowground is temperamental, to put it mildly. Below-ground reserves, even though adjudged 'proven' by the most experienced and competent geologists, sometimes prove to be far less than estimated. I, myself, have brought in wells that gushed 15,000 barrels for a few days, then suddenly and inexplicably went dry.

Then, every oilman is acutely aware of the First Axiom of the petroleum industry: whatever crude prices may be today, they may be far, far different tomorrow. At present, crude is selling for what seem to be high prices. (The high cost is more apparent than real, as I'll demonstrate elsewhere in this book. All the same, in terms of dollars, pounds sterling, Deutschmarks, Yen or any other currency, crude oil is much more expensive than it was three years ago.)

Will the prices hold?

Another good—and for the oilman, anxiety-creating—question. Crude prices have often plummeted abruptly and drastically in the past, and no oil producer on the face of the earth has any guarantee that history will not repeat itself.

The record—as shown by a few random examples—speaks for itself.

In May, 1903, Oklahoma crude was worth $1.03 a barrel at the wellhead. Exactly two years later, the price fell to 52 cents a barrel—and by 1915, was down to 40 cents and even less per barrel. World War One and its aftermaths reversed the trend. The 1920 base price for crude was up to $3.50 a barrel, with better grades commanding high premiums. Some of my own wells were then producing oil that sold for $5.25 per barrel at the wellhead.

What had gone up came down. In January, 1920, the crude price nosedived to $1.75 a barrel, soon slumping further, to $1.25. After the great East Texas oil fields were opened up in the early 1930s, the flood of 'new' oil was catastrophic to the price structure. Enormous quantities of crude were sold for as little as *ten cents a barrel.**

---

* *Editor's note:* 42 U.S. gallons comprise a 'barrel' of crude oil or petroleum products. This is an international standard of measure.

An oilman seeking to compute his wealth in terms of belowground crude reserves is dealing with imponderables. Another unpredictable factor is the policy and attitude of governments. Some countries have greatly increased taxes on crude production or have sharply reduced depletion allowances. Others plan to follow suit. Yet others have imposed—or say they intend to impose—restrictions on the quantity of oil that may be produced. Some governments have simply nationalized the holdings of privately owned oil companies, while more indicate they are moving in the same direction. And—but I see no need to continue the recital.

The best any businessman—especially any oilman—can hope to obtain from his accountants is an approximate paper-estimate of his worth as represented by his invested wealth. On the other hand, in these days of government agencies, powerful taxation authorities, securities analysts and investigative reporters, it is impossible for a legitimate, active businessman to keep his *rated* wealth secret.

For example, the Getty Oil Company—of which I am president—issues detailed annual reports and financial statements. Its 46th Annual Report, covering the calendar year 1974, showed the company and its subsidiaries as having a shade less than $2 billion in stockholders' equity. Before anyone seizes on that figure, he should remember what I tried to make clear earlier. The *net realizable assets* of any company may be less (even far less) or, for that matter, more (even far more) than what is reflected by figures prepared according to standard accounting procedures. He should also remember that assets—save for the total that is in cash—are 'spendable' only if and when they are sold (and, again, it is the market and innumerable other factors that determine what price they bring at sale).

All this leads to direct confrontation with the question of 'how rich' I 'really' am, and I am impelled to reiterate that I do not know with any degree of accuracy because there is no way for me to know.

I can say that, of this writing, my personal, all-in *rated* net worth is certainly above a billion dollars. The additional *rated* net worth of the Getty Family interests—including that of the Sarah Getty Trust, of which I am only the trustee—is about twice again as much.

There is only one means by which the true, cash-in-hand

money-value of my and the Getty Family holdings could ever be established. This would involve dissolution of the Getty companies and sale of their assets.

Before carrying this line of reasoning further, I must point out that disposing of the four million shares owned by me or the nearly eight million shares of Getty Oil Company stock in the Sarah C. Getty Trust by sale in the open market or otherwise would be foolish. The current market price per share probably would not be attained and any such sale would take more years than I have left. Also, the underlying asset value per share is undoubtedly more than the market price. Then there would be the problem of finding good new investments. Events current at this writing show that tax-exempt bonds are risky. Other bonds are too. Again, it would take many years to reinvest properly and the end result would be the payment of tremendous expenses plus taxes ending with a much smaller trust. History on the other hand shows that, over the years, the present assets in the Trust have done rather well.

The end result of any sell-off of assets would depend on economic and market conditions and a host of other unpredictable considerations. It could be that such a sale might realize only a part of rated values. Conversely, in a super-perfect economic and business climate, the sweeping sell-out could leave the Getty Family with ten billion dollars—or even twenty billion, for that matter. (Not for long, though—not for any longer than it would take the tax-collecting hordes to descend on the scene.)

But the tax-men have no cause to poise themselves for a sprint. The Getty interests are not about to sell off their shares or dissolve their companies. Those companies have been built into a large and thriving family business. I continue to be an active businessman and, as head of the Getty Family am qualified to act as its spokesman. The Gettys are going to keep their family business operating—energetically, efficiently and with a view to even further growth.

3

THE PREVIOUS CHAPTER has, I hope, clarified the demarcation lines between my admittedly considerable personal wealth and the much greater wealth I *control* during my lifetime. For those who are interested in what will happen to my personal share-holdings after my death, the bulk of them will go to charity. Control of the share-holdings of the Sarah Getty Trust will go to the successor trustee or trustees as my mother—at whose insistence the Trust was originally established—intended.

A word about comparative financial influence may be in order at this point. Yes, as a private individual I *do* control a very large amount of wealth. On the other hand, it must be borne in mind that there are numerous corporations having many times the assets of the Getty Oil Company. The heads of these corporations—and they may be salaried presidents with only tiny (or, conceivably *no*) share-holdings in their companies—*control* greater wealth and can exert greater financial influence than I do.

The crux—for the sake of those not conversant with corporate organizations—is this. The Getty companies are a family business, with the Getty Family interests owning more than two-thirds of the shares in the company. Actual ownership of the giant corporations is, in most instances, much more dispersed. There are, for example, multibillion-dollar corporations in which no single investor owns more than two or three percent of the outstanding shares.

* * *

Sizeable segments of our present-day society have been conditioned to believe that the rich are racked by guilt-feelings over their wealth. It may be true in some cases, but not—I'm willing to wager—in overly many, and most certainly not in my own. I suffer no guilt-complexes or conscience pangs about my wealth. Nor do I have any defensive feelings because I happen to be so much richer than most people. The Lord may have been disproportionate, but this is how He—or Nature, if you prefer—operates.

Anyone viewing life with a realistic eye recognizes that certain inequalities are—and always have been—evident in the overall scheme. Given a group of ten—or a hundred— prize-fighters, all of much similar build and weight and with more or less the same amount of training, one will become the champion. The others will be runners-up, in descending degrees of success, with a tailend Charlie at the bottom.

We are all aware that large numbers of artists—painters, sculptors, pianists or ballet-dancers—initially display equal talent in their respective fields, work equally hard and are equally persevering. Yet, one or two or three in each field will achieve success, fame and wealth. The others will not.

It is no different with, say, writers or politicians. The random, inexplicable factor of Nature's tendency to be disproportionate operates with them, too. The rewards they receive are not evenly distributed. Some writers produce excellent works—yet barely eke out an existence. Others whose literary talents are no greater will earn hundreds of thousands—and, what with motion picture and television rights—even millions.

Most of us have known political aspirants who were gifted, of impeccable character, immensely likable and who laboured unstintingly to achieve their goals. However, despite having every imaginable plus-factor, they were unable to attain anything but minor posts such as membership in a town council. At the same time, other much less gifted or industrious individuals rose rapidly through the political ranks and became Senators, Members of Parliament, Cabinet Ministers, Governors of States or even Premiers or Presidents. It could be argued that the successful aspirants had some charismatic quality that captured the fancy and loyalty of the public. This is undoubtedly true in some instances—but hardly all. Certainly, whatever our nationality, we have all seen inarticulate, clay-lump clods elected to high office by landslide majorities as Nature's perverse penchant for inequity manifested itself.

So it is with business and businessmen and their successes and rewards. Nevertheless, it is a popular pastime to sniff that a businessman's wealth is tainted and that it taints by virtue of its very existence. (The exercise enjoys particular favour with followers of the 'Down With Up' School of social philosophy.)

Let anyone who wishes, recoil with horror at my heresies, but I reject the proposition as absurd, baseless and stemming from the garish green envy which the success of others inspires in the inept, the lazy and the chronic malingerer. Furthermore—and anyone so inclined is free to consign me to the tumbrils—I take pride in the creation of my wealth, in its existence and in the uses to which it has been and is being put.

At no given moment has even one percent of my rated wealth been available to me personally in readily spendable cash or chequeing accounts. The other 99-plus-percent is not buried under a tree or squirreled away in my mattress. It is invested and at work. Among other things it makes possible the production of goods and services for millions of consumers and provides well-paid employment for some 12,000 people in the United States, Great Britain, Europe, the Middle East, Japan and other parts of the world. And that is *direct* employment for men and women on the payrolls of the Getty companies, their subsidiaries and affiliates. It does not include many thousands of other jobs which are created when those companies build additional plant capacity, order tankers, buy drilling rigs—or, for that matter, issue purchase orders for paper towels or paperclips.

What's more, Getty companies are spending enormous sums as risk capital to discover and develop new and additional supplies of oil and other energy-sources. As an example, the Getty Oil company is exploring and drilling in many onshore and offshore areas of the U.S. and other portions of the globe. The search goes on endlessly. Getty Oil has recently participated in the discovery of a new oilfield off the coast of Spain in the Mediterranean and two fields in the South China Sea. It will take years of toil and the expenditure of fortunes in supplementary capital before any earnings may be expected from these fields. A key project undertaken by the Getty Oil

Company in consortium with Occidental Petroleum, Allied Chemical Corporation and Thomson Scottish Associates is in the United Kingdom sector of the North Sea. During 1975 and 1976 Getty Oil will spend more than $250 million on these North Sea operations alone. No one can estimate how long it might be before the company may hope to realize a penny of profit on this quarter-billion-dollar-gamble.

Then, my companies pay and generate very significant sums of tax-money. These go to national and local governments which—presumably—use the revenue wisely and well for the good of their citizenries. In 1974, Getty Oil and its subsidiaries paid $316 million to various governments in income taxes and $209 million in other taxes such as excise, property and so on. This means that Getty Oil—which ranks 17th in size among U.S. oil companies—alone contributed over half a billion dollars to public revenues in a single year. Beyond this, the company's executives and employees—myself included—paid taxes on their personal incomes, property and all the other items and transactions on which taxes are levied. The company's shareholders also paid their *double* share of taxes.

The original bite came when company profits were taxed, reducing the net profits and thus the amounts that could be distributed as dividends. Then, those receiving dividends had to pay personal income taxes on them to the Federal and in most instances their State and finally, in certain cases even their City, governments.

Observe what this implies. The U.S. Federal Corporation Tax is 48 percent. Thus, a company earning an annual net profit of $1 million is taxed $480,000, leaving an after-Federal-tax profit of $520,000. If that entire sum is distributed as dividends to investors, those individuals in the top Federal Income Tax bracket are taxed again—at the rate of 70 percent. It is therefore quite possible that Federal taxes alone reduce the $1 million profit to as little as $156,000 (with even further bites usually being taken by State and City governments).

Indeed, the leading part that business plays—and pays—as a financier of governments and their spending programmes is very often overlooked or ignored. By a coincidence in no way odd, the blindest eye is usually turned by those politicians who are the most strident business-baiters. They see business as a limitless bonanza from which public revenue may be mined without end or limit—and do not hesitate to legislate accordingly.

Although always aware that business foots much of government's cost, I did not realize the full extent until Vice President Nelson Rockefeller visited me at Sutton Place in July, 1975. After lunch, we sat together in my drawing room and discussed a wide range of topics, eventually focusing on the American economy and its problems. A remarkably intelligent—I would not hesitate to say brilliant—man with a vast store of knowledge about all aspects of economics, domestic and international, Vice President Rockefeller spoke to me frankly and openly. He deplored the growing tendency of politicians to use business as a vote-getting whipping-boy, and he underlined the degree to which government is dependent on business.

'Eighty-five percent of what the United States Government spends comes from business,' he declared.

Eighty-five percent!

I hadn't known the proportion was that high. The implications stunned me for a moment. In Fiscal Year 1974, U.S. Government outlays exceeded $300 billion. This means that over $255 billion of the spending was financed out of money provided by American business firms—a bit of statistical data that impels me to digress. Private enterprise is by no means perfect. Privately owned companies make many mistakes, sometimes costly ones, and there are those which occasionally (or frequently) fail to make a profit. Some even go into bankruptcy. Yet, in the main, most companies manage to meet their payrolls and other bills, pay their taxes and show a profit at the end of the year. If properly managed, they plough a substantial part of the profit back into the business and use it for expansion, research, plant modernization and whatever else will contribute to growth. As the noted economist, Otto Eckstein, has said, free-enterprise business 'is the only engine that has been developed so far that encourages people to be highly innovative, to develop new products and processes.'

Today, in many countries still to greater or lesser degree 'capitalist' there is a growing demand by politicians for 'socialization.' They argue that nationalization of all (or almost all) business and industry is the failsafe panacea for every economic ill. As everyone knows, nationalized industries are notorious for their inability to operate at a profit.

Even some of socialism's supporters have to admit this. One of these is English academician Professor Wilfred Beckerman, who has declared: 'Socialists have always recognized . . . that some industries cannot both operate at socially desirable levels and charge prices that will yield profits . . . Certain industries need to be nationalized *in order to be able to run them at a loss.*' (The italics are Prof. Beckerman's.)

His words ring with a faint echo of that ultimate monstrosity of doublethink uttered by some addled American Army officer during the Vietnam War: 'The village had to be destroyed so that it could be saved'!

There are many who feel that the United States Postal Service—a Federal Government Monopoly and in effect a nationalized industry—operates very far below a 'socially desirable level.' Since it was established in 1971 (to replace the old Post Office Department, increase efficiency and cut deficits) postal rates have soared and efficiency has fallen. As for deficits, they have zoomed. In Fiscal 1975, the Postal Service lost $869 million—*despite* a whopping $1.6 *billion* Federal subsidy. In the meantime, private enterprise mail delivery services have sprung up. They operate at a most 'socially desirable' level, save their customers time and money—*and* earn satisfactory profits (even though they spend extra money for neat plastic bags in which to deliver the day's mail).

Last summer, British newspapers revealed the heavy losses sustained by all the nation's nationalized enterprises save for the National Coal Board, which somehow managed to take in more money than it spent. Mr. Harry Fieldhouse, editor and political expert, made this trenchant comment:

'If nationalized monopolies cannot be run at a profit, a Socialist State becomes impossible. It must either go bankrupt or it must preserve and cherish a profitable private sector big enough to subsidize the public losses.'

It is intriguing to speculate what socialist politicians will do if they have their way and nationalize all business. The capitalist goose that lays the golden tax-eggs will be transmuted into a money-losing socialist crow. Who will provide the funds for the salaries—and the secretaries, chauffeured cars, globe-hopping junkets and other perquisites—of senators, congressmen, Members of Parliament and the bureaucratic hordes? The prospect is one that might be profitably pondered by professional business-baiters and by all who reject Abraham Lincoln's dicta: 'You cannot help the wage-earner by pulling down the wage-payer. You cannot help the poor by destroying the rich.'

Flawed as it is, the free-enterprise system still remains the most viable and efficient economic system. No one has yet developed a substitute that approaches, much less surpasses, its longterm, consistent capacity to provide the greatest good for the greatest number. Capitalism does result in inequalities—no argument over that. But, as I said earlier, Nature is disproportionate—so how could systems operating within its grand scheme be different? Economist Otto Eckstein declares that 'some injustice is inescapable if the (capitalist) system is to perform.' I submit that injustices and inequities are inescapable if any form of economic or political system is to perform.

The Chairman of a socialist National Coal Board receives much higher pay, infinitely more perks and lives in a far better and more elaborate house than any miner who toils at the coal-face. The Commissar heading a textile trust in the USSR is chauffeured from his spacious Moscow apartment to his office and then to his comfortable country *dacha* in a ZIS limousine. The clerks in his office—to say nothing of the spinning machine operators in the factories—live in cramped one- or two-room flats and ride to work aboard jammed trolleys or buses (or walk). Many millions of Chinese workers pedal their bicycles to and from work—but I'm inclined to doubt that either Chairman Mao or the late Premier Chou en-Lai rely on bicycles for transport.

Whether in a Western democracy or an Iron Curtain country, every city has a best hotel, and the hotel has a best room—and there is usually someone occupying it. By the same token every city—Capitalist or Communist—has a worst hotel, and that hotel has a worst room, and there is usually someone occupying it, too.

I've stated that I have no guilt-feelings about being rich. On the other hand, if I thought that by giving 99 percent of my wealth to the poor or some government I would help abolish poverty and human ills, I would not hesitate to do so. But suppose I did and every man, woman and child in the world received even as much as a dollar. What lasting good would it do? The answer is none—and I would have nothing left to invest in productive enterprises that filled certain human needs and requirements even while creating jobs and paying salaries and taxes.

No, I repeat. Nature is not impartial and even-handed. If it were, human nature—and human foibles—would swiftly redress the imbalances and create disproportions and inequities.

Am I a cynic? Perhaps, although I prefer to consider myself a realist. Choose whichever label you desire. I'll accept and wear either as I contend that if all the money and property in the world were divided up equally at, say, three o'clock in the afternoon, by 3.30 p.m. there would already be notable differences in the financial conditions of the recipients. Within that first thirty minutes, some adults would have lost their share. Some would have gambled theirs away and some would have been swindled or cheated out of their portion (thereby making some others richer). The disparity would increase with growing momentum as time went on. After ninety days, the differences would be staggering. And, I'm willing to wager that, within a year or two at the most, the distribution of wealth would conform to patterns almost identical with those that had previously prevailed.

Call it Fate, luck, natural law or what you will. Some individuals will rise to higher levels of recognition than others. A Harold Robbins, Agatha Christie, Anthony Burgess, Georges Simenon, Irving Wallace or Jorge Luis Borges will write books that sell more copies than the books of hundreds of other writers combined. Scores of political contenders will fail—while a great man like Franklin Roosevelt or, on the other hand, a mediocrity like Lyndon Johnson, will become President.

Yes, and some businessmen will be more successful and amass greater wealth than others. Why should they—or I—feel any sense of guilt, especially when the accumulated wealth is deployed and employed constructively and productively.

The late Max Aitken, First Baron Beaverbrook, was a man I admired immensely—as a person, as an astute businessman and as a realistic philosopher with a piercing insight into life, human nature and the world as it is. I consider it an honour and a highly rewarding experience to have established a warm and close friendship with him. Among his many grand qualities, Max possessed rare wit and could say volumes in a single sentence. I mention him now because he once summed up all I have been seeking to express in this chapter with a classic one-line remark.

'You know, Paul,' he said. 'I've always felt that I had a reserved seat in life.'

It's entirely probable that Max here hit on the most valid explanation for the disparities and disproportions one encounters in life. Be it generaled by a Power, a mysterious X-factor or merely a combination of circumstances, it does seem that some people do have reserved seats in life. If they do, it would be foolish and a needless waste for them to be guilt-ridden about it and move back and lose themselves among the standees.

4

ANY ATTEMPT TO deny that my own seat in life was reserved for me would be ridiculous. However, I was rather tardy in realizing that the reservation had been made. I was almost 22 before I took any particular interest in business or a business career. Until then, my ambitions alternated between a desire to become a writer and a wish to enter the U.S. Diplomatic Service.

When I first went into business, I did so somewhat reluctantly. In spite of this, by the time I was 24, I had made my first million dollars. Satisfied that this would suffice me for a lifetime, I retired.

But I am getting ahead of myself. While the story of my early life and business career has been told in detail elsewhere, a brief outline of it here will serve to establish some base-reference points and provide perspectives.

My father, George F. Getty Sr., was a highly successful attorney in Minneapolis, Minnesota, where I was born. He and my mother, Sarah MacPherson Risher, were married in 1879. The following year, they had a daughter—my sister, Gertrude Lois, whom I never knew, for she died during a typhoid epidemic in 1890, two years before my own birth. I was thus an only child.

By 1903—when I was eleven—my father's net worth exceeded $250,000, a very large sum in those days and easily equal to a million dollars or more in the shrivelled currencies of our present time. Wealthy as he was, that year—1903—was the crucial turning point in my father's career. It was then that the future course of the Getty Family's fortunes was set.

A client's legal problems sent George F. Getty Sr. to Bartlesville, Indian Territory, in what later became the State of Oklahoma. Arriving in Bartlesville, he found a new oil boom getting underway in the area. He transacted his legal business, winning the case for his client—and became infected with oil fever.

Father bought the oil and gas lease on 'Lot 50', an 1,100-acre tract located in the Osage Nation, and incorporated the Minnehoma Oil Company. Several men were associated with him in the venture, including: W. F. Bechtel, W. A. Kerr, Frederick V. Brown, John W. Bell and P. D. McConnell. But my father was the principal stockholder and president of the corporation, and he made the drilling contracts and was present on the site during all well completions. I mention this for good reason—as will be seen presently.

There are men—albeit they are few and far between—who seem to have an uncanny affinity with oil in its natural state. By some mysterious instinct, they appear to sense its presence even when the pool is thousands of feet below ground. T. N. Barnsdall, a fabulously successful American oil industry pioneer, vowed that he could 'smell crude' if it existed below the surface of ground on which he walked or stood. Lyman Stewart, founder of the Union Oil Company, is another man who is said to have had the 'wild talent,' as Charles Fort would have described it. I'm inclined to think my father had a touch of this instinct or talent, too. Forty-three wells were eventually completed on Lot 50. Of these, 42 were producers; only one proved a dry hole. The record is remarkable by any standards.

After the first well was brought in on Lot 50, Father took Mother and me to Bartlesville. He wanted us to see his new enterprise for ourselves and share the triumph of his initial success and the excitement of drilling a second well with him. As a boy, I faithfully kept a daily diary. My early diaries—along with those from later years and up to the present—are intact. Here is a selection of entries I made during January, 1904:

'Sunday, Jan. 17: We are going away to Indian Territory Tuesday night.'

'Tuesday, Jan. 19: Tonight at 8:30 we got on the train for Kansas City . . . we go on the Northwestern to Council Bluffs, Iowa.'

'Wednesday, Jan. 20: We traveled through Iowa and Missouri and got to Kansas City about 5:10 and went to the Midland. This is one of the largest hotels.'

'Thursday, Jan. 21: We took the 12:15 train for Bartlesville. We got there late so it was dark and I couldn't see anything. We went to the Midway Hotel.'

As written, the entries convey nothing of the sense of adventure and taut expectation I felt. An eleven-year-old, I was striving to be an 'objective reporter' and believed that a daily diary should record only unadorned facts. I suppose among youngsters of the 1970s this would be called 'keeping my cool.' However, as I read the words even now they evoke sharp, clear memories of my emotional responses. I can feel again the elation I felt when told I would be going to Indian Territory—and the disappointment I experienced because we arrived in Bartlesville 'late . . . and I couldn't see anything.'

Disappointment—and disillusionment—were bitter the next morning as my fantasies of seeing war-painted Indians, gunslinging cowboys and galloping cavalrymen crumbled. Seen in daylight, Bartlesville was a dreary, primitive boomtown, with mainly clapboard buildings—a few false-fronted to give the impression of being two-storeyed—and sagging wooden sidewalks. Some men did carry heavy revolvers strapped to their waists, but they were oilfield workers and not cowboys—and the Indians I saw were neither painted nor very picturesque figures. There was a modicum of compensation a few days later—in the dining room of the Midway Hotel. As I noted in my diary:

'Sunday, Jan. 24: Fine day . . . We had a fine dinner. There were ten great Indian Chiefs that sat near us. They had blankets and feathers and were on their way to see Roosevelt.* One Chief called Two Keys had two keys of gold in each ear.'

---

* *Editor's note:* Theodore Roosevelt, then President of the United States.

Visits to Lot 50, where drilling on Minnehoma Oil's No. 2 well was underway, fascinated me. Quickly picking up oilfield jargon, I learned that a drilling crew's work-shift is called a tour, but pronounced as 'tower,' and could soon talk with what I considered impressive authority about bull wheels, Samson posts and shooting wells with nitroglycerine. Much of the fascination was of the sort almost every young boy feels for things mechanical, be they fire engines, steam rollers or pile-drivers. Yet, in retrospect, I think I was already—at some level—responding to the lure of oil. No, not to the business or profits aspects of petroleum industry operations, but to the challenge and adventure inherent in field operations, in the hunt—the exploration and drilling—for oil.

On March 2, 1904, I first experienced the unique thrill of being on the scene when a drilling crew reaches pay sand and strikes oil. Still—as it were—keeping my cool, I recorded the event with this stolid entry in my diary: 'We all went to see the No. 2 well come in. It came in at 1,426 feet below the surface.'

My parents and I started back to Minneapolis two days later. On March 10, I was once again in my classroom at the Emerson Grammar School—'for the first time in six weeks,' I remarked in my diary, careful not to reveal what a monumental letdown it was for me. I added that 'In the afternoon Harry, William and I played marbles for keeps. I skinned a flint.' That particular win was not, I fear, due entirely to my superior marble-playing skill. My friends Harry and William, asking endless questions about my experiences in Indian Territory (and much distracted by my somewhat embroidered tales), failed to play with much concentration on the game.

I made another trip to Bartlesville with my parents in October, 1904. We detoured *en route* for a memorable ten-day visit to the fabled St. Louis World's Fair. (Its official designation was 'The Louisiana Purchase Centennial Exhibition,' but some colossal bureaucratic blunder caused the anniversary date to be miscalculated by a year.)*

Editor's note: At the beginning of the 19th century, France had an 827,000-square-mile colony, known as the Louisiana Territory in North America. The United States bought the entire territory from Napoleon Bonaparte for slightly more than $15 million—hence the American name, 'The Louisiana Purchase' for the transaction. It included areas that later became the States of Louisiana, Oklahoma and Missouri. However, the purchase was made in 1803—and, consequently, were it not for the curious error Mr. Getty cites, any 'Centennial Exhibition' should have been held in 1903, not 1904.

We went on to Bartlesville, staying there ten days. By then, three producing wells had been completed on Lot 50. A fourth (actually No. 3, but there had been drilling delays) was near completion. Still not yet twelve years old, I none the less felt myself a much travelled and sophisticated man of the world, especially of the oil world. I considered myself qualified to pass judgements and record them along with technical data in my diary, as witness my entry for October 17:

'In the morning we got up at six o'clock . . . and started for the lease. We got there at ten o'clock and walked around to see the four wells, all good. No. 3, the poorest of the lot, was shot last night at 10:15 with 100 quarts of nitroglycerine. We saw the column of oil from the drilling shoot 100 feet in the air and keep it up for five minutes.'

That same day, my father marked the location where he wanted the fifth well drilled. As it happened, this was the only one that turned out to be a duster among the 43 total he was to drill on the Lot 50 lease.

We went back to Minneapolis again—briefly. My mother and father had decided they would like to move to Southern California. Father thought a preliminary reconnaissance trip was in order. We left Minneapolis in February, 1905. After looking over San Diego (Father thought it too small a town), La Jolla (it was remote and isolated), Santa Monica (a straggly seaside hamlet) and some other towns, my parents concluded that they liked Los Angeles best. Although we once more returned to Minneapolis, shortly after my graduation from the Emerson Grammar School in 1906 we moved to Los Angeles permanently.

My father bought a corner plot on Wilshire Boulevard at Kingsley Drive. He had a large Tudor-style house built. It became our new home.

George F. Getty's business flourished and expanded during the next three years. The Minnehoma Oil Company—by then, he and my mother held 72 per cent of the stock—bought other leases on which it conducted successful wildcatting operations and which it further developed. The company still held the Lot 50 lease in Oklahoma, though, and production was gradually increased as my father had more wells drilled on the property. In 1909, although not yet 16, I asked my father if I could spend my summer vacations from school working in the field, on Lot 50. Father's reply was characteristic.

'It's all right with me—if you're willing to start at the bottom.'

That meant I would be employed as a roustabout—an oilfield labourer whose job it was to perform the heaviest (and usually the dirtiest) work on a drilling site. My father was explicit about the terms under which I would be employed. I was to receive the roustabout's going wage, three dollars a day for a 12-hour tour. I could expect no preferential treatment because I was the Boss's son. I would have to hold my own with the other men, take my share of the orders and do my share of the work. I accepted these conditions—if for no other reason than that, having asked for a job in the first place, I risked losing some of my father's respect if I refused or quibbled.

I had long enjoyed the advantages and comforts that might be expected to go with being a wealthy man's only son. To my astonishment—and, I imagine, that of my parents—I adapted readily to the abrupt transition. I not only took bunkhouse living and grub-shack eating in my stride, but enjoyed both. Big for my age—almost six feet tall, weighing a fat-free eleven stone five and in excellent physical condition, I found I could handle a roustabout's often backbreaking work without complaint. (That is, I could after the first week or so, when the blisters on my palms had begun to toughen into protective callouses.)

Having proven myself, the other men labouring on the drilling sites accepted me as one of their own. Among other things, this meant I was addressed as 'Red'—because of my hair-colour—or 'Paul,' rather than as 'Hey, you.' It also meant I was expected to contribute my share in the payday-night donnybrooks between drilling crews—and each crew considered itself a rival of the next. These mêlées were fuelled by the muriatic acid which Oklahoma bootleggers palmed off on the thirst-parched as whisky.*

Editor's note: The sale of alcoholic beverages was forbidden by Oklahoma State laws long before the United States as a whole went 'dry' under the 18th 'Prohibition' Amendment to its Constitution.

During the three years that followed, my time was divided between college terms in California and summer vacations spent working on Lot 50. And, I was working my way up. In those days of cable-tool drilling, the drilling crew proper on any given rig consisted of only two men. These were a driller and a tool dresser—or 'toolie.' While the tool dresser assisted the driller in many ways, his principal responsibility was to sharpen and retemper dulled drilling bits and keep all other drilling tools in optimum working order.

The toolie had to be a crack technician and an expert, highly specialized blacksmith. The quality of his work at his rigside forge and anvil could make or break vital drilling bits—and in time, even the entire drilling operation. I decided I wanted to learn the tooldresser's craft—more an art, if the truth is to be told. I did—thanks to the patience and efforts of a leathery, veteran toolie who agreed to take me under his wing and be my mentor. I regret that I am unable to remember his Christian name, but I can never forget his surname, Grizzle. While accurately suggesting his physical appearance, its connotations were at sharp odds with his helpful and outgoing nature and personality. Grizzle taught me all he knew, not only about dressing and maintaining drilling tools, but about virtually every phase of field operations—and his knowledge of these was encyclopaedic. Such was his reputation in the fields that when he pronounced that he considered me a qualified toolie, it carried more weight than any dozen university diplomas.

In May and June, 1912, I went to Japan and China as a tourist, returning to the United States to spend the summer working on the Lot 50 lease. In November, I went to England, where I read political science and economics at Oxford, rooming with Magdalen men. Completing these studies, I toured Europe and parts of the Middle East and North Africa until September, 1914, when I returned to the United States.

My father then asked the question most fathers ask sons who have completed their formal educations but have not decided on the careers they would follow: 'What do you intend doing now?'

Study at Oxford and travels abroad had tipped the scales of my ambivalent ambitions (literary versus service in the Diplomatic Corps) in favour of the latter. I said as much. Among the very many positive qualities for which George F.

Getty was widely liked and admired was his unfailing habit of presenting any arguments in a calm, wholly reasoned yet always tolerant manner.

Having heard me out, he presented what he frankly admitted was his 'side of the case.' It began with a reminder that he headed an oil business worth some millions of dollars, that he was nearing the age of sixty, and I was his only child.

'I've built what I hoped would be a family business,' he said and, after a pause, continued. 'You're only twenty-one, Paul, and can easily afford a year-long detour before trying for the Diplomatic Service. Would you be willing to consider it?'

I allowed that I might—depending on the nature of the detour.

'Try your hand as an independent operator in the fields,' Father urged. 'If the experiment doesn't work out or you're unhappy when the year is over, you can do whatever you wish. I won't say another word.'

Although I still aspired to become a member of the *Corps Diplomatique,* the idea of prospecting for oil as a wildcatting operator did have its appeal, and I could easily spare a year. I accepted my father's suggestion and agreed to the terms of his offer.

He would provide me with $100 per month for living expenses while I scouted for low-cost leases on properties that either instinct or my knowledge of surface geology told me might bear oil. Once I found a promising lease, Father would furnish the capital for its purchase and for exploratory drilling and development costs. Profits—if any—would be divided: 70 per cent going to my father and 30 per cent to me.

I had obtained all my field experience in Oklahoma. It stood to reason I should begin there, on familiar ground. I went to Tulsa, lived in a six-dollar-a-week room at the Cordova Hotel and had my meals at a boarding house a short distance from the hotel. The other boarders were also wildcatters on slender budgets hoping to make their big strikes. Some did. I particularly remember R. A. Josey, with whom I became great friends. Always good natured—and an inveterate player of practical jokes—he later made spectacular finds and earned millions.

My days were spent scouring the countryside in a third-hand Model T Ford. Although aesthetic monstrosities and decidedly uncomfortable, Model T Fords provided the principal means of transport for oilmen in those days. Apart from horse or mule drawn waggons, they were the only vehicles capable of negotiating the primitive, unpaved tracks that passed for roads in Oklahoma.

Long months went by without result. Successive large-scale oil strikes had created a classic boom climate. Prices that property owners demanded for oil and gas leases were insanely inflated. I was frequently on the verge of giving up. That I did not is due in large part to the warm-hearted encouragement and advice I received from older, seasoned oilmen like John Markham and R. M. McFarlin.

I owe a very special debt of gratitude to McFarlin. A multimillionaire and part owner of the McMan Oil Company, one of America's most successful oil producing firms, he went out of his way to befriend me. He bolstered my sagging morale, gave me invaluable counsel and passed on knowledge and lessons he had learned through long experience. Next to my father, R. M. McFarlin was probably the individual most influential in shaping my character and business philosophies.

The detour-year was nearing an end, and I had nothing to show for my efforts as a would-be wildcatting operator. Then, I learned that a half-interest in a lease on a Muskogee County property was to be sold at public auction. I inspected the property—known as The Nancy Taylor Allotment—and felt an immediate positive reaction. Unfortunately, so did numerous other independent operators, many of whom were established and had large financial resources. My boarding-house table-mates speculated that the auction price would surely reach $15,000 and probably more.

My father had set a limit on what I could spend for a lease, and it was far short of any such figure. It seemed useless for me even to enter the competition—and then I had an idea. What if the other bidders were made to feel as I did—that they were up against unbeatable opposition?

The game was worth a gamble. I asked a friend, a locally prominent bank vice-president to attend the auction, bid for me, but not reveal that he was acting on my behalf. The ruse was effective. Seeing the bank official at the auction, the other contenders automatically assumed that he was representing some major oil company and any offers they might make would be topped. They did not even bother bidding. The

Nancy Taylor Allotment prize became mine at the astoundingly low price of $500.

A company was promptly formed to explore and develop the lease. I began drilling operations. My impatience, suspense—and anxieties—increased daily as the derrick was built, the drilling rig installed and the bit began boring into the ground. In all, an interminable month passed until, at the very beginning of 1916, the well was completed, coming in for 700 barrels a day initial production.

My last sentence should be punctuated with whole rows of exclamation marks. But even they—or volumes of words—cannot adequately describe the elation and triumph one experiences when he brings in his first producing well. The feelings do not diminish when it is the tenth—or hundred and tenth—well that comes in a producer. Nor are the responses entirely—or even largely—money-oriented.

All veteran oilmen—I among them—have brought in wells that produced, say, 500 barrels a day during periods when crude prices were down to 25 cents (or even less) a barrel. Obviously, the $125-a-day gross income this production represented could cover only a portion of daily operating expenses, let alone provide any return on original capital investment. None the less, the sense of elation and triumph was—and is—always there. It stems from knowing that one has beaten Nature's incalculable odds by finding and capturing a most elusive (and often a dangerous and malevolent) prey.

The completion of my first well changed my luck from bad to good and it grew better at an astonishing rate. A rapid succession of profitable lease transactions and additional oil strikes followed. It all happened so fast and on such scales that by mid-1916, my accrued share of profits from my wildcatting operations totalled slightly more than a million dollars.

A $1,000,000 figure and the term 'millionaire' have their own peculiar magic, a mesmerizing—almost mystical—implication. Anyone who starts from scratch—even someone like me, who started from scratch but with family wealth behind him—is likely to regard the figure and the label as ultimates and ends in themselves.

Having accumulated the magical sum and qualified for the magical cachet with such brain-boggling speed, I viewed them as full-stop ends. Perhaps, being not yet 24, I lacked the maturity to grasp what—to play loose with Emmanuel Kant— might be termed a categorical imperative. In order for it to have substantive meaning, wealth must be regarded as a means; the true measure of any wealthy person is shown by the broader ends toward which he directs the means.

And so, snug (and not a little smug) with my million, I stopped working. Completely.

I retired.

But, as so often happens in life, circumstances provided a convenient rationalization. In this particular instance, prevailing world conditions were the excuse I could give for abandoning all constructive activity and choosing a life of total indolence.

5

IN THE SUMMER of 1916, Europe had been at war for two years. To many Americans, the conflict was something taking place 'over there' and 'none of our business.' My perspectives were different. Friends I had known at Oxford or during my travels on the Continent were at the Front. More than a few had already fallen. Believing that America's entry into the war was merely a question of time, I thought it wise to make a headstart in preparing myself for the eventuality.

Some years before, during my pre-college schooldays in Los Angeles, I had attended the Harvard Military Academy, where military training was limited to primer-level square-bashing. At the same time, I heard imaginative young reserve-officer instructors predict that 'aeroplanes' would play important roles in any future wars. By 1916, their prophecies were being proven deadly accurate at the war-fronts.

I had 'gone up' as a passenger and was enthusiastic about flying. (A quarter-century would pass before I developed my much-publicized, phobic fear of air-travel.) Having retired, and being without occupation or responsibilities, I made formal application for pilot-training in what was then the tiny 'Air Service' of the United States Army. The application was duly acknowledged by a form-letter stating that there were presently insufficient training facilities and aircraft. Applicants for pilot-training would be called up when more of these became available.

The United States declared war on April 6, 1917—whereupon

aspiring pilot-trainee J. Paul Getty and the United States Army began a memorable pen-pal relationship. My file of official form-letters grew. Their gist: All applicants would have to wait until the Air Service could absorb them into its training programme; in the meantime, they were earmarked for training and frozen—which meant they could not enlist in other branches or even be conscripted.

This comedy of military muddling continued right up to the Armistice—and after. In early 1919, I received a letter written on the richly-embossed stationery of the U.S. War Department. Bearing the facsimile signature of Secretary of War Newton D. Baker, it was a paean to my 'outstanding display of patriotism' in having applied for pilot-training in 1916. It went on to express regrets that 'exigencies of the military service' had prevented my being called to active duty.

I learned that such letters had been sent out by the thousand. It was comforting to know that I was by no means the only victim (or, quite possibly, lucky beneficiary) of the Army's bureaucratic bungling.

Ironically, my cousin, Howell 'Hal' Seymour (who had filled out no applications) was taken into the Field Artillery and sent to France with one of the earliest American Expeditionary Force contingents. Hal, who had manned close-support 75-millimetre field guns for months on the Western Front, received thank-you letters from no one: But stay-at-home civilian J. Paul Getty was inundated with praise and gratitude by no less a personage than the Secretary of War.

'You ought to frame this and hang it on your wall,' Hal muttered with justifiable sarcasm when I showed him the letter. I wanted to say that I could think of a far more appropriate use for it, but I restrained the urge.

I had remained in Southern California throughout my precocious retirement (and my wait for the trumpet to sound). The hiatus lasted more than two years, and I cannot help but look back at it with mellow nostalgia for it was a period during which I literally did nothing but have a good time. When I came out of retirement, there were to be no replays of this carefree play-period. I state as fact, not as grievance, that there has not since been a solid week—let alone a month or year—during which I would (or could) be able to avoid work or grappling with business problems.

The Southern California of 1916–19 was an ideal place for anyone seeking to enjoy himself. Urban sprawls, Freeways, smog and other notorious Southern California blights lay two decades in the future. The year-round climate was incomparable. There were magnificent, uncrowded beaches (and I have always loved sun, sea and sand), breathtaking scenic wonders, forested and lake-studded mountains, desert-land—all and more within easy driving distance. (I had long since traded up from my Model T to a gleaming Cadillac roadster.) Even in those days, there were excellent restaurants, supper and nightclubs. The social atmosphere was casual, relaxed, friendly. Above all, Southern California, then as later, abounded with exceedingly attractive—and largely unattached—young women.

A man in his mid-twenties who had both time and money to spare could have scarcely hoped for more. He could (and I most certainly did) take a Total Immersion course in practical application of the pleasure-principle. But it was spouting oil and not a sated Id that led me to emerge—or, more accurately, suddenly decide to leap—out of retirement in 1919.

By that year, American oilmen were focusing increasing attention on Southern California. Great new producing areas were being discovered and developed; yet another epic Oil Rush was in the making. I was forced to concede that my success in Oklahoma and magical million had only caused my oil fever to abate and lie dormant temporarily. It flared again as I observed the rapid growth of new derrick-forests in beach-areas, on hillsides and amidst orange groves. Other men were boring down into pay sands, bringing in gushers, opening up new fields. For my part, I lolled on sandy beaches and opened up nothing that could possibly gush except for far too many champagne bottles. This state of affairs first nagged, then gnawed and finally became intolerable.

I un-retired.

My father said nothing, not even 'I told you so,' but it hardly required ESP on my part to perceive that he was much pleased. Others who knew me took note of my decision with varying reactions and comments. Among them was Bill Roeser, a friend who had also come to California from Oklahoma in 1916. Bill was a colourful and flamboyant wildcatter, famed throughout the industry for his habit of wearing a fresh, crisp $10,000 banknote as a boutonnière. Not much older than I,

Roeser had already made and lost two large oil fortunes and was rapidly amassing his third in the California fields. Learning through the industry grapevine that I was about to resume my own wildcatting operations, Bill immediately telephoned me.

'Hey, Paul, how does it feel to dig up toward the surface instead of drilling down below it?' he asked.

I said the question made no sense.

'The hell it doesn't,' Roeser declared, sounding his most dead-level serious. 'Since I hear you finally up and disinterred yourself, I figured you're the only oilman in the business who knows the answer.'

Like many people, I sometimes swing from one extreme to another. Having been supremely indolent, I went back to work in two capacities simultaneously. On the one hand, I picked up where I left off in 1916 conducting joint ventures with my father and his Minnehoma Oil Company. On the other, I undertook independent enterprises, which I financed entirely with my own private capital.

The first of these private ventures proved a dismal failure. I acquired a lease on the Didier Ranch near Puente, California. Because joint father-son projects kept me busy and shuttling back and forth between California and Oklahoma, I retained a drilling contractor to drill an exploration well on the Didier Ranch lease. Unfortunately, I didn't enquire very closely into the contractor's bonafides. Seven months after the well was spudded in, I found that my cheques paid out in fees to the contracting firm totalled nearly $100,000, and the drillers had managed to get down only 2,000 feet. The time-cost-depth ratios set something approaching a record low for that era. I halted drilling operations, abandoned the well and relinquished the lease to the owner of the property.

The Didier Ranch fiasco was not, I am happy to say, an augury of things to come. Wells I drilled elsewhere in California and in Oklahoma and New Mexico came in producers, some yielding truly spectacular quantities of crude. My costly experience with the drilling contractor proved a bargain because of the lesson it drove home. During the A.D.—After Didier—period, whether operating in association with my father or on my own account, I acted as my own drilling superintendent. I spent most of my time in the field, working alongside my crews on the drilling sites. Around-the-clock stints were commonplace—and, on one occasion, during a crucial stage in drilling operations, I worked straight through for 74 hours.

There were many reasons for my choosing to be, rather than to hire, my drilling superintendent. Not the least of them lay in what, whether innate or acquired, has always been a key (if not altogether meritorious) facet of my nature. It is all too familiar to anyone who has worked with or for me. Members of my family were particularly aware of it, as may be illustrated by a conversation I had with another of my cousins, June Hamilton, in the late 1930s.

June was a close friend of President Franklin Delano Roosevelt and his wife, Eleanor, and a frequent guest at the White House and the Roosevelt family home in Hyde Park, New York. While I had met FDR a few times, I could claim no more than a bare acquaintance with him. Being one of Franklin Roosevelt's great admirers and staunch supporters, I was eager to know more about him. June Hamilton was able to provide accurate insights from her firsthand observations and impressions.

'How do you find FDR as a person?' I asked June. 'Is he easy to get along with?'

'He's the easiest man in the world to get along with—as long as you do exactly what he wants,' she replied, pausing and giving me a dry look before adding, 'that's one thing you and he have in common.'

I hastily changed the subject—consoling myself with the thought that my tendency to be autocratic (which I had long recognized in myself) was a trait I shared with the President of the United States.

Yes, I chose to be my own drilling superintendent because it was the only way I could be sure that my crews did exactly what I wanted. On the other hand—and paradoxical as it may seem—it gave me a unique sense of independence and self-sufficiency. I never had to search further than myself when seeking to lay final blame for mistakes or wrong decisions. Having dropped one President's name, I might as well drop that of his successor, Harry S. Truman, who provided the clearest and most succinct explanation of what I mean with the sign he kept on his Presidential desk: 'The Buck Stops Here.'

When the man in charge—of a candy factory, a drilling operation of a nation's government—accepts direct, final responsibility, he makes full advance payment for the rewards, prerogatives and privileges he receives. He is released from any need to feel beholden or indebted.

It should also be noted that during the first three decades of this century, an oilman who was a 'Working Boss' enjoyed a distinct advantage. Oilfield workers—whether roughnecks, derrick riggers or expert drillers—were (and still are) a fiercely proud and clannish lot. In those days, before the era in which vast, impersonal corporations came into their full, structured and organization-charted own, oilfield workers viewed pinstripe-suited home-office executives as outsiders and objects of contempt. They maintained (with greater or lesser justification) that such lubbers couldn't tell the difference between a kelly and a crown block and were better fitted to be perfume salesmen or doily-designers.

When a 'Boss' knew his way around a rig (and, when necessary, would perform any task from riding the hook during latching up operations to sharpening dulled bits) oilfield workers accepted him as a full member of their exclusive fraternity. It didn't matter that he was worth one million—or one hundred million—dollars. He was an 'Honest-to-Gawd' oilman and provided he abided by oilfield codes of fairness and (sometimes elemental) justice, employee morale and efficiency soared.

Even today, I take pride in the fact that men like Walter Phillips, Oscar Prowell and 'Spot' McMurdo asked to sign on with me. They were known to be among the finest drillers in the U.S. oil industry. Their services were sought after avidly by every American oil-producing company. What gives me still greater pride is that the three men remained on my payrolls despite the strenuous efforts of other companies to lure them on to their own.

While I'm boasting, I must offer two more chest-expanding examples. Ernest B. Miller Jr., began his career as a roust-about with the Tidewater Oil Company in 1934 (by then, I owned a substantial interest in Tidewater and later gained full control). Ernie Miller stayed with Tidewater and my companies until January 1, 1975, when, after forty years of truly distinguished service, he retired—as a director and the executive vice-president and chief operating officer of the Getty Oil

Company. His successor in all three posts, Harold E. Berg, no less an outstanding executive and genuine oilman, started with Tidewater in 1937.

The loyalty of men like Ernie Miller, Harold Berg—or Walter Phillips, Oscar Prowell and 'Spot' McMurdo—cannot be bought with bonuses, fancy fringe-benefits or company-paid vacations in Miami or Marbella. It has to be earned, even (perhaps especially) by autocrats.

In a 1974 article on the Getty companies, *Forbes* Magazine told its readers:

'Getty's executives are a tight, closemouthed band of longtime employees who toil energetically and anonymously . . . there is a strong sense of loyalty and the close team feeling of "it's Getty challenging the big oil giants." '

I submit that such an assessment made by hardnosed financial writers and editors is an accolade. In 1923, my net worth had increased to about $3 million, almost all invested in oil-producing ventures. My father's fortune was in the neighbourhood of $15 million—and also at work in the form of investment in the business of finding and producing oil. (My father's personal bank balances totalled less than $100,000; my own total was far below that amount. But we kept our companies highly liquid and made only minimal use of their credit.)

The Roaring Twenties were the period of that Great American Prosperity which was built on shaky, if not outright chimerical, foundations. My father and I were far from alone in recognizing this. In 1926, Bernard Baruch, whom I knew personally (never dreaming that one of his nieces would become my fifth wife some thirteen years later) was already writing to Mark Sullivan: 'Now let me make a prediction to you. Business has undoubtedly reached its zenith . . .'

Some months later, Baruch wrote to Winston Churchill: 'Business conditions in America are not as good as the newspapers make them.'

My rated wealth increased threefold during the Roaring Twenties, but the October, 1929, Stock Market Crash made American balance-sheets—business and personal—virtually meaningless. All market-values crumbled as stock-prices plummeted. Even if they had been held at conservative levels, the rated values of any asset—plant, real property or whatever—had to be revised downward, and sharply. Even then the resulting figures were largely academic. Those who sought to liquidate assets were unlikely to find buyers at any price.

Despite the bad—and rapidly worsening—economic situation, the Gettys and their business enterprises were quite safe and secure. Neither my father nor I had succumbed to the stock-speculation madness of the Twenties; the Wall Street Crash caused us no direct personal losses. And, as I noted parenthetically above, our companies had substantial reserves and were practically debt-free.

In 1923, my father had suffered a stroke, from which he made a remarkable recovery. In April, 1930, when he was nearly 75 years old, he suffered another. Although he fought with the courage and determination he had shown in all things during his life, he lost the battle five weeks later.

I've purposely refrained from discussions of my relationship with my father and mother and details of my personal life and feelings, for these belong elsewhere in this book. However, I must state here that the love, respect and admiration I had—and still have—for my father were boundless. His death was a blow that the passing years have only numbed. Not long after he passed on, I wrote these words—they were from the heart, and remain so:

> His loving kindness and great heart, combined with a charming simplicity of manner, made George F. Getty the idol of all who knew him. His mental ability was outstanding to the last. I, his son and successor, can only strive to carry on to the best of my ability the life work of an abler man. This is said in no sense as eulogy, but as an impartial appraisal of the facts.

Long before, my father told me that he had built what he hoped would be a family business and reminded me that I was his only child. I was 37 when he died—and no longer had any freedom of choice over what I would do with the rest of my own life.

6

MY MOTHER WAS named the principal beneficiary of my father's will and thus became the controlling stockholder in his companies. Reflecting post-Wall-Street Crash value erosions, official appraisals set the value of George F. Getty Sr.'s estate at $15.5 million—approximately the same as his net worth in 1923.

Knowing that I had my own fortune, Father left me $500,000, and I became the president of the Minnehoma Oil and Gas Company and of George F. Getty, Inc., roles in which I found myself considerably restricted. My mother and the executors of my father's will were deeply worried about the economic situation, and they advised drastic retrenchments and curtailed operations. My own views were in direct opposition.

Convinced of eventual economic recovery and firmly believing in the business dictum, buy when prices are low, I urged a programme of expansion. Stocks in publicly owned companies with huge (if temporarily undervalued) assets were selling at prices that made them barely believable bargains. There were shares selling for as little as a twentieth of their net underlying asset value. Anyone who purchased them was, in effect, buying $20 for every dollar he spent.

The Getty companies—my father's and my own—were primarily engaged in oil exploration and production. Their crude had to be sold to refineries or pipeline companies. I reasoned that with share prices being where they were, the time was ideal to obtain control of a company (or companies) with refinery facilities and marketing outlets. In other words, economic conditions created a unique opportunity to put together an integrated, well-to-consumer oil company at a cost within our resources.

'The Getty companies have the cash and the credit—let's use them,' I argued.

When my mother and the executors hesitated, I decided to go ahead on my own, using my own capital. I set my sights on the Tide Water Associated Oil Company, and in March, 1932, I took the first step in what would prove to be a two-decade-long campaign (and battle) to obtain clear-cut numerical control. I bought 1,200 shares of Tide Water Associated stock at $2.50 per share. During the next six weeks, I bought an additional 39,000 shares. Little more than a year later, these holdings had jumped to 734,000 shares—impressive, but still very far from a controlling interest.

Incidentally, there was much comment by press and public in 1972 when I appeared in a television commercial for the stock-brokerage firm of E. F. Hutton & Company. Many theories (some quite absurd) were advanced as to why I had agreed to 'plug' the firm. The truth is simple: it was part-payment on a long-standing debt of gratitude.

E. F. Hutton & Company had been my brokerage firm almost from the time I began my business career, and for decades my principal brokers with the firm were Gordon Crary (a former classmate at the Harvard Military Academy) and Ruloff Cutten. While conducting the Tide Water campaign, it was often necessary to ask that my brokers carry me. Any brokerage firm would have done so had I been able to offer Standard Oil of New Jersey or General Motors shares as collateral. But E. F. Hutton & Company had faith in the underlying value of Tide Water shares and in the company's future, and they knew I would liquidate my other assets to protect them against loss if this—by any chance—ever became necessary. Hutton and Company carried me for sums ranging into many thousands of dollars during the most crucial periods in the contest for control of Tide Water. It has consistently proven itself to be a fine stock-brokerage house over the more than half century I have been one of its clients. Thus, appearing in the television commercial was only a small gesture of thanks on my part to the firm.

I certainly needed all the help I could get in the Tide Water campaign. William 'Billy' Humphrey, president and board chairman of Tide Water, and the company's incumbent management were fiercely determined to stop me. Billy Humphrey was a resourceful and relentless opponent. Yet, despite proxy-fights and other (often gloves-off) battlings against each other, I came to like and respect him greatly.

Abruptly, in the midst of it all, I learned that the controlling interest in Tide Water actually belonged to Standard Oil of New Jersey—which, in turn, was controlled by the Rockefeller interests. Had I known this originally, I would never have begun buying Tide Water shares—for a pigmy independent operator such as I was could hardly stand a chance against one of the world's largest and most powerful major oil companies. But, by the time I discovered the truth, I was too deeply committed to withdraw from the fray.

It was against this bleak background that, in 1933, my mother turned her controlling interest in George F. Getty, Incorporated over to me and she received, among other things, $3,000,000 in notes of that company. Later in 1934 she placed most of those notes in the Trust we created and named me as Trustee.

The grotesque constructions some have placed on this strictly-business transaction between Mother and me would be hilarious were it not that they totally disregard her motives. Although nearing eighty, Mother was clear-minded and farsighted. Her strong protective maternal instincts demanded she make certain that I, my children and their children would be secure, no matter what turns financial and economic trends took in the future. The notes went into a 'spendthrift trust' that Mother and I established jointly. That done, Sarah Getty felt content; she had made ample provisions for me, her grandchildren and great-grandchildren.

Obviously, as I now exercised full control over George F. Getty, Inc., I had a free hand in directing the company's operations and in utilizing its resources. My prospects of winning the 'impossible' Tide Water battle were a shade less dark. They were soon to be brightened by a completely unexpected development, but in order to relate it properly, it's necessary to sidetrack briefly.

For some years, I had lived in a beach house I built near Santa Monica, California. The infinitely grander house next door belonged to the film star, Marion Davies. It had been built for her by the multimillionaire publisher, William Randolph Hearst.* Although Hearst was fiercely jealous of Marion, she and I became the best of friends. I was a frequent guest in her home and on numerous occasions met William Randolph Hearst there. In December, 1934, he invited me to spend the New Year holidays at his San Simeon estate. I accepted gladly, eager to see the famous fantasy-world he had created.

On the evening of my arrival, dinner was served in the great dining hall, draped with the priceless Siena banners Hearst had collected. There were two dozen or so other house-guests, many of them prominent personages, and I was seated next to Marion Davies—who, of course, had her customary place at Hearst's side.

Now, Hearst had stuffy prejudices against what he considered 'excessive' drinking. No guest at San Simeon was permitted more than one cocktail before a meal. This included Marion Davies, *de facto* mistress of the estate, who liked to drink. The customary single cocktail having been placed beside each plate, Marion quickly downed hers and saw that I hadn't yet touched mine. Speaking softly but with the slight stammer that I and other men—Charlie Chaplin and David Niven among them—found to be one of her irresistible charms, Marion asked me: 'If you don't want your drink, Paul, may I have it?'

Unfortunately, Hearst overheard. 'No!' he said, frowning.

Editor's note: The romantic relationship between Marion Davies and William Randolph Hearst began in 1917 and lasted until his death in 1951. It was one of the more open—avidly-discussed—secrets of the era. Incidentally one of the publisher's sons by his wife, Millicent, is Randolph A. Hearst, the father of Patricia 'Patty' Hearst whose kidnapping in 1974 and its aftermaths have received worldwide publicity. A compulsive spender, William Randolph Hearst was particularly lavish with his gifts to Miss Davies. The Davies-Hearst house to which Mr. Getty refers had more than a hundred rooms and is described by one of the publisher's biographers as 'a pile that made the neighbor's places seem like summer cottages.' In it were 37 fireplace mantels Hearst had bought from the owners of stately English homes. The main dining room, reception room and drawing room came from Burton Hall in County Clare. Hearst had them dismantled, shipped to the United States and re-assembled. Paul Getty, reminiscing in his diary on April 4, 1963, estimates that the Hearst-Davies house at Malibu Beach 'cost $3 million,' and adds, 'my own house cost $100,000.' Other sources claim Hearst spent $8 million to build this beachside palace for Marion Davies.

'Please give me the drink, Paul,' Marion pleaded.

My dilemma was acute. Should I be rude to my lovely friend, Marion Davies, and refuse her? Or should I risk angering my host? I reached for my glass indecisively and, entirely by accident knocked it over, spilling the contents. Hearst later complimented me on the diplomatic manner in which I resolved my predicament. When I protested it had been accidental, he refused to believe me.

On New Year's Day, a servant told me I was wanted on the telephone—a long distance call from New York City. Jay Hopkins was on the line. (Hopkins in later years was to be the founder of the General Dynamics Corporation.)

'Glad I managed to track you down—Happy New Year,' Jay said. He went on to tell me that Jersey Standard had transferred its Tide Water shares to a 'Mission Corporation,' a Nevada holding company, and intended to distribute Mission Corporation shares to its own stockholders on a pro-rata basis. The tactic would disperse Jersey Standard's Tide Water holdings so widely that control of the company would be out of my reach forever.

My spirits slumped—only to soar a moment later.

Hopkins informed me that John D. Rockefeller Jr.—who had evidently been kept in ignorance of the reasons lying behind these moves—was willing to sell his rights to Mission Corporation stock at 10 1/8 ($10.125) per share. John D. Jr. owned about 16 per cent of Jersey Standard's common. Purchase of his pro-rated Mission Corporation rights meant acquiring another large bloc of Tide Water stock. This would be a huge leap forward for me.

'I'll buy the rights,' I declared emphatically, then grew worried. 'Jay, suppose Jersey Standard's management hears that Rockefeller intends to sell. They'll try to talk him out of it.'

'Not a chance,' Hopkins assured me. 'He's aboard a train bound for Arizona. They can't reach him, and I have his authorization to sell.'

The transaction, involving close to $1.8 million, was closed then and there, over the telephone.

Years afterward, when he headed General Dynamics, Jay told me the amusing sequel to the story. It seems that when he returned to New York City from Arizona, John D. Rockefeller Jr. had a meeting with Messrs Farrish and Teagle—

respectively board chairman and president of Jersey Standard. Farrish and Teagle informed John D. Jr. that they had a proxy-fight on their hands over Tide Water and asked that he not sell his Mission Corporation share-rights under any circumstances.

'But they've already been sold,' Rockefeller said.

'Sold? To whom, Mr. Rockefeller?'

'Someone out in California. I understand he's a nice young man.'

'His—his name isn't Getty by any chance?'

'Yes. As a matter of fact, I believe it is.'

The reactions of Farrish and Teagle may be left to the imagination.

Armed with John D. Jr.'s assignment of rights, I approached other Jersey Standard stockholders—with predictable results. Many of them felt that if a Rockefeller thought it wise to sell his Mission Corporation rights so far in advance of actual share-distribution, they would be wise to do the same. Whenever they expressed willingness to sell, I bought, making appreciable increases in my Tide Water holdings.

But the Billy Humphrey-Farrish-Teagle team unlimbered other weapons. These were effectively countered by the tireless efforts of my close friend and brilliant attorney, David Hecht. A meeting of Mission Corporation directors was held in Reno, instantly spawning a series of court actions. Dave Hecht won them—and the day. The Getty interests had their control of the Mission Corporation confirmed, thereby gaining a strong voice in the management of Tide Water plus some extremely valuable surprise bonuses—about which more later. The Tide Water campaign itself was not yet completely won, though. Final, clearcut numerical control of that company was not achieved until 1952.

When the Japanese attacked Pearl Harbour on December 7, 1941, I sent a telegram to James Forrestal, a personal friend, who was then Assistant Secretary of the Navy, volunteering my services. I could not go to Washington myself because my mother fell gravely ill. Physicians advised against moving her to a hospital, but urged me to remain near her. On December 25, Mother took a sudden turn for the worse; I wrote in my diary: 'Christmas Day was a sad one because of Mama. She is very ill and has, I admit, little chance to recover. I was hopeful until this afternoon, but then became alarmed. Mama took three cups of water from me. She kissed me. Afterwards, I went out of the room and cried.'

Sarah Getty died on December 26. She was almost 89, and to the last a loving and wonderful person, a great lady. My diary entry two days later was brief—'How I miss her! No one ever had a better mother.' Even now, looking at the words recalls my sorrow and anguish as sharply as if they had been written yesterday.

On January 6, 1942, I took—and passed—a Navy physical examination and went to Washington. My first stop was at Jim Forrestal's office. I reminded him that I was an experienced yachtsman (the largest vessel I had owned was the 260-foot *Warrior,* with a crew of forty) and a qualified navigator. Forrestal countered that I was 49 years old.

'We can give you a commission and an administrative job ashore,' Jim said. 'But sea duty is out of the question.'

It so happened that Forrestal knew of the surprise bonuses I had received when acquiring control of the Mission Corporation. Its eyes solely on Tide Water, Jersey Standard's management somehow overlooked the fact that Mission Corporation also held a 57 percent interest in the Skelly Oil Company, a large U.S. midcontinent oil company headquartered in Tulsa. Thus, by gaining control of Mission, I also gained control of Skelly. Furthermore, among its holdings, Skelly Oil owned the Spartan Aircraft Corporation.

Spartan had two branches. One was an aviation school that gave flight training to thousands of young air cadets under contracts with the U.S. armed forces, the RAF and RCAF. It was an unqualified success.* The other branch of Spartan was supposed to manufacture training aircraft and components and sub-assemblies for prime-contracting companies making combat planes. It, Jim Forrestal told me glumly, was a disaster.

Navy Secretary Frank Knox, with whom I was personally acquainted, confirmed what Jim said. He recommended that I forget donning a Navy uniform and take personal charge of

---

Editor's note: More than 1,500 Royal Air Force cadets were sent to the United States for training at the Spartan School of Aeronautics. Captain Maxwell 'Max' Balfour, who had been a combat pilot with a U.S. pursuit Squadron in France during World War One, was the school's Director of Training. In 1946, Captain Balfour was awarded an Order of the British Empire for his services to the R.A.F.

Spartan's manufacturing operations instead. I said I would think it over. That same evening, and by sheer coincidence, I ran into Jake Swerbul, head of Grumman Aircraft, in the lobby of the Mayflower Hotel. Jake practically turned livid when I mentioned Spartan.

'It stinks!' he rasped. 'We've had to reject practically every God damned thing it's produced for us on sub-contract!'

The next morning I told Knox and Forrestal that I would do what they had asked.

My oil companies were staffed and managed by men fully capable of operating them on their own. I moved to Tulsa and, as president of Spartan Aircraft, took direct charge. The first step was to sweep out incompetents, replace them with qualified personnel and tighten up operations even while implementing an expansion programme. Soon streams of vitally needed components and subassemblies manufactured to rigid specifications were flowing to Grumman, Douglas, Boeing, Lockheed and other prime contractors. Factory space was increased seven-fold. The number of employees—originally in the hundreds—increased to over 5,500.

I spent the war years at Spartan and became very much involved in the company, its activities and future. And I felt deep obligation to the employees who had won Spartan so many commendations for efficiency from the U.S. Government and prime-contracting companies. After V-J Day, I stayed on to convert Spartan's operations into peacetime manufacture of house-trailers and mobile homes. Only when these began coming off the assembly line did I revert my attention to oil.

In 1948–49, Getty interests obtained the oil concession on Saudi Arabia's undivided half-interest in the so-called Neutral Zone lying between that country and Kuwait. Four years and tens of millions of dollars were spent before a drop of crude was brought to the surface. But, by 1954, it was evident that the Neutral Zone had immense oil reserves.

Getty companies had done considerable international business before. Neutral Zone finds and production transformed them into truly global enterprises. Much work and capital and sweeping organizational restructurings were needed to make this new business empire viable. Tankers—then super-tankers—

pipelines, storage facilities, refineries had to be built. The list of 'things to be done' was awesome, but they were done. The empire has thrived and expanded further.

Today, Getty companies—operating on their own or in consortium with other companies—are exploring for and producing oil onshore and off in many parts of the world. These include several States of the Union, the United Kingdom sector of the North Sea, Peru, the waters off the Spanish coast, the Java and South China Seas—and other areas. Getty Oil owns a shade less than half of the Mitsubishi Oil Company, Ltd., the fourth largest petroleum company in Japan. Skelly Oil is operating in the Persian Gulf waters between Sharjah and Iran. And this is only a quickskim sampling of Getty-Company operations and activities that extend into numerous other fields—petrochemicals, uranium, oil shale and agriculture among them.

In short, the Getty Family fortune is hard at work as invested capital, being used to the utmost as a means toward achieving ever more productive ends.

An American financial journal recently observed that I have been an active businessman for more than sixty years and said, 'Paul Getty still minds the store . . . his hand is never far from the throttle.'

The similes are mixed but apt enough, I suppose, and they serve as a satisfactory coda for this broad-stroke outline of my still-continuing business career. With the business-oriented base-reference points established, I can proceed with my broader theme—of how I see (and have seen) myself, my private life, other people and the constantly changing world around me.

7

I HAD BEEN living at Sutton Place in Surrey, England, for more than a year when, as my diary note for August 15, 1961, shows, I 'received a letter from Ruth Hill, my first dream girl'. Ruth and her husband were touring England and asked if they could drop by and see me. Of course they could, I replied, and looked forward to their visit.

My diary entry six days later:

'Ruth Hill and her husband, Frank Leslie, to lunch. Ruth sat across the aisle from me at the Emerson Grammar School in Minneapolis. We graduated in 1906. I went to California shortly afterward and we hadn't seen each other since. We talked of school days and schoolmates. Ruth has naturally changed in looks since 1906, but is still the same sterling character and wonderful person. I was thrilled to see her. She and Frank were married in 1916. I am still thinking of my grammar school days.'

I think back to my childhood often. The diaries I kept as a boy of eleven and twelve recapture the flavour of a tranquil and uncomplicated era.

'Sunday, March 27, 1904: In the morning I read *Napoleon Bonaparte* and went to Sunday School. In the afternoon I played with Harry and Ruth'—yes, the same

Ruth Hill—'In the evening I read and counted my stamps. I have 300 and 200 traders.'

'April 18: I got a nickname at school today. It is Hippo.'

'July 4: I got up at 5:00 o'clock in the morning and fired off some of my firecrackers. After breakfast I saw a parade of the Dog and Pony Show. In the afternoon I and Aunt Nettie and Uncle Travis went to the Dog and Pony Show. It was fine.'

'September 10: In the morning I played football. In the afternoon I went out nutting and got a flour sack half full of hazelnuts. In the evening I read.'

But then, in 1904, Dr. Sigmund Freud was virtually unknown outside Vienna, and Dr. Benjamin Spock was only a year-old diapered infant in New Haven, Connecticut. The Age of the Neurotic Child had not yet dawned. Children were just that and not potential case-histories to be compiled by $50-an-hour child psychiatrists.

My father—I called him Papa—was a tall, broad-shouldered man with lively blue eyes, a keen mind and a kind, straightforward nature. My mother——Mama—had large, lustrous eyes and handsome, expressive features. Her carriage was almost regal, and her patience and sense of humour were almost inexhaustible. My parents were an ideally balanced couple and devoted to each other. Theirs had been a partnership in every equal-sharing, two-way sense of the word ever since they met and married while still attending college, where they studied for teaching degrees. Indeed, after my father became a schoolteacher, it was with my mother's encouragement and financial assistance that he was able to quit and go through law school.

My parents knew the now-apparently-lost art of showing their child great love and affection without being overly indulgent or permissive. My school report cards invariably received close scrutiny. Comments on them—whether of praise or censure—lost no force because they were made quietly, without melodrama.

Father concerned himself with the development of my character and the more practical aspects of my early education and training. Mother looked after the softer sides—from table-manners to awakening and guiding my cultural interests. It was at my father's behest that I took boxing lessons, and at my mother's that I studied the piano. (I did considerably better at the former than the latter.)

Papa's concepts of child-discipline were based on the assumption that reason and reasoning should prevail, and the withholding of privileges was the cure when they did not. On occasion, I left him no choice but to depart from his rules and use more drastic measures. I recall one incident all too clearly.

My first dog was a brown mongrel, 'Jip', that attached himself to me when we went to Bartlesville, Indian Territory, in February, 1904. Jip and I shared many adventures together. My parents were glad to let me keep him—with one proviso. Jip could not sleep in my room at the Midway Hotel, where we stayed. One night I sneaked Jip into my room. It was reported to my father by the hotel chambermaid, and— but my diary tells it best:

> 'February 17: Papa gave me a whipping for saying he was a doggoned fool and the chambermaid had better go and soak her head in Jip's mouth.'

Even Jip got the message. From then on, he was content to sleep on the carpet of the corridor outside my room.

George and Sarah Getty believed in the work-ethic (which, I fear, has precious few adherents nowadays). Their son had to learn that money was something to be earned:

> 'June 17, 1904: In the afternoon I earned 35 cents by cleaning books for Papa.' (Not as simple a task as it may sound. Father had hundreds of heavy, dust-collecting volumes on the shelves of his law-library.)

Or:

> 'December 15, 1904: In the afternoon I sold the *Saturday Evening Post* and got 50 cents.'*

* *Editor's note:* The *Saturday Evening Post*, long one of America's most popular weekly publications, used boys as door-to-door salesmen, paying them part of the 5-cent-a-copy price as commission.

Withal, I was hardly any paragon of virtue, as became apparent when we moved to Los Angeles and I went to Polytechnic High School. The low marks I received in my studies—and the black marks I received for my deportment—convinced my father that I needed a turn of the disciplinary screw. I was therefore enrolled as a day-student at the Harvard Military Academy. (Located in Los Angeles, it had no connection with Harvard University.) American 'military schools' being loosely patterned after the U.S. Military Academy at West Point, I found myself in a stricter and more regimented environment than I had ever before encountered.

. Gordon Crary was a classmate—and, in later years, he would be my principal stock broker at E. F. Hutton and Company. Gordon and I were originally drawn together by a shared dislike for boot and button polishing and other military school bull. We consequently saw much of each other on punishment fatigue-details. The close friendship we formed lasted until his death in 1962—and has carried over into the friendship I have formed with his son, Gordon Crary Jr.

I gradually adapted to Harvard Military Academy regimen and rules—bar sporadic transgressions, one a memorable milestone. Another classmate and I played truant—went AWOL, in military school jargon—for a dalliance with two willing damsels we had met the previous week at a fiercely chaperoned dance. In my classmate's words, this initiatory experience was everything it was cracked up to be—and then some. I agreed wholeheartedly.

It strikes me that the contrast between theoretical codes of sexual morality and actual practice might be likened to the contrast between Ancient and Modern Greek. Ancient Greek, no matter how well and fluently spoken, is incomprehensible to the people of Greece who speak the modern version. By somewhat the same token, the strait-laced codes of sexual morality we learned by rote when I was young were incompatible with prevailing everyday realities.

I once—in 1964—said as much to Hugh Hefner, the publisher of *Playboy* Magazine (for which I had written a number of articles on business and finance). Hefner, who takes great pride in asserting that his magazine has been a strong influence in liberalizing public attitudes toward sex, was—I fear—chagrined by my remarks. I grinned inwardly, recognizing the reasons for his reaction. Hefner was still in his 30s; I had passed my 71st birthday. Younger people are discomfited by the suggestion that members of their swinging generation are not, after all, the first to have enjoyed amorous adventures while still in their teens.

Graduation from the Harvard Military Academy in June, 1909, completed my high school education. My first summer stint in the oilfields followed. Then my father made a sudden decision to take Mother and me on a tour of Europe. We sailed from New York aboard the S.S. *Baltic*. Stored in the vessel's hold was a new Chadwick touring-car; Father preferred to motor through England and Europe.

Landing in Liverpool, my father hired a chauffeur whose accent was such that at first we were unable to understand anything he said. Slowly, we learned to translate such renderings as 'lookerts' and grasp that this meant 'law courts.'

It was the Edwardian Period, a Golden Age. Passports and visas were unknown; currency-exchange problems did not exist. Wherever we went, there seemed to be a high level of prosperity. There was peace, and people appeared content. The most talked-about subjects were Admiral Robert Peary's conquest of the North Pole and Louis Bleriot's flight across the English Channel from Calais to Dover. True, some wealthier Britons were up in arms over proposed 'soak the rich' taxation measures to finance social security programmes. Seen in retrospect, these were as nothing compared to present-day tax-levies. But in those times, 'thems't 'ave'—as our Liverpudlian chauffeur put it—saw them as sure to cause wrack and ruin.

We made the customary sightseeing trips in England, including one to Oxford, and this was to have a decisive—if delayed—effect on my life. The Gettys and their Chadwick proceeded on to the Continent, touring France, Germany, Holland and Switzerland for three glorious months.

The Chadwick sailed with us for New York and was shipped to Los Angeles by rail. My father let me drive it in the daytime, when he wasn't using it himself. At night, he kept the car in a garage at the back of our family house on Wilshire Boulevard and Kingsley Drive.

In those days, the parents of daughters seemed to feel that 'double-dates' were safe. Young men, as a result, made it a point to hunt in pairs, wherever possible. Their chances of making conquests on their double-dates were greatly enhanced if one or the other had an automobile. (Lest anyone think I am making claims to have been a precocious demon-lover, I hasten to add what is hardly an original observation. The female of the species is far cannier than the male. Men are not seducers; they are only seduced into believing they are.)

My mother and father made a habit of retiring comparatively early in the evening. Some male friend or another and I having made dates with two girls, I would wait until my parents were in bed, steal into the garage and push the Chadwick out into the street, which sloped slightly. Climbing into the driver's seat, I'd allow the car to coast a hundred feet or more until I was far enough from the house so that my father could not hear me start the engine—and I was off.

Returning home—usually in the predawn hours—I parked a block from our house, walked to the garage and opened its doors. Going back to the car, I would start it up again and gather sufficient momentum so that I could switch off the engine and coast silently into the garage. Having previously re-filled the fuel tank to its original level, I turned back the odometer, closed the garage doors and tiptoed into the house.

I did all this on several occasions without my father becoming any the wiser. Such luck could not last indefinitely. Automobile tyres of that period had a life of about 3,000 miles. One day, Father noticed that the Chadwick's tyres were wearing out even though the odometer showed he had driven barely more than a thousand miles.

'They must be faulty,' he said and complained to the dealer from whom he bought the tyres. The dealer made an inspection and opined that the wheels must be out of line. A mechanic checked the wheels and found them to be in perfect alignment. Father confessed he was baffled.

I failed to heed the warning signals. A friend and I had what contemporary idiom described as a double-heavy double-date the following night. I followed my usual procedure, 'borrowing' the Chadwick. My friend and I took our girlfriends to a nightclub. When we left it, we bought a bottle of red wine to take with us. At some point during the return-drive (or, more probably, during the side-of-the-road parking interlude *en route)* one girl spilled wine on the seat covers. I tried to remove the stains without avail, and crossed my fingers hoping my father would never notice them.

Father said nothing the next day, and I relaxed. Obviously, I reasoned, he hadn't seen the wine-stains. I had another double-date scheduled for that night. When my parents had gone up to bed, I went to the garage—where I found the Chadwick's wheels chained to the concrete floor.

After what might be termed a decent interval, I tried a new tack. I doubted that my father would give me the money to buy myself a car, but guessed he would finance me if I built one. I broached the subject to him—careful to avoid mentioning that I intended building a racer—and he approved and agreed to foot the bills.

Renting space in a repair-garage, I bought a Continental engine, Fedders radiator and Apperson clutch and propellor-shaft. (I considered shaft-drive superior to the chain-drive used on many makes of automobiles in those years.) I designed and built the body myself, did my own chassis welding and bolting and even made the wheels. The final product, assembled with a mechanic's help, was a fast, two-seated racer with a very low centre of gravity. Driver and passenger sat with legs out-stretched. For reasons that elude me now, I named the car a 'Plaza Milano.' Father was pleased with the results, and I noted with surprise, a bit envious.

Because of its design, my racer could be made to spin like a top on a wet street. I needed only to put the car in second gear at about twelve miles per hour, cramp the steering wheel and depress the foot-throttle to put the car into a whirling spin.

A family named McNair lived a few doors from our house. There were three McNair daughters. Edith, the oldest, was ten years my senior, but became my particular girlfriend. I considered it a singular distinction to be going out with a woman so much older than I. She was a very sophisticated person, had travelled much abroad, and spoke French. (Her friends, on the other hand, teased her mercilessly that she was a 'baby-snatcher.')

I soon took Edith McNair for a drive in my Plaza Milano, and telling her to hold on tight, demonstrated the spinning trick. Somehow, Edith lost her grip and was thrown from the car. Although she had on a thick lambskin coat, she was wearing a corset—all women did in those days—and as she rolled on the pavement, the stays bruised her black and blue. She was otherwise unhurt, but her parents none the less banned her from riding in my car.

On New Year's Eve in 1910, the ban was finally lifted. I took Edith to the popular Ship Cafe in Venice, a seaside town southeast of Los Angeles. On the way home, I drove at high speed and, while long familiar with the road, forgot about a very sharp curve until it loomed dead ahead. To make the turn was impossible so I held the steering wheel steady, continuing straight ahead. My Plaza Milano handily jumped a ditch and went into a ploughed field beyond.

'Made it!' I exclaimed with relief—a split second before a front wheel snapped off and Edith McNair was again thrown out of the car, to roll head over heels in the ploughed earth. Once more, she was unhurt—except for bruises caused by her corset stays. My car suffered no damage beyond the broken axle. It was towed to a garage the next day and repaired. Edith and I walked to the edge of the road. Minutes later, some friends who had also been to the Ship Cafe drove up, saw us and gave us a lift home. When I delivered Edith to the door of her house, her parents took one look at her dishevelled and dirt-streaked coat and dress—and withered me with their glares. From then on, Edith McNair was permanently and irrevocably banned from riding in any car driven by me.

Automotive escapades aside, I devoted myself to trying to obtain a higher education—first at the University of Southern California in Los Angeles, then at the University of California at Berkeley. I applied myself to the task and obtained good marks, but I was disappointed, bored and felt that I was getting nowhere.

The problems stemmed from faults and flaws in the American—and especially Californian—educational systems. University undergraduates were treated and taught as though they were retarded and totally irresponsible children. We were checked in and out of lecture-rooms—'de-merits' being awarded for absence or tardiness. Our movements and actions in school or out were monitored and closely supervised. Yet the pervasive atmosphere was that of the playground. If one shouted rah-rah loudly and waved pom-poms vigorously at football games and joined the 'right' fraternity or sorority, he or she conformed, fitted and was accepted. As far as I could see, learning was considered an incidental by-product.

What made it worse for me was that I was intent on studying economics and political science. At the time, the United States was still insular, isolationist. The nation had tremendous industrial capacity and sold its products to the entire world, but otherwise it largely ignored what transpired beyond its borders or, at very most, outside the Western Hemisphere.

After all, hadn't George Washington warned America against becoming involved with foreign powers?

Besides—American Indians excepted—weren't all Americans immigrants or the descendants of immigrants? Why had immigrants left their homes in the British Isles and Europe and come to America? Because they wished to enjoy greater freedom and a better life, that's why. Hence, it stood to reason that the Old World was bad—and as long as the bad was on the other side of an ocean, it could be easily disregarded.

Consequently, economics courses focused on American economics and were, for the most part, designed to prove that the American Way had no peers. As for political science, both textbooks and instructors tended to be equally chauvinistic and even more naive. The typical professor's *Weltanschauung* encompassed little beyond Canada, Mexico and our own—and but recently acquired—colonial empire. (Needless to say, we Americans piously avoided calling it that.)

In April, 1912, I threw in the towel. I told my parents that I felt the kind and quality of education I wanted was only available abroad—at Oxford University, then by far the leading centre of learning in the English-speaking world. My father and mother conceded that I might be right.

'But I'd like to get the feel of the Orient first,' I added.

In May, I left for a two months' tour of Japan and China, a trip to which I'll refer again. July through September were spent working on the Lot 50 lease in Oklahoma. In November, I sailed for England.

As an amusing postscript, just before I left Los Angeles for New York, my father confirmed my suspicion that he was envious of my Plaza Milano. He asked if he could drive it 'every now and then' during my absence. I naturally said yes. And so, to the consternation of all who knew him, for two years George F. Getty Sr. drove to and from his office daily in the snazzy, low-slung racing car I had built.

8

IT NEVER CEASES to amaze me that there are still so-called 'educators' who view the University of Oxford as (to quote words they've used in my hearing) 'an academic anarchy' and 'a miscellany of colleges in search of a university.'

A distinguished American university official who visited me not long ago on a fund-raising mission went even further.

'We operate our institution with a tightly controlled organization,' he boasted. 'Our administration is governed by rules very much like those of an efficient corporation. There's none of the lax management that characterizes so many universities— Oxford being an extreme example, as you probably know, Mr. Getty.'

'Interesting,' I said, my hackles rising, but refrained from carrying the issue further. By then, my main interest was to have this particular visitor take his leave with all possible speed.

True, the University of Oxford scarcely exists apart from its constituent colleges, each enjoying almost total autonomy within an administrative framework whose main substance is tradition. This, paradoxical as it may seem, imparts strength rather than implying weakness. At the Oxford I knew, there was complete academic freedom, and the student was afforded unparalleled opportunity and latitude to learn.

To learn—not to be taught.

That was the secret.

Under Oxford's tutorial system, the student received every encouragement and aid to investigate, seek out information, then to absorb and digest it and make his own interpretations and reach his own conclusions. This led not merely to acquisition of knowledge. It provided stimulus and means for the student's overall intellectual development. In short, he was not taught *what* to think, but given guidance in learning how to use his mind. I owe much to my two terms at Oxford.

I desired to read economics and political science. Some of the leading tutors and lecturers in these fields were at Magdalen College. I went there with a letter of introduction and recommendation signed by President William Howard Taft, who was a friend of my father. I suspect it was the first time Warren, the President of Magdalen,* had an American appear in his office carrying a letter from the President of the United States. However, I have strenuous doubts that this played any part in influencing the brilliant—and unflappable—Herbert Warren's decisions regarding me. He read the letter, nodded politely, and put it aside.

'Umm—well, now,' he said. 'Suppose we have a chat.'

The 'chat' proved to be a masterly, low-keyed—but indepth—probe into my knowledge level, motivation and general attitudes. Naturally, tea was served during our dialogue.

I matriculated as a non-collegiate student at Oxford. My tutor was at Magdalen and although I had rented digs located above an antique shop at 14 The High, it turned out that I more or less lived at Magdalen.

Many people seem to have a greatly distorted picture of Oxford University. They imagine it to be a sort of superfinishing school for snobs, prigs and decadent aristocrats. Certainly this is not true now, and it wasn't true in my time, either. Indeed, from some viewpoints, Oxford seemed much more democratic than the University of California at Berkeley, an institution supported entirely by public funds.

There were many social divisions and much class-consciousness in the two California universities I had attended. The major and impenetrable barrier separating the Ins from

---

* *Editor's note:* (Thomas) Herbert Warren was president of Magdalen College from 1885 until 1928 and Vice Chancellor of Oxford University from 1906 until 1910. In 1914, he was knighted, being awarded the K.C.V.O.

the Outs was the 'Org'—'Non-Org' line. Those who belonged (more properly, could afford to belong) to fraternities and sororities were socially IN. All others were OUT. Beyond this, there was much further stratification. One's social standing depended largely on the relative status (determined by the exclusivity and expensiveness) of the fraternity or sorority to which one belonged. (I, incidentally, had stayed 'Non-Org,' but then, I have never been much of a membership-card collector.)

While social life at Oxford was far more formal than in American universities, snobs and snobbishness inspired contempt. This was reflected in a doggerel verse jeeringly recited by Oxford students. It began: 'I am George Nathaniel Curzon/A very superior person/I dine at Blenheim once a week . . .'

More to my personal point, it must be remembered that I was an American and—save for a brief brush in 1909—unfamiliar with Britain and British manners and mores. None the less, the men at Magdalen accepted me as one of their number and on my own merits. The fact that I was the son of a wealthy man had no bearing. In the first place, my father had set strict limits on my budget. In the second, many of my fellow-students came from families with infinitely greater fortunes than my father then had. Finally, it was not simply a social gaffe but THE unpardonable sin to talk about the wealth of one's own family—or that of any other student and his family.

The first close friend I made at Magdalen was George Dawson-Damer, brother of the present Earl of Portarlington. I was to feel a deep sense of loss when, a few years later, George fell on the battlefield in France.

Underscoring the genuineness of the absence of class-distinctions at Oxford was my introduction to His Royal Highness, the Prince of Wales, who was also at Magdalen. We—for some reason—took an instant liking to each other and were to meet frequently at luncheons, dinners and social affairs of one kind or another. We called each other 'David' and 'Paul' and formed a close, warm friendship that was to endure for almost half a century. It lasted through the years when he became King, abdicated to marry Mrs. Wallis Simpson (by odd coincidence, I knew her husband, Ernest Simpson quite well) and to the end of his life as the Duke of Windsor. There is a great deal I will have to say about the

Duke of Windsor in a later chapter; at the moment, I had best return to Oxford.

I made many friends at Oxford—but that was a long time ago, and most of them are now gone; some, like George Dawson-Damer, were fated to die soon after leaving the University in the 1914–18 war. I enjoyed a full and exhilarating social life with these friends. We often went to London together—attending the theatre, dinner-parties, balls. I was frequently invited to the homes of my fellow-students. Their homes were frequently stately country manors which, in that last blaze of the Edwardian era, were still at the height of their splendour. I even visited Blenheim Palace—but, unlike George Nathaniel Curzon in the verse, can lay no claim to having dined there at all, much less once a week.

Did I fall in love with England and the English way of life at that point in my life? No, I can't honestly say my responses were that strong. But there was no question in my mind that I liked England and the English people. Perhaps their strongest attraction and appeal was that they were so highly civilized. Although the Britain of today is a far cry from that of 1912, much of that civilized quality remains—at least in comparison to the rest of the world. It's as Arthur Koestler stated recently. Britain's 'atmosphere still contains fewer germs of aggression and brutality per cubic foot in a crowded bus, pub or queue than any other country in which I have lived.'

Oxford was, for me, an ideal place to study. Students were considered and treated as mature, responsible individuals, not as untrustworthy adolescents. The underlying philosophy was that if a student desired an education, he would obtain it without constant, niggling supervision. I remember my surprise that tutors recommended—or merely suggested—attendance at certain lectures, but this was not mandatory.

'If you're brilliant enough to pass your examinations without once attending a lecture, fine,' my own tutor told me during our first discussion. 'Even better than fine,' he added dryly. 'Since no one has ever quite managed that trick before.'

Responsibility for making a success or failure of my studies lay entirely with me. It was powerful incentive, and any serious student quickly developed the art of self-discipline—something I, for one, have found invaluable ever since.

There was much emphasis on sports at Oxford—but again, no one pushed or pressured. After my experience at two California universities, it was refreshing—and a relief—not to be constantly exhorted to 'go out' for this or that sport or 'get on' some kind of team. Students could enjoy sports for their own sake. In this spirit, I could cheerfully engage in my own favourites: swimming, boxing and weight-lifting.

The British Empire was at the peak of its power. Britain exercised control over a very large segment of the world's population and land area, and its influence was felt far beyond its dominions and colonies. And Britain—or, more specifically, London—was the financial, commercial and shipping capital of the world.

Men like Henry Palmerston, Benjamin Disraeli and William Gladstone—and their illustrious predecessors and successors—had refined the art of international politics to the peak level that had not only built Empire but created *Pax Brittanica*. British economists, financiers and businessmen were accustomed to thinking in global terms, and they had a clear comprehension of economic forces and factors.

It followed that Oxford textbooks and lecturers could and did offer the broadest, yet most sharply focused, view on international politics and economics. My interest in the subjects turned into fascination, which caused my capacity for absorbing information to soar. The more I learned, the more strongly I wished to enter the U.S. Diplomatic Service. Of course, I was to become a businessman rather than a diplomat, but what I learned at Oxford has been used to great advantage throughout my business career.

Taking my examinations in June, 1913, I passed them and received a non-collegiate diploma in Economics and Political Science. Now quite sure of my Diplomatic Service ambitions, I recognized a once-in-a-lifetime opportunity to observe at first hand how the theories I had learned worked in actual operation. I wrote my father telling him I wished to take a long trip across Europe, on into Russia, then down into the Balkans and parts of the Middle East. I wanted to visit political capitals and industrial and commercial centres—as well as get the 'feel' of the countries and gain insight into their people.

Father replied, approving. He enclosed a bank-draft for $200, the sum he set as my monthly allowance. Additional drafts would be sent each month to the American Express office in whichever city was indicated in my itinerary. Soon afterward, I left for the Continent.

Many years later, I read this passage in James Hilton's book, *Lost Horizon:*

'When the High Lama asked him whether Shangri-la was not unique in his experience, and if the Western world could offer anything in the least like it, he answered with a smile: "Well, yes—to be quite frank, it reminds me very slightly of Oxford." '

Hyperbole?

Perhaps.

But then hyperbole is defined as rhetorical exaggeration designed to emphasize, not to deceive.

9

BERLIN, THE FIRST stop on my Continental itinerary, had a pervasive air of chip-on-the-shoulder arrogance. Prussian *offiziers* swaggered far more insolently than I had seen four years earlier. Soldiers and civilians alike talked incessantly of an imminent 'day of reckoning' and of Germany's 'sacred right to a place in the sun.' At first, I shrugged it all off as merely echoing Kaiser Wilhelm II's widely-publicized bellicose utterances, which most of the world ridiculed as empty bluster. Then I travelled through Germany. Military uniforms were ubiquitous. In Hamburg and the main German naval base at Kiel great numbers of new warships were in evidence, and shipyards were feverishly building more.

'Willie Hohenzollern may, after all, have something up the sleeve of the arm he keeps hidden behind his back,' I wrote to my former tutor at Magdalen. I imagine he considered me both callow and cheeky. Who was I to cast doubts on the conventional wisdom that there could be no war in the enlightened Twentieth Century?

Denmark, serene and prosperous, was a powerful antidote for pessimism. The Danish social and political systems were democratic, and they functioned smoothly and efficiently. The friendly and hospitable Danes were industriously engaged in peaceful pursuits.

Coincidence dogs anyone who travels much and lives long. In the early 1960s, largely at the behest of the Danish Government, the Getty interests built, and for a time operated, an oil refinery in Denmark. It was located at Kalundborg on the island of Sjaelland—by a quirk of fate, on the site where I enjoyed a picnic lunch with Danish friends in the summer of 1913. The area was then an open, unspoiled beach; the needs of Danish economy later transformed it into an industrial zone. This, in microcosm, reflects the dilemma causing so much friction between environmentalists and industrialists (who, I feel constrained to say, are by no means all inveterate Nature-rapers).

Such use of virgin lands is regrettable. But there is no alternative if industry and governments are to satisfy rising consumer demands. New industrial plants—be they oil refineries or candy factories—can only be built on land that is available, has ready access to transportation facilities and is zoned for the purpose.

Sweden provided more refreshing revelations. It is one thing to read textbooks and study statistics, quite another to see the realities they describe. Even in 1913, the Swedish educational system was one of the world's best; there was virtually no illiteracy in the country. (By sharp, shocking contrast I have recently seen figures which suggest that *today* the United States may have a five per cent actual, and a fifteen per cent functional, illiteracy rate.)

I marvelled at the remarkable industrial structure the Swedes had fashioned out of their three chief natural resources: timber, iron-ore and water power, and at their ingenuity as farmers. Although less than one-eighth of their land area was arable, the level of their agricultural efficiency was astonishingly high. And, sampling the famed Swedish aquavit, I unhesitatingly conceded its potency to surpass even the strongest 'White Lightning' made by Oklahoma moonshiners!

Crossing the Gulf of Bothnia to Abo, Finland (then an autonomous grand duchy of the Russian Empire), I continued on to Helsingfors. While the Finns were no less industrious than the Danes or Swedes and there was outward calm, one could sense underlying dissatisfaction. Fiercely independent, the Finns chafed at being even nominally under Russian control.

*   *   *

In those days, Russia was the only European country that required foreigners to have passports and visas for entry. I had both and went to St. Petersburg, where I remained while learning the rudiments of Russian and forming my first impressions which, overall, were not encouraging. A national inertia was apparent, due more to Tsarist bureaucracy than Tsarist autocracy. The bureaucratic apparatus exerted a pernicious influence in every sphere of Russian life. It sapped the Empire's vitality with its rules and regulations, its forms and stamps and seals and by the incredibly slow pace at which it operated. It is not, I might glumly parenthesize, too difficult to find dishearteningly close parallels in many countries in our present day and age.

There was much discontent in Russia—yet, at the same time, a marked and universal resigned acceptance. I began to comprehend what so many observers meant when they spoke of the Russians' 'brooding fatalism' and *'Nichevo'* philosophy. None the less, the Russians were lavishly generous.

At one end of the scale, this was demonstrated by a young Russian Prince who was my travelling companion on a long steamer voyage down the Volga. When we arrived in Baku, I was low on funds; my monthly allowance cheque was snagged in some postal service bottleneck. My friend insisted on lending me money so we could continue our travels together. I demurred; there was no telling when my cheque would catch up with me.

'Nichevo,' he shrugged, thrusting a large wad of rouble-notes into my hands. Not until I reached Vienna weeks later did I get my father's forwarded cheques and only then was the loan repaid.

At the other end of the scale, endemic Russian generosity was displayed in the Volga towns and villages where I went ashore. Being a foreign visitor, I was deluged with invitations to visit homes and eat and drink. Whenever I left, gifts of food and vodka were pressed on me—on the all-too-valid grounds that these were essential supplements to the dull and skimpy fare served aboard the limping Volga steamer.

The most lasting souvenirs I collected during this trip through Russia were the traditional songs I learned. Long afterwards, I became friends with Prince Felix Youssoupoff,*

* *Editor's note.* Widely credited with having led the group of Russian noblemen who assassinated the notorious 'monk', Gregory Rasputin, on December 31, 1916.

who had a limitless repertoire of Russian songs. I last met him in Paris on April 28, 1959, and as my diary entry for the day shows: 'Had a real Russian dinner with Prince Felix. He is 73, but doesn't look or act it. He played the balalaika and we sang old Russian songs for hours.' It delighted Prince Felix—and astounded me—that I still remembered the words and melodies.

Incidentally, I made another visit to Russia—in 1935, but there was precious little singing to be heard then. The country had suffered through war, then revolution, then civil war and famine to become the Union of Soviet Socialist Republics. I have dismal memories of my introduction to this supposed egalitarian paradise in a grim, indescribably depressing Moscow. One incident out of many illustrates why I became quickly disillusioned by the Wave of the Future.

There were almost no ordinary passenger automobiles to be seen. Paradoxically there were goodly numbers of chauffeured limousines—by some perverted twist of egalitarian doctrine, almost all allocated to Party officials and government functionaries. However, a State-owned agency had a few which it rented to foreign tourists. I hired one.

The streets were awash with icy slush, mud and water. My Russian chauffeur seemed to derive sadistic pleasure from driving so that he would splatter—better yet, drench—pedestrians with this muck. None—not one—of the victims ever changed expression, much less shouted protest or shook a fist. Terror had been laminated on to Russian fatalism. No Muscovite dared show anger out of fear that I, the limousine's occupant, might be a commissar or a secret police official.

Still, there was much in the nature of the ordinary Soviet citizen that inspired admiration, respect and confidence—and I said so in 1941, when the Nazis invaded Russia. Predictably enough, some of my Russian emigré friends considered this rank heresy. David Mdivani (of the 'Marrying Mdivanis') was among them. He prophesied a quick Russian defeat and collapse of the Communist regime. I disagreed, with the results shown by these two diary entries:

'September 13, 1941: David Mdivani offered to bet me $100 that the Nazis would be inside Leningrad within a month. I took him up on it.'

'November 19, 1941: Ran into Mdivani. He paid the $100

on our bet. I'm not sure if he's disappointed because the Reds haven't been beaten or secretly proud of the stand they're making.'

Baku, Yalta and eventually Vienna. Once more the language was German, but spoken in soft accents. Once more military uniforms, but the men wearing them were a far cry from the Prussians in Berlin. I suppose it was only appropriate that their attitudes made one think they were all from the cast of a Johann Strauss or Franz Lehár operetta. *Gemütlichkeit* was the Austro–Hungarian Empire's way of life; not many wished to see the happy pattern disturbed.

Budapest was even more carefree—and since all the world seems to enjoy Hungarian stories, I'm moved to contribute a few of my own.

Some days after arriving in Budapest, I dined with a party of Hungarian Hussar subalterns and several lovely young ladies; all spoke English ranging from the fair to the fluent. At one point, a girl unexpectedly asked her escort, a lieutenant in full aigleted regalia: 'What would you do in a war, Lasalo?' The question stunned him.

'War?' he almost gasped. 'Why, that would ruin everything for everyone!'

Another officer raised his glass. 'I know what I shall do if there is ever a war,' he declared solemnly. 'I will set an example of courage for my men by drinking myself to death—heroically.'

The young woman I was with laughed. 'Now you see the truth,' she said. 'We Hungarians are all quite mad.'

Not very long ago, I related the story to Zsa Zsa Gabor.

'But of course, darling,' Zsa Zsa nodded, keeping her beautiful face straight. 'Madness is the Hungarian national conceit.'

Which leads me to a further Magyar detour. The Hungarian-born actor, Béla Lugosi, and I were guests at a Hollywood party given by my friend, composer Igor Stravinsky in—if memory serves—1939.

'How is everything with you?' Igor asked Lugosi.

Lugosi gave him a morose look. 'Terrible,' he said in his famous Count Dracula accent. 'The studios are not satisfied that I am a Hungarian and a genius. I must also act in their films.'

But then, I know another Béla who blandly avows himself to be a 'professional Hungarian.' He says it is a lucrative occupation.

Belgrade, Bucharest—and the Black Sea port of Constanza, where I booked passage for Constantinople. I spent several weeks in Turkey, the centre of the Ottoman Empire that included Syria, Lebanon, Iraq, Jordan, Palestine, Arabia and Yemen. Sultan Mehmed V ruled, but the Empire was shaky, sustained mainly by memories of past glories.

Again, coincidence. During the 1950s, Aristotle Onassis and I formed what grew to be a close friendship and association in several business ventures. When I told Ari that I had been in Smyrna, a Turkish city with a very large Greek population in December, 1913, and reminisced about my favourite cafe there, he did a classic double-take. He had lived in Smyrna until 1922, Ari said, adding: 'As a kid, I went by that cafe several times a day—yes, even in December, 1913.'

Very probably, the young Aristotle Onassis often passed within feet of the window-table where I sat sipping Turkish coffee or *raki*. From Smyrna to Greece, a country in perpetual political ferment. But my attention was drawn from politics by the breathtaking beauties of Ancient Greece and especially of Ancient Greek sculpture. It was the beginning of a life-long passion. After I became an established businessman, I could afford to buy and collect Greek sculpture—including examples of the Elgin Marbles. Among them was *Myttion*, a unique and exquisite 4th Century B.C. sepulchural stele, and one of the few pieces of art known to arouse great emotional reaction in that dean of art historians and critics, Bernard Berenson.

A guest at *I Tatti*, near Florence, in 1953, I showed Berenson a photograph of *Myttion*. He studied the photograph, fascinated.

'Come here—hurry!' he called to one of his associates. 'Here is a magnificent piece! I only wish that I owned it!'

I spent December 15, 1913—my twenty-first birthday—aboard a decrepit 3,000-ton Rumanian steamer bound for Alexandria, Egypt. The ship ran head on into one of those particularly savage storms that strike without warning in the Mediterranean during winter months. Captain and crew were hopeless incompetents; the vessel often came close to foundering, but somehow survived, although its lifeboats were torn away and the inside of the ship was a waterlogged shambles.

Two months were scarcely sufficient to view properly the awe-inspiring monuments and relics of ancient Egyptian civilizations, but in February, I sailed for Gibraltar. The experience aboard the Rumanian hulk still very fresh in my mind, I decided to play safe and I took the large, superbly equipped and manned Cunarder, *Franconia*. From Gibraltar, I made an overland tour of Spain—which, much to my surprise, extended into April.

Now, as a schoolboy, I had learned about Inquisition and Armada, *Conquistadores* and their exterminations of Aztecs and Incas. I was exposed to the virulent anti-Spanish propaganda that inundated the United States during—and for years after—the 1898 Spanish–American War. Even in 1905, one of my Minneapolis schoolteachers was constantly reciting such lines as these from Tennyson's *Revenge:* 'I should count myself the coward, if I left them, my Lord Howard/To these Inquisition dogs and the devildoms of Spain.'

Perhaps it was reaction against such propaganda (or a distaste for Tennyson's treacly verse). In any event, like countless others, I fell in love with Spain and its people. The country has a quality—frequently remarked—that intrigues and fascinates. Its landscapes are no less beautiful for often being stark and severe. The people have an inner strength; Spaniards in all walks of life possess pride and dignity and a strong sense of honour. In these regards, I believe them to be closer lineal descendants of the Ancient Romans than any other Mediterranean races or nationalities.

April, 1914, in Paris was all that the song written much later proclaims April in Paris to be. The main—indeed, almost sole—topic of conversation was *l'affaire* Caillaux, the juiciest scandal France had known for decades.

Gaston Calmette, editor of *Le Figaro*, had publicly accused the French Finance Minister, Joseph Caillaux, of financial irregularities in office. Caillaux denied the charges and fought back, filing legal actions against the editor. Calmette, who apparently did not have evidence to back the accusations, felt cornered. Desperately seeking an escape-hatch, he resorted to blackmail. He had some lurid letters Joseph Caillaux's wife had written. He informed Mme. Caillaux he would publish these unless she prevailed upon her husband to withdraw the legal actions he had started. Whereupon—on March 16, 1914—Mme. Caillaux went to Gaston Calmette's *Figaro* office and, taking a pistol from her handbag, shot him dead.

Naturally, she was arrested for murder—and all Paris breathlessly awaited further revelations (and on days when there were none, invented them). As anyone acquainted with Gallic mentality and temperament would guess, Mme. Caillaux was later tried and acquitted—to the plaudits of the multitudes.

The Caillaux case aside, nothing marred the Spring or first week of summer—even the weather was the best in any Frenchman's memory. I readily succumbed to the general euphoria, savouring all I could of Parisian life.

In the third week of June, my mother and father arrived in Paris. They planned another European tour, with me as their guide to show them some of what I had discovered during my year of roaming. They intended a long stay in Paris, though, and I took them to theatres, concerts, art galleries and museums. Then, on Sunday, June 28, I left them to their own devices and went with a group of friends to see the running of the Grand Prix at the Bois de Boulogne race-track.

We had an excellent box, only about twenty yards distant from the one occupied by M. Raymond Poincaré, the President of France, and his party. The third race on the card had just been run when there was a considerable commotion around M. Poincaré's box. My friends and I watched with great interest as a messenger, flanked by uniformed *gendarmes*, handed the President an envelope encrusted with wax seals. M. Poincaré opened it, read the message inside and, his face paling, hastily left his box.

Such was the temper of the times that my friends and I—and all who had seen the tableau—agreed that there must have been some spectacular development in the Caillaux case. What else could be *that* important?

'Madame Caillaux has committed suicide—I'm sure of it', one young lady in our party theorized.

'Nonsense!' another disagreed. 'It must be that they've found proof that Joseph Caillaux is really guilty of what Calmette claimed!'

The speculations continued until the next race began. Then

we turned our attention to horses and track and forgot the incident. Only when we saw the headlines in the late afternoon newspapers did we learn what was in the message delivered to M. Poincaré. The Austrian Crown Prince, Archduke Franz Ferdinand, and his wife had been assassinated by Serbian terrorists in Serajevo.

Even then, patterns of life remained normal and complacent in Paris. During the weeks that followed, stories on *l'affaire* Caillaux and Mme. Caillaux's trial took precedence over dispatches indicating a growing threat of war.

'*La guerre? C'est impossible!*'

That was the consensus.

One month—to the day—after the assassinations in Serajevo, Austria declared war on Serbia. On August 1, Germany declared war on Russia, two days later on France. The next day, when Germany refused to guarantee Belgian neutrality, the British Government reluctantly issued a declaration of war against Germany.

The impossible had happened. Europe was at war. Now there was a new consensus—the same on each side. Having begun, it was impossible that the war would last more than six months. The enemy—whichever the enemy was—would be completely crushed by then, if not sooner.

My parents and I went to England. We waited there through the unbelievable days in which German armies blasted their way across Belgium and deep into France. It was not until September 12, 1914, that we sailed for the United States. By then, the First Battle of the Marne had been fought, and it was obvious the war could not end in six months. But no one yet dreamed it would last more than four years.

10

No RATIONAL PERSON today doubts that the responsibility for starting the 1914–18 war lies squarely with Kaiser Wilhelm II and his ministers and advisers. Even such eminent German historians as Fritz Fischer have conceded this. The overwhelming mass of evidence was recently summed up by Hugh Trevor-Roper in these words: ' . . . in 1914, Germany alone showed a consistent will to aggressive war and had consistent plans of conquest.'

Unfortunately, once the Allies won the war, they demonstrated a consistent lack of will to make a just and lasting peace and their consistent policies and actions made World War Two inevitable. Granted that it was Hitler's *Wehrmacht* that invaded Poland and went on to ravage and destroy one country after another. In that immediate sense, the guilt for World War Two lies with Nazi Germany. But the original sins were committed at Paris, Versailles and Geneva by the governments of France, Italy, Great Britain and the United States—or, more properly, by the men heading those governments.

U.S. President Woodrow Wilson framed his Fourteen Points as a basis for peace. An ivory-tower academician with little if any grasp of political realities, Wilson went to the Paris Peace Conference after the Armistice with high hopes and ideals. He was totally incapable of standing up against tough, cynical men like French Premier Georges Clemenceau and British Prime Minister David Lloyd George. Clemenceau,

David Lloyd George and Vittorio Orlando, the Italian Prime Minister, were bent on taking vengeance against Germany and thereby gaining political credit in their own countries. They looked upon Wilson as a woolly-headed amateur who could be manipulated with ease.

Before Wilson arrived, David Lloyd George asked Clemenceau and Orlando: 'Should we not make it clear to the German Government that we are not going in (to the Peace Conference) on the Fourteen Points?'

Georges Clemenceau's documented comment: 'We will squeeze Germany until the pips squeak.'

Wilson was no match for such 'allies', particularly since he was greatly influenced by 'Colonel' Edward M. House. Even Bernie Baruch, one of Woodrow Wilson's most indefatigable apologists (Baruch was a member of the American delegation to the Peace Conference) was forced to admit that House was a '. . . mysterious, always controversial figure . . . who became the *eminence grise* of the Wilson Administration.'

When the Paris Peace Conference began, Germany had taken its first, faltering steps toward becoming a democracy. The first German Chancellor in the new Weimar Republic was Friedrich Ebert, a Social Democrat and a pacifist. Practical considerations alone would have dictated that the Allies support Ebert, give him latitude and means to bring order out of postwar chaos in Germany and nurture a true, strong democracy. Tragically, the 'make the pips squeak' approach prevailed among the Allies. Wilson, intimidated and out-manoeuvred by Clemenceau, out-talked by David Lloyd George—and nagged by Col. House—allowed the key provisions of his vaunted Fourteen Points to be discarded.

The end-product of the Peace Conference was the Versailles Treaty, which was presented to Chancellor Ebert on a take-it-or-leave-it basis. If he left it, Ebert was informed, the Allies would reopen hostilities. Germany signed.

The Versailles Treaty was vindictive. Impossible reparations payments were imposed on Germany. The sum went into the billions of gold marks; even the most obtuse student of economics could have readily seen this was certain to wreck completely the already barely functioning German economy. Worse, the punitive provisions of the treaty guaranteed violent nationalistic reaction inside Germany. A gallant and determined leader, Friedrich Ebert managed to suppress the early manifestations—including the Kapp *Putsch* and Adolf Hitler's first (1923) attempt to establish a dictatorship in Bavaria.

Ebert could excise tumours. He could not remove the poisons that caused them. These were injected into the German mainstream by the Versailles Treaty, and Germany's lunatic-fringe extremists took full advantage. Although Hitler was jailed for nine months, upon his release he began to attract more and ever more converts to his National Socialist German Workers'—Nazi—Party.

By 1932, the Nazis had gained considerable strength, but were still well short of a majority in the German *Reichstag*. Many German politicians and outside observers foresaw the grave threat the Nazis posed. Were they to gain power, Germany would become an even greater menace to world peace than Wilhelmine Germany. Most concerned of all was the then-German Chancellor, Heinrich Bruning—who, like Ebert, was a moderate, a pacifist and a firm believer in democratic principles.

A Disarmament Conference was convened in Geneva in 1932. History was to repeat itself, but with a different cast of characters. The main power-players now were French Premier André Tardieu, British Prime Minister Ramsay MacDonald and Italian Foreign Minister Dino Grandi. The wartime Allies now had a second chance to insure peace.

German Chancellor Bruning knew he could kick the props out from under Hitler and his Nazis by obtaining a few concessions for Germany at Geneva. He purposely kept his proposals modest, but was certain that even these would be sufficient to reverse the German political trend. In German eyes, success would be seen as a major triumph for the democratic government Bruning headed—and if democracy could obtain results, what need was there for Nazis and Nazism?

The second—and last—chance the Allies had was lost. The delegates to the Geneva Conference—most particularly André Tardieu—rejected the German proposals. Bruning returned to Berlin empty-handed.

Hitler and his supporters made immense political capital out of Bruning's 'failure'. They derided him as inept, impotent and thundered that they could do better. Heinrich Bruning resigned as an alternative to being thrown out of office.* Franz von Papen was briefly installed as a puppet Chancellor— and then Adolf Hitler took over. The moment he was in power, Hitler thumbed his nose at the Allies—and the entire world—and seized infinitely more than Bruning had ever dreamed of obtaining. What followed needs no detailed recounting here. Hitler and his Nazis went from one power-grab— and one horror—to another until they finally plunged the world into the holocaust of the second, and truly global, war of the Twentieth Century.

I contend that a more reasonable and just peace than that imposed by the Versailles Treaty would have enabled a firmly democratic system to develop and thrive in Germany between 1919 and 1932. It certainly would have made the emergence of a Hitler and a Nazi Party improbable, if not impossible. I further maintain that, having missed the boat once, the Allies could have caught it the second time around at Geneva. Had they granted Bruning even minimal concessions at Geneva, Hitler would never have become Chancellor—and then dictator.

While this is a statement of my personal convictions, it is also in the nature of a preface to some very definite and unequivocal remarks I have long desired to make publicly about my friend, the Duke of Windsor. The connection will become apparent presently.

Millions of words have been written about the Duke of Windsor, the vast majority by people who did not know him—in most cases had never so much as seen him in person, much less met and talked with him. In recent years, it has become fashionable to cast aspersions on his nature, character and personality. A favoured sport practiced by some sources with motives most charitably described by that omnibus adjective, ulterior, has been to suggest that he was not only somewhat less than a patriotic Englishman, but that he was a pro-Nazi.

It is conveniently forgotten that David—as Prince of Wales—served with the B.E.F. in Flanders, in France and on the Italian Front during the 1914–18 war. It is even more conveniently forgotten that during 1919–1925, he toured the world,

---

* *Editor's note:* Ex-Chancellor Heinrich Bruning went to the United States a few years after his resignation. From 1939 until 1952 he taught Government at Harvard University. He returned to Germany for a period and taught at the University of Cologne. His last years were spent in Norwich, Vermont (in the United States), where he died in 1970.

visiting almost fifty countries, a roving ambassador who greatly enhanced Britain's image abroad and made countless millions of friends for Great Britain. Nor do his detractors choose to recall the squalid, behind-the-scenes machinations that forced his abdication on the pretext that he intended marrying Wallis Warfield Simpson, a—heaven forbid!—divorcee. There is ample evidence to indicate that he was not wanted as King Edward VIII because he would have been much too popular a monarch to suit the purposes of certain political wire-pullers. My friend, Max Aitken—Lord Beaverbrook—was one who fought against the abdication, and as he told me:

'Some of the scurviest figures in British politics wanted to be rid of David. They were afraid of the great appeal he had for people of every social level in Britain and the Colonies. Churchill and I did all we could—but the political leadership of the time forced the issue.'

As I have previously mentioned, David and I became friends at Magdalen, when he was Prince of Wales. At this point, I fear I must take issue with some self-appointed 'experts' on the life of the Duke of Windsor. He is alleged to have thrown his weight about at Oxford, demanding that he be addressed as 'Sir'. I never witnessed—nor even heard of—any incidents to support such a claim and, needless to say, they would have been much discussed by other students if they had occurred. As for David's purportedly less-than-brilliant showing at Oxford, there is another side to the coin. Even then, he displayed an uncanny clarity of vision—and wisdom—in the field of world affairs.

In our many conversations, often lasting until three a.m. or later, David showed himself to be a remarkable—if, in his own land unheeded and unhonoured—prophet. Among all the Britons I knew in 1912–13, he alone recognized the menace posed by his cousin, German Kaiser Wilhelm II. (David called him 'a braggart capable of any outrage to bolster his self-esteem and prestige.')

I was astonished one evening in 1912 when David grimly predicted: 'I'm afraid there will be war. Europe is moving steadily toward it. The politicians refuse to see the obvious.'

Although I was to remember the words later, at the time, I wrote them off as products of an overactive imagination, for no one else held even vaguely similar views before June, 1914. But, in retrospect, such statements explain why Oxford dons gave as their verdict that the Prince of Wales 'would never be a British Solomon.' David's ideas and perceptions did not conform to those fixed by consensus—an offense permitted to eccentric undergraduates, but unpardonable in a Prince of Wales, who was expected to be the very embodiment of the Establishment.

David's foresight was no less clear at the time of the 1918 Armistice. He sought to lobby for a just peace settlement with the new, democratic Germany. In a constitutional monarchy, he could do no more than that—lobby, seek to persuade. Even this was adjudged excessive meddling in some quarters. Indeed, there is basis for belief that the Prince of Wales was originally sent off on his global goodwill missions to prevent him from spreading such heretical gospels further in David Lloyd George's Britain. The tactic backfired, for his tours gained the Prince of Wales enormous personal popularity at home and abroad. Unfortunately, this in turn aroused yet greater resentment against him among cynical and self-seeking politicians.

David fully comprehended the implications of Allied intransigence at the Paris Peace Conference and the Geneva Disarmament Conference. Many years later, he and I both happened to be in the South of France and spent considerable time in each other's company. He had strong feelings on the subject even then.

'We made dreadful mistakes, bungled horribly in Paris and Geneva,' he said to me. 'When I became King, I was helpless to undo any of it, for all policies were made and carried out by the elected government. Whenever I dropped as much as a hint, Baldwin* got his back up. Then, after I abdicated, I resolved to make every effort possible as an individual holding no official position.'

A bit of explanation is in order here. David had a great affinity for Austria (not Germany, as has been so widely misrepresented). He loved Austrian music and food and spoke German fluently, with a perfect Austrian accent. Now, it must be remembered that Adolf Hitler was an Austrian rather than a German and known to unbend with anyone who

---

* *Editor's note:* Stanley Baldwin (First Earl Baldwin of Bewley); British Prime Minister, 1935–37. Generally conceded to have been one of the prime-movers behind the abdication of Edward VIII.

spoke Austrian-accented German and was intimately acquainted with Austria and its customs. Furthermore, as the record shows, until about 1938, Hitler viewed the British Royal Family with something approaching reverential awe. David decided to capitalize on these elements.

'In October, 1937, I went to Germany. My purpose was to establish communication with Hitler personally. I hoped he might—just might, mind you—be made to see some reason. At the very outside, I thought such a dialogue could buy time before Hitler moved against Europe and Britain, as something more than mere instinct told me he would, sooner or later.'

It is significant that Stanley Baldwin had been urged to do the same, confer with Hitler, by members of his own party. But Baldwin did not like to travel outside the British Isles. Lord Beaverbrook once voiced his theories about this to me.

'Baldwin feared that if he left Britain for even a few days, his cronies might add their own seasonings to the personal political fish he was eternally frying.'

The Duke of Windsor continued his account.

'Another consideration uppermost in my mind was the plight of Germany's Jewish population. It seemed imperative to me—if not, I'm afraid, to anyone in Whitehall at the time—that something had to be done toward saving them from Nazi persecutions.'

Again, I feel justified in interjecting my own comments. The most scurrilous charge levelled against the Duke and Duchess of Windsor is that they harboured anti-semitic feelings. Were it not so grave, the accusation would be hilarious. David had close ties of friendship with the English, French and Austrian branches of the Rothschild—and many other Jewish—families. He was a man totally devoid of racial or religious prejudice. (Indeed—I've been told by sources I consider highly reliable—David was too much so to suit the tastes of the then Archbishop of Canterbury, who saw himself as a defender of the one and only true faith.)

As for the Duchess of Windsor, I met her only after she married David. However, I knew her former husband, Ernest Simpson, quite well. A man whose code was one of fair play toward all, Simpson would have seen any show of racial or religious intolerance as a major character flaw. And, when I got to know Wallis, I detected absolutely no trace of any such prejudice in her.

'Did Hitler listen to you when you spoke with him?' I asked David.

'Yes, I think so. The way was opened—ever so slightly— for further progress. Had there been any proper follow-through action in London or Paris, millions of lives might have been saved.'

Although David never said as much to me, I have reason to suspect that he was not acting on his own when he went to Germany and spoke to Hitler and other Nazi leaders. It would not surprise me if one day a musty EYES ONLY file is fished out of some top-security vault and new light is thrown on the episode. Hunch—if nothing else—tells me it might reveal that the Duke of Windsor acted with the necessarily secret support of political figures who were not as blind to the Hitlerian menace as those then in power in Britain and France.

'But the Press carried accounts that you returned Hitler's Nazi salute and made statements highly favourable to Hitler and his regime,' I said. 'Were those invented stories?'

'No,' David said without hesitation. 'They were true.' He gave me a long look. 'There are times when it's necessary to do or say certain things—and then allow them to remain on the record.' He smiled. 'Wallis and I both have broad shoulders. We can bear the load.'

David said he had gone to Germany hoping that 'at the outside' he might buy time for Britain and Europe. Whatever time he succeeded in buying was not utilized by those for whom he bought it. The political leaders of France and Britain had thrown away two opportunities to prevent the rebirth of aggressive militarism in Germany. They showed no inclination to make a third try, even to avert war and save untold numbers of lives. Instead, they sought to buy off Hitler by allowing him to invade Austria, occupy the Czech Sudetenland . . .

Another reminder to put the Duke of Windsor's story in proper perspective. When war began in 1939, he immediately made urgent requests to London, asking that he be placed on active service in the British Army as a line officer. He wanted to fight the Nazis—the same Nazis, I might point out, with whom he had been accused of 'sympathizing'. Mysterious political forces again went to work. His request was refused. He was offered only far-behind-the-lines staff posts—and was finally appointed Governor and Commander-in-Chief of the Bahamas.

My November 28, 1963, diary entry includes this notation: 'David comes to visit me at Sutton Place. He remembers many visits here between 1919 and 1936, but this is his first since 1936.'

There is far more for which I had no space in a daily diary entry. David took nostalgic delight in coming to Sutton. He and his brother—King George VI—often played tennis on the covered courts of the estate when it was owned by the Duke of Sutherland. David and I sat in my study, reminiscing about our days at Magdalen, events great and small that had transpired since and speculating over what the future held for the world. One evening our conversation again turned to Germany, Hitler and the World War Two era. David grew pensive.

'You know, Paul, Hitler and his thugs planned to kidnap Wallis and me,' he said. 'The story's been told often enough, Lord knows—usually in distorted form, as one might expect. Every now and then, I wish they'd succeeded. It's a pleasant fantasy to think I might have managed to see Hitler again alone—and somehow found a way to finish off the bugger.'

I had wanted to ask David something for a long time.

'Do you think Hitler was insane?'

'Clinically insane, yes. I never doubted it. But there are many kinds and degrees of insanity, Paul. Remember the Versailles Treaty and Geneva . . .'

And that brings me full circle. I have little to add save that Winston Churchill risked his political future in 1936 by bitterly opposing Edward VIII's abdication, declaring: 'I feel bound to place my personal loyalty to him on the highest plane.' And, I might cite Churchill's later remark: 'It's better to jaw-jaw than war-war.'

It is my admittedly partisan belief that my friend David would have been an exceptionally wise and courageous monarch and that his efforts to 'jaw-jaw' with Adolf Hitler have never received the recognition and appreciation they so richly deserve.

11

ANY MENTION OF the Duke of Windsor automatically brings to mind the saga of his romance with Wallis Simpson. In his public abdication speech on December 11, 1936, David declared:

'. . . I have found it impossible to carry the heavy burdens of responsibility and discharge my duties as King . . . without the help and support of the woman I love . . .'

He and Wallis Simpson were married the following June. Many predicted the marriage would be shortlived, that they would separate within six months or a year at most. Even after more than a decade some doom-watchers remained undaunted; rumours of an impending break between the Duke and Duchess of Windsor were perennial gossip-column items. I, among the others who knew them, believed otherwise, as is reflected by a 1952 diary note I made in Paris:

'Nov. 1: Dinner at Dorothy Spreckels' lovely apartment at 12 rue Murillo. Dorothy—tall, blonde, slender— looked most attractive, but all eyes were on the Duke and Duchess of Windsor. They are devoted to each other. People will still be talking and reading about this fascinating couple and their ideal marriage a century from now, when most other celebrated figures of today will be long forgotten. She'—the Duchess of Windsor— 'gazed at David lovingly while he told me of an elephant hunt in Kenya and how much he enjoyed playing golf . . .'

The marriage of the Duke and Duchess of Windsor lasted thirty-five years, until his death on May 28, 1972.

Whatever my other flaws and weaknesses, I have never been given to envy—save for the envy I feel toward those people who have the ability to make a marriage work and endure happily. It's an art I have never been able to master.

My record: five marriages, five divorces. In short, five failures.

A hatred of failure has always been part of my nature and, I suppose, one of the more pronounced motivating forces in my life. It is not that I love success for its own sake. However, once I have committed myself to any undertaking, a powerful inner drive cuts in and I become intent on seeing it through to a satisfactory conclusion. In most fields of endeavour, I have been successful more often than not. When my efforts resulted in failure, I did everything possible to insure that my mistakes were not repeated.

Obviously this has not been true of my marriages.

How and why is it that I have been able to build my own automobile, drill oil wells, run an aircraft plant, build and head a business empire—yet remain unable to maintain even one satisfactory marital relationship?

It is one hell of a question. I have pondered it long and frequently—and discussed it at endless length with my wives, intimate friends and parents (and with more than a few attorneys and divorce-court judges).

My father disapproved of divorce. During his lifetime I was married three times, divorced twice, and my third marriage was already coming apart before my father died. In his opinion, I was simply irresponsible.

My mother lived to see me go through four divorces and marry for a fifth time. She maintained that I made my mistake in marrying women much younger than myself—all my wives were ten to twenty years my junior. (Of course, my mother— like most mothers with a son for an only child—could never quite bring herself to believe that *any* woman was really 'good enough' for me!)

While there is something to be said for Mother's argument on the age difference, there were reasons—and they seemed to me good ones—for marrying much younger women. I remained a bachelor until I was 31. Most women close to my own age were already married. Those I met who were, say, in their mid-twenties and still single generally had flaws in their natures, temperaments or characters—otherwise they would not have remained single. (It must be remembered that all my marriages were in the 1920s and 1930s when, social conditioning being what it was, most women's main—if not sole—aim and ambition in life was to marry. And men were conditioned to believe that any woman who had passed the age of 23 or so and remained unmarried was a sort of factory second, a reject. The idea may have been both unfair and totally false—but there it was.)

Then, it was my experience that as unmarried women became older, they tended to be much more peevish and fractious than younger ones. A good example—from among many—was provided by a young woman I'll choose to call Ellen. She was 26 to my 29, and we dated regularly for two months. I was almost ready to propose. Then, one evening, we were driving to a nightclub in my Cadillac which—for those days—had excellent, cushioned wheel-suspension. Even so, when I drove over a bump in the road, Ellen was jolted forward and her head just barely struck the windscreen.

'Why don't you look where you're going?' she demanded furiously. 'You might have killed me!'

That sounded an alarm bell. The incident was too slight to deserve an acid comment; a younger woman would have laughed it off. During the next week or so, I took a much closer look at Ellen. I saw the huffy, pettish cracks behind the charming façade she maintained and soon stopped dating her. She later married someone else, dropped the façade completely, and became her real, nagging and shrewish self.

Most of my ex-wives cite my preoccupation with business as a major factor that interfered—and in each case eventually led to a dissolution of our marriages. I'll grant there is good basis for the charge, and I will plead guilty to it. But there are at least two sides to any story, and the *Rashomon* principle applies nowhere more than it does in marital squabbles that end up in the divorce courts.

I might as well recount the stories of my marital failures. Generally speaking, the versions of these that have appeared in the public press are totally unrecognizable to either my ex-wives or to me. Perhaps I can correct some of the most glaring distortions even though my version cannot help but be a biased one—tinged with my own notions and judgements.

My first wife was Jeanette Demont, an exquisitely beautiful dark brunette with a vibrant and magnetic personality and a remarkable degree of intelligence. She was eighteen, making her thirteen years my junior. I had known her for some months, and in October, 1923, we eloped to Ventura, California, where we were married.

What motivated me to even consider marriage in the first place? The answer could well be that at some deepdown level, I was tired of being a bachelor. Probably a need for feminine companionship more lasting and meaningful than that provided by casual romances and the usual single man's ration of philandering had long been stirring inside me. And I sometimes conjecture that the fact my father had recently suffered a stroke might have had a bearing on the matter. Although Father recovered, his illness may have brought home to me the realization that man is mortal. The only means by which he can pass on what he has built—or any part of himself—is through his children.

Despite all of this, it always seemed to me—and the observation is hardly original—that my wives married me; I didn't marry them. I don't think I ever made a conscious evaluation or clearcut decision that the women I married were superior to some others I knew and didn't marry. I was a bachelor, and I was friendly with various women, and—at that time—most of them wanted to get married.

Yes, of course. The decisive factor was love—or what at the given moment I believed to be love. It certainly was the reason that I decided to marry Jeanette Demont.

We rented a comfortable house on Wilshire Boulevard in Los Angeles. For a time, it appeared that Jeanette and I would make a success of marriage. A high point was reached seven or eight weeks after our elopement when Jeanette became pregnant with my first son, whom we were to name George Franklin Getty, II, after my father.

The idyllic interlude however was brief. Cracks appeared in our marital structure even before George was born. They did not appear spontaneously; they were caused—by both of us.

My business interests created problems. I was drilling several wells in Southern California, and it was by no means uncommon for me to stay on the sites overnight or even for two days or more. I also travelled extensively to the oilfields in Oklahoma and New Mexico, and I refused to take my pregnant wife with me on such trips. Then, of course, a man who remains single until the age of 31 finds it extremely difficult to change many of his habit patterns overnight merely because a marriage licence has been signed and sealed.

Jeanette was a woman of strong and sterling character, and she had an idealized concept of marriage and marital relationship. She was also markedly—and outspokenly—jealous. On many occasions when I was home we would go out for dinner—to the Brown Derby, Coconut Grove, or some similar spot where I would often see people whom I knew, and inevitably many of them were women.

'How could you say hello to that little slut?' Jeanette would demand.

Or she might challenge:

'You had an affair with that blonde bitch you waved to, didn't you?'

My protests or denials had little effect, and by that curious paradox familiar to most men, all the less so when the complaints were totally unjustified. Only two months after George was born, Jeanette informed me that she found our life together intolerable. She left me and filed suit for divorce, which was granted on February 15, 1925, the marriage having lasted only eighteen months. At first stunned and dismayed, I quickly regained enough of my common sense to appreciate that the major responsibility for the breakup was mine. Once the acrimony that accompanies any divorce was dispelled, Jeanette and I re-established a friendly relationship and have remained friends since. She remarried many, many years ago. I am greatly pleased that her marriage has been happy and lasting. I only wish I could say the same for my second try.

A particularly long and arduous period of business activity paid off handsomely in 1926. Several of my wells came in, producing large quantities of oil. My business affairs were in good shape—good enough so that I could supervise them by keeping in touch with my associates and employees by mail, telegraph or telephone. Having always loved Mexico—and,

ever since my 1914 trip to Spain having yearned to learn
Spanish—I went to Mexico City. I enrolled in a summer
course to study the language and Mexican History at the
University of Mexico.

How can I explain what happened next?

I might say it was a delayed rebound from my marriage to
and divorce from Jeanette. Or perhaps I had simply con-
tracted 'matrimonial fever'. Either or both might fit, but they
are far from being definitive.

Among other students enrolled in my Mexican classes was
a tall, slender and brilliant young woman, Allene Ashby. She
was seventeen, the daughter of a Texas rancher. Very much
an outdoor person, Allene excelled as an equestrienne. Our
flashfire romance developed after we began horseback riding
together. She being young and inexperienced and I being much
too enchanted by her, neither of us recognized an essentially
summer romance for what it was.

One morning, we drove to Cuernavaca and were married.

The act was impulsive and, as we both realized within only
a few weeks, a serious mistake. Once away from the University of Mexico and the romantic Mexican setting, we discovered that we had almost nothing in common. So we separated
and somewhat later, Allene got around to suing for divorce.
The decree did not become final until 1928—but as will be
seen, by then I was once more deeply involved in a romance
that would lead to my third marriage.

In 1927, I decided to spend seven months each year in the
United States and five months in Europe; this became a
regular annual pattern until 1939. The months in Europe were
not to be vacations, although they would serve to get me
away from the immediate stresses and pressures of my American business interests. I continued working and I kept in
constant touch with my companies. At the same time, I
embarked upon and conducted a variety of business ventures
in the European countries.

I made the 1927 trip abroad with my parents. They—and
I—were dismayed by the changes that had taken place since
our previous tours in 1909 and 1914, and it was the last time
my beloved mother and father were to see Europe. We were
accompanied by Father's devoted Japanese valet, Frank Komai.
Usually laconic, Frank maintained an inscrutable silence about

his impressions as we spent two weeks in London, a week in Paris, then went to Strasbourg, Baden-Baden and Innsbruck. Only when we reached Venice and took a gondola to the Royal Danieli Hotel did Frank Komai make his first—and only—comment regarding anything European. Staring around him in wonderment at the Venetian canals, Frank issued his verdict: 'I thinking this very funny place—nothing like same in Japan.'

In August, my parents and Frank Komai returned to the United States. I remained in Paris, renting a *petit meuble* at 12 rue St. Didier—it served perfectly as a twice-divorced bachelor's pad, the now-current term that could be used to describe the apartment and imply the uses to which it was put.

Then I decided to keep the flat as a base and travel a bit. I went to Vienna . . .

12

AT MANY LEVELS, the Vienna of 1928 was barely recognizable as the city it had been in 1913, when I was last there. There were no signs of the prosperity and the exuberance that had characterized the Austro-Hungarian Empire's capital. Friends I sought to find were—like so many in England and France—gone. Many had been killed in the war. Others had simply vanished. Yet, Vienna still somehow retained vestiges of its gaiety—and at the Grand Hotel, where I stayed, the service, food, wines and furnishings were as superior as they had been before the war.

Dining one evening in the hotel restaurant, I saw two young women seated at a table with a much older couple. While both the girls were attractive, one—a flaxen-haired blonde—was ravishing. I couldn't take my eyes off her. Later, a tip to a waiter provided the information that the young blonde woman was Fraulein Adolphine Helmle. The older couple were her parents, the other girl a friend who had come to Vienna with the Helmles. Dr. Otto Helmle, Fraulein Adolphine's father, was an engineer who headed the Badenwerk industrial complex in Karlsruhe. He was in Vienna to attend an engineer's convention.

I had watched the party leave its table and go to the elevators. Adolphine made a striking figure. Five-feet-ten, she was not only beautiful, but her lively face and every movement radiated vitality and vivacity. What followed two

nights later is best told in Adolphine's—or to use the nickname she preferred, Fini's—own words.

'My girlfriend and I shared a bedroom and one evening a
waiter brought a visiting card inviting "the young ladies" to
join a Mr. J. Paul Getty downstairs. My friend and I were
eighteen, on our first grownup trip abroad, and we were
intrigued. We pleaded a headache to my parents saying we
were going to lie down and we met this Mr. Getty in the
writing room.

'He invited us to dinner. I didn't dare look at my girlfriend
when I accepted as we had just eaten one dinner. He ordered
the most expensive meal and wine and by the time I finished
everything, I really had a headache. My girlfriend and I
returned to our room. Minutes after we were inside it, a
waiter knocked on the door and said, *"Pardon, Fräulein,* but
here is the bill."

'I was furious but paid with money my parents had given
me the same day to buy clothes. When Paul tried to speak to
me in the lobby the next afternoon, I refused to listen to him.
I thought he was a crook. Then he discovered the waiter had
made a colossal blunder by bringing the bill to me. Actually,
it had also been added to his hotel account, as he told the
headwaiter to do. The amount was refunded to me by the
hotel with the manager's profuse apologies. Once the muddle
was straightened out, I thought it hilariously funny.'

Fini had captivated me. When, a short time later, she
introduced me to her parents and we told them we wished to
marry, they expressed strong disapproval. Dr. Helmle snorted
that I was 36, twice his daughter's age. Besides, he was
something of a German chauvinist. He did not want his
daughter to marry an American and leave Germany.

Fini rebelled against her father's *diktat.* My previous wife,
Allene, obtained her final decree in October 1928. Despite
the opposition of *Herr Doktor* and *Frau* Helmle, I arranged for
Fini to meet me in Havana, Cuba, and we were married
there. After our honeymoon, I took her back to Southern
California.

Fini spoke little English and, since the demands of my
business were pressing again, I did not want to leave her
alone in what for her was a new and alien environment. For
these reasons, we stayed with my parents at the beginning.
My mother and father were charmed and delighted by Fini.

Mother thought I had at last found a wife good enough for me. She even went so far as to admit that perhaps the difference in our ages didn't matter.

'Paul's parents treated me like a daughter,' Fini has declared publicly. 'I loved them and I believe they loved me.'

There was no evidence that Fini's parents showed any similar feelings toward me. The knowledge that their daughter had married against their wishes continued to rankle. Fini was bombarded with letters from her parents. It must be remembered that she had been brought up in a Germany where all children—especially daughters—were programmed to accept their fathers' word as law.

I believe that the Helmles' parental pressure is what caused my marriage to Fini to come apart. Fini became pregnant in 1929. Dr. Helmle was adamant that *his* daughter—not my wife, understand, but his daughter—bear the child in Germany. By then, Fini's loyalties—and nerves—were shredded. Convinced she had been—and was being—a traitor to her parents, my wife declared she wanted both of us to return to Germany.

My business affairs were in a crucial state at the time. I could not leave until several important matters were cleared up. Fini said she would go on alone; I was to follow as soon as possible. She sailed in late summer, 1929. By mid-October, I had cleared up the most pressing of my business problems and left for New York. I was there on October 23, when the great Wall Street crash began. This demanded a delay until I could formulate plans for my brokers and attorneys to follow. Then I sailed.

I was with Fini when she had our baby in Berlin, a boy we named Ronald, but who was quickly nicknamed Ronnie. My joy at being a father for a second time was crushed by Dr. Otto Helmle's stiff, stern ultimatum. Either I would agree to live permanently in Germany with Fini and our son—or he would insist that Fini divorce me. I made frantic efforts to achieve some sort of compromise. Then, on April 22, 1930, I received a cable informing me that my own father had suffered a second stroke and was in very serious condition.

There were no transatlantic flights in 1930. I took the first available ship. Radiograms kept me posted on my father's condition, which grew more grave each day. All domestic flights in the United States were grounded due to foul weather when I arrived in New York. I took the fastest train to Los Angeles, arriving in time to see Father, who lingered for thirty days. His death was the heaviest blow, the greatest loss, I had suffered in my life. Yet, even while suffering my own grief and comforting my mother in hers, I had the unpleasant task of dealing with government tax agents. I wonder if any of them realized the ghoulish quality of their actions when they swept in, very shortly after my father's funeral, pressing for 'estate valuations' on which to base inheritance tax levies.

As 1930 drew to a close, it became obvious nothing could be done to save my third marriage. Dr. Otto Helmle meticulously directed the attorneys who brought divorce proceedings against me on Fini's behalf. Although Dr. Helmle was *korrekt* in the way only Germans can be, he was a hard, shrewd bargainer. He adamantly demanded a large financial settlement for his daughter. The divorce became final in August, 1932.

Fini has never remarried, and we have maintained close touch and are good friends. She visits me often; her last trip to Sutton Place was in 1974. Ironically, Fini has long lived in Southern California. I believe that had it not been for the interference of Dr. Helmle, her father, things between us might well have worked out much differently.

After his sixth marriage, Cornelius Vanderbilt, Jr. said: 'In my view we much-married people are the idealists, the romantics, the searchers for an ideal of happiness that seems to elude us in this life.'

Mmm. Maybe—but the line strikes me as being a shade pretentious and more than a little defensive. In my own case, I see my marital patterns as a violation of Cicero's maxim: 'To stumble over the same stone twice is a proverbial disgrace.' Yet I doggedly persisted in tripping over the same boulder.

On December 2, 1932, Ann Rork and I were married in Mexico. I was 40; Ann exactly half my age. The daughter of Sam Rork, the Hollywood producer-director who made Clara Bow a topflight screen star, Ann was a lovely and vivacious brunette who aspired to become an actress herself.

We lived in the beach house I had built for us in California. For a time, all went well. Ann gave birth to my third son,

Eugene Paul (who would eventually change his name to Paul Getty, Jr.). Our home life was pleasant. Then the demands of business created problems. Ann complained that I was away from home too much. Since I was rich, why should I have to work, she demanded. We had another son, Gordon. After his birth, Ann grew restive. She wanted to have her own career in motion pictures. Frictions increased and our relationship deteriorated very rapidly.

Ann filed for divorce. As she subsequently described it, the suit was 'noisesome'. If asked to give my own descriptions, I would use much stronger terms, but it was all long ago. It should suffice to say that I had many more problems and difficulties over this divorce than any of the others. Looking back at it, I feel that little if any of the clamour, the claims and the charges raised and broadcast was Ann's doing. I believe the responsibility lay with the legal representatives she was prevailed upon to retain. They were recommended to her by other aspiring actors and actresses for whom any event, even a divorce, was an opportunity to strive for maximum dramatic effect and the widest publicity-play.

And so, by 1935, I was again a bachelor—a four-times-divorced bachelor. My marital fever should have been cured, permanently. It wasn't. Business reasons compelled me to move to New York City for a considerable period of time. I leased a penthouse apartment there from Mrs. Frederick A. Guest.

Betsy Beaton was a successful stage actress in New York. I had known and dated her frequently a few years before, when she lived in Hollywood. (Her father was K. C. Beaton, a well-known writer and syndicated newspaper columnist.) Betsy was starring in a play when I moved into my newly-leased apartment. I telephoned her and asked that she drop by whenever it suited her to see the place, which Mrs. Guest had furnished with magnificent antiques.

Betsy came by one afternoon with one of her close girlfriends, Louise Dudley Lynch, a niece of Bernard Baruch. When I saw Louise, my first thought was, 'this is THE girl.' A Junoesque, auburn-haired beauty, she had immense charm and wit. I soon learned she also possessed no small degree of talent. Louise was one of the first of what the newspapers of the time called 'Society Chanteuses,' talented social-register young women who sang in exclusive supper clubs.

She had a remarkable voice-range—from contralto to coloratura soprano—and yearned to be an opera singer. Her talent was considered good enough for such judges as Eugenie Leontovich and Amelita Galli-Curci to recommend that she take operatic lessons.

Being related to multimillionaire Bernie Baruch did not mean that Louise was rich. Baruch had left her side of the family to fend for itself. She had only her—admittedly four-figure—weekly salary as a singer. I offered to finance her lessons—on a loan basis. She would repay me from her future earnings.

Unfortunately, some 'expert' or other felt the name Louise Lynch was not quite distinctive enough for opera and convinced her to adopt a professional name, Theodora Lynch. (It sounded more 'classical,' the advisers claimed, pointing out that Enrico Caruso had been born Errico and Rosa Ponsell began life as Rosa Ponzillo.) Louise allowed herself to be convinced, but insisted that off concert programmes and three-sheets, she be called 'Teddy.' It is the nickname by which she is known to her friends, and the name by which I will refer to her from here on in this book.

Teddy went first to London, studying there under Blanche Marchesi. Then she moved to Rome, taking more advanced lessons—and also working as a correspondent contributing feature pieces to the New York *Herald Tribune*.

By then, I was hopelessly smitten. I followed Teddy to Rome.

My diary entry for November 14, 1939:

'Teddy and I were married at noon in a romantic setting, in a palatial room in the Campidoglio.'

Although World War II had begun, Italy still remained neutral. I went back to the United States. Teddy decided to stay and continue her studies. She was not to return to the U.S.A. until June 1, 1942—for in the interim she was arrested by Italian Fascists as a suspected spy and, for a time, imprisoned. She was finally repatriated aboard the Swedish ship, *Gripsholm*, along with American diplomats who had been interned when Italy declared war on America.

Teddy was 23 when we were married, and I was 43—another

twenty-year gap. At least, as my cousin Hal Seymour remarked, I persisted in being consistent in the generation gap.

Our child, Timothy—'Timmy'—was born on June 6, 1946.
I was then fifty-three, with four other sons by my previous
wives, but I still took great joy and pride in fatherhood. By
contrast, Teddy has stated: 'Paul really didn't understand
fatherhood until Timmy came along.' Possibly that is how it
appeared to her. I can't deny that I was doubtless more
demonstrative with Timmy than I had been with my other
sons when they were infants.

Teddy and I were happy. At last, I thought, this was a
marriage that would last. Then problems began to arise. The
first stemmed from my insistence on remaining in Tulsa,
Oklahoma, while the Spartan Aircraft Corporation was re-
converted to peacetime production.

Teddy has been quoted as saying: 'Paul was a good husband and father, but his first love was business. When there
was a new business venture, he couldn't resist.'

There was nothing 'new' about the Spartan 'venture.' It
was a sense of wanting to see what I had built during the war
thrive in peace—and a sense of obligation to the people who
had helped me build it. However, it is extremely difficult to
explain such concepts to the full satisfaction of a woman who
is your wife and the mother of your child.

Then, Teddy herself was eager to resume her own career.
She appeared in concerts, recitals, operatic productions and
motion pictures. I think the clash of career-interests was an
element adding to the increasing difficulties of our married
life.

The Getty interests' oil explorations and discoveries in the
Neutral Zone proved the *coup de grâce*. I had a global
business—and in order to oversee it properly, I had to be
centrally located, midway between the United States and the
Middle East. I went to Europe in 1951 knowing I would have
to stay there for some time. Teddy and Timmy were with me
for a while. Then Teddy issued what—from her standpoint
and Timmy's—was a reasonable ultimatum.

'Timmy is an American. He should be brought up in
America—and I want to go back to the States and live there,
too. Come home with us.'

'Is that an or-else?' I asked.

'I'm afraid so, Paul,' Teddy nodded.

Teddy obtained her interlocutory decree in 1957. It became final the following year. My fifth marriage—like all the others—was ended, over; another failure.

None the less, a strong bond of friendship remains between Teddy and me. We stay in communication with each other. In fact, as I write these words, I am expecting her to visit me at Sutton Place within a matter of weeks.

I have only this to say in my own defence. I did not divorce any of my wives. Nor did I demand or request a divorce or institute divorce proceedings in any of my marriages. A marriage contract to me is as binding as any in business, and I have always believed in sticking to an agreement. It was always my wives who invoked the escape-clauses.

Unfortunately, it seems to be true that a marriage licence can ruin a relationship between a man and a woman faster and more completely than anything else. Before marriage, many couples are very much like people rushing to catch an airplane; once aboard, they turn into passengers. They just sit there.

A friend once said to me: 'Paul, you're basically a moralist—otherwise you wouldn't have been married five times.' Perhaps there is a grain of truth in that—but then, what about all the women I *didn't* marry?

Even so, five wives can't all be wrong. As one of them told me after our divorce: 'You're a great friend, Paul—but as a husband, you're impossible.'

In one way, I consider myself lucky—luckier than most divorced men I know. Once the marriage licences were torn up, my ex-wives and I became friends again.

13

I, J. PAUL GETTY, do hereby solemnly swear:

That I am neither a homosexual nor a eunuch, nor have I ever taken any vows of chastity.

That I have always enjoyed the company of women and have formed deep and long-lasting friendships with many of them.

That I will, if called upon, fight to the death for women's rights to enjoy the same privileges and prerogatives of citizenship as those extended to males of the species.

BUT . . .

In recent years, there has been a global upsurge of feminism, best known as the 'Women's Liberation Movement.' It has attracted adherents by the millions. They range across a spectrum from wild-eyed extremists to the most intelligent and rational of females like Princess Ashraf Pahlavi, twin sister of the Shah of Iran. A close friend of mine for several years, Princess Ashraf is a completely feminine woman and possesses a remarkably fine intellect.

Princess Ashraf has become an active force in the 'women's movement.' She served as consultative chairman—or should that be chairperson?—of the preparatory committee for the 1975 International Year of the Woman. She headed the Iranian delegation to the United Nations sponsored conference on women's role in society. In June, 1975, she was interviewed by *Newsweek* Magazine. Greatly as I like and admire

Princess Ashraf, I was badly unnerved by this statement attributed to her:

'In this age of decolonization, women are the last colony left to male imperialism.'

Good God, I thought. Images of Feminist Freedom Fighters manning—womanning?—barricades came into my mind. I glanced nervously toward the door of my study. For a moment, I considered the possibility that my trusted and indispensable aides, Mrs. Barbara Wallace and Mrs. Elaine Mellish, might burst through it wearing tiger-striped combat uniforms and brandishing machine guns. Taking a firm grip on myself, I resumed reading.

'I am not interested in war between the sexes,' Princess Ashraf was quoted as saying. 'We need the support of men in our struggle for equal rights. Besides, neither of us can get along without the other.'

My relief was indescribable. The prospect of seeing my friend, the lovely and magnetic Princess Ashraf at the head of an opposing army in a war between the sexes should strike terror into any male heart. Much more harrowing is the vision of a world in which one sex tries to get along without the other. Even so, just to be safe, I resolved that henceforth I would address Mrs. Wallace and Mrs. Mellish as 'Ms.'—until the last of my fear receded and I remembered that I have long called them both by their first names.

I must confess that in many ways I am a nineteenth-century man—which helped wreak havoc with my marriages by creating anachronistic mélanges, for my wives were all very much twentieth-century women. Overall, I tend to agree with what Henry Litton once said in a conversation we had when he was more than a hundred years of age.

'What do you think of modern women?' I asked Henry.

'I admire them,' he replied, 'but I think they have lost something. When I was young, we could always tell a lady and when a lady appeared, a man would always take off his hat. Women then had much more respect than they have today, and that was a valuable influence on our society.'

I believe that in terms of true equality of influence, importance of their role, the respect they received and their sense of identity, the position of women a century ago was superior to what it is today. Of course, there were class differences; all women weren't 'ladies'. But all men weren't gentlemen, either. The inequalities and injustices that prevailed then had far more to do with economics and the caste system than they did with the sex of an individual.

None the less, and whether we like it or not, men and women are not the same in nature, temperament, emotions and emotional responses. Parenthetically, I—for one—do not believe that the differences in their physical strength and endurance is very great. In Russia—and elsewhere—I have seen women handily performing the heaviest and most gruelling manual labour. I imagine there are women in Russia and other countries who are physically stronger than the roughest, toughest policemen on the London, New York, Munich or Paris police forces.

The differences I consider fundamental and definitive lie in other directions. By and large, I have observed that men incline to be more objective and women more subjective, especially in any situation where personalities may be involved. Assume that John and Mary are co-workers sizing up Tom, a new colleague.

John is most likely to say: 'Tom seems to know his job.'

Mary will be much more inclined to say: 'He's nice.'

Ask a man a question, and he will usually concentrate on the question. At its simplest, the principle is expressed in the ancient wheeze: 'Ask a man where he got the steak he's serving for dinner and he'll reply, ''From Jones, the local butcher.'' Asked the same question, a woman will respond by demanding, ''Why, what's wrong with it?'' '

My own nature is such that I am able to concentrate on whatever is before me and am not easily distracted from it. A few years back, an exceptionally pretty girl I knew learned that I intended to spend the afternoon viewing the Wallace Collection. She asked me to take her along. I refused—politely but firmly.

'Why not?' she pouted.

'Frankly, because you're a little spoiled,' I told her. 'If I took you with me, you'd expect me to concentrate on you rather than on the collection. You'd want to compete with it for my attention. If the collection won, you'd be annoyed. If you won, I'd be annoyed—and would consider my afternoon wasted.'

She refused to speak to me for weeks afterward, and that

leads me to another quality I have very frequently observed in women. They have phenomenal memories. They rarely forget (or fully forgive) any real or imagined slight or any failure of a man to carry out a promise—or what women choose to interpret as promises. The prudent male therefore watches his words carefully—not that it does him much good.

I know a couple—call them Bob and Helen—who, though not married, have been living together quite contentedly for some years. They paid me a visit recently, and our conversation turned to this subject. Bob grinned and nodded his head toward Helen.

'We can give you a perfect example,' he said, chuckling. 'One Saturday night about four years ago, I was feeling pretty good, and I suggested to Helen that we might go to her favourite hotel restaurant for brunch the next day. As it turned out, we slept late on Sunday morning and it was raining heavily, so I announced we'd stay home. Helen was furious over that for months . . .'

'I still am!' Helen snapped, and she wasn't joking. 'After all, you promised . . .'

Bob merely groaned.

When I actively headed the Spartan Aircraft Corporation, a third or more of the 5,500 factory workers on the payroll were women—and, I want to emphasize, they were efficient, conscientious and loyal. Because I spent much of my time on the shop floor, personally supervising operations, I had a unique opportunity to study the differences between male and female workers.

One of the more surprising discoveries I made was that women were completely honest and straightforward about their capabilities and limitations. Asked to perform some task beyond their ability and experience, they would openly admit they could not do it and ask to be taught or shown. Not so the men. They could not bring themselves to confess ignorance or ineptitude. Instead they would usually claim full understanding and try to bluff their way through—making very costly mistakes and blunders in the process.

Roles reversed when it came to taking criticism. Male workers accepted criticism of their work matter-of-factly, taking no personal offence. Women almost invariably reacted to any critical remark about their work as though it was an all-out attack on them as individuals. Their eyes would fill with tears or they would burst out crying or flee into the women's restroom. Afterwards, they were likely to sulk for hours—or days—or even quit entirely.

Women's libbers are by now doubtless labelling me as an archetypal chauvinist, but that's how I've seen it. Rhetoric and dialectics can't change what I have learned from observation and experience. At the same time, I want to make it clear that nothing I have said is intended as a putdown of women or an implication that they are lesser creatures than men. I am simply making an appeal to reason, making my puny contribution to the cause of bringing the roles and relationships of the sexes into something approaching a realistic perspective.

Men have their male faults, flaws and weaknesses. Women have their female defects. The sum of each does not make either sex better or worse. Neither sex is perfect, nor a paragon of virtues as compared to the other, and in this sense they are certainly equal.

My marriages provide some kind of textbook examples. I was anything but the ideal husband, with a full measure of male faults. I'm afraid I gave more time and attention to oil wells and proxy-fights than to home and fireside. My autocratic tendencies were no less apparent in my personal life than in business. I was often short-tempered, brusque. I forgot birthdays, anniversaries, dinner-engagements. While I did not purposely start romances with other women, I did have a philosophy that many men have, but which is anathema to their wives. I had many good women friends, and I felt that just because I was married was not a reason for me deliberately to avoid those women.

These are admissions enough for any all-woman jury to find me guilty on the spot (and sentence me to be burned at the stake, I imagine)!

Is the condemned man permitted to say something in mitigation?

Each of my wives was jealous and resentful of my preoccupation with business. Yet none showed any visible aversion to sharing in the proceeds of that preoccupation. Possibly I was stone-deaf throughout all my marriages; which would explain why I never once heard any suggestion such as this:

'Give up working, Paul. We'll get rid of the servants and cars, move into a small apartment and live on a modest scale.'

Then, there is the matter of alimony—not child-support, alimony.

John Barrymore—whom I knew in Hollywood—went through his share of divorce-proceedings. Tallying up the astronomical sums he had paid out in alimony, he made this sour—but classic—remark to Gene Fowler:

'I realize a man has to pay the piper—but why is it that I have to subsidize an entire symphony orchestra?'

Looking back over the years—and five divorces—I can think of a total of several million reasons why my sympathies are with Jack Barrymore's attitude on the subject.

By some process of idea-association, that reminds me of Aristotle Onassis. In 1954, Ari told me it cost him about $30,000 a month—$360,000 a year—to own and operate his famous yacht, the *Christina*. It's safe to guess that by 1975 the cost had at least doubled, being somewhere around $750,000 annually. According to published reports, Ari left his widow, Jacqueline Onassis, an income of $250,000 a year—plus half ownership of the *Christina*. Knowing Ari's sense of humour . . .

Nevertheless the successful—or success-oriented—businessman has and presents his own peculiar patterns and problems *vis-à-vis* women, wives and sex. These have been the topic of endless controversy and conjecture. Sixty-plus years of experience are, I believe, adequate credentials for adding my own views.

14

FOLLOWERS OF THE famed dream merchant, Dr. Sigmund Freud, look upon businessmen and entrepreneurs with a fastidious shudder and label them 'Homo Economicus,' a breed apart. Freudians say Homo Economicus possesses the 'capitalist spirit' that and this is a repression of normal erotic impulses, a sublimation of sexual drive.

Never having felt the urge to sprawl on analytical couches, I have no first-hand knowledge of what revelations Freudians seek to dredge from a businessman's unterbewusstsein in order to reach their conclusions. I do, however, know that I've never observed any link between my own capitalist spirit and erotic impulses. And having known businessmen and entrepreneurs almost all of my life, I am yet to note any discernible relation between their drives to achieve success and their sexual drives. Some businessmen are highly sexed. Others are in whatever one might care to consider an average category. Yet others would most certainly rate nearly zero on any sex-drive scale.

Of course, there is no end to psychiatric theories about sex-drives and success-drives. Theodore Reik rejects the Freudian position outright, declaring that 'the primal sex-drive is entirely incapable of being sublimated.' The Adlerian School holds that the 'strongest life-force' is not sex at all, but 'the will to power.' Dr. Sofie Lazarsfeld, a leading Adlerian, has written:

'It depends on the individual's courage whether he adapts

102

his personal destiny to the requirements of the community or not. If he does so adapt himself, he attains psychological health and balance and engages to the best of his ability in the three great life-tasks relating to the community, sexuality and profession.'

Lazarsfeld adds that all human actions are 'to a very considerable extent dependent upon whether the individual is prepared to take the responsibility for them, or whether he is possessed with an anxiety which causes him to refrain or thrust the responsibility on other people or on some factor that is supposed to be beyond his control.'

I submit that the successful businessman must and does take the responsibility for his actions. It is the mediocrities and the outright failures who blame everyone and everything but themselves for whatever goes wrong. That is why they are mediocrities or failures.

My own experience makes me laugh at the repression/sublimation/compensation and other sexually-oriented theories that attempt to explain an individual's urge to achieve, accomplish and attain. The tangle of psychiatric hypotheses reminds me of an ancient vaudeville skit. The curtain rises on two engineers standing near a huge wooden crate. They manipulate slide-rules and mumble calculations as they try to determine the best means for moving the crate. One suggests a ramp, rollers and a truck. The other insists that a crane is needed. Their argument builds, and they babble about the laws of physics and recite algebraic equations. At this point, a man in coveralls ambles onstage. He gives the engineers a contemptuous glance, handily lifts the crate and carries it into the wings.

'It's an empty,' he says over his shoulder.

Worth no more than a muted snicker as humour, the skit does have a moral applicable to the subject under discussion. Being super-specialists wrapped in their doctrinaire theories, psychiatrists are often blind to the obvious. Whatever degree of erotic motivation there may be in a man's drive to achieve, it is primer-level simple to understand.

Male penguins lay shiny pebbles at the feet of female penguins; it was for Eve that Adam munched on the apple. Males have always been motivated to some extent or another by a desire to have women, please them and bask in their praise, love and devotion.

Instead of proffering apples, modern Eves consume Everests of lobsters, filets mignon and crêpes suzette and oceans of Dom Perignon. They also like to do more than just windowshop at St. Laurent and Cartier. Rather than being a sublimation, the capitalist spirit unquestionably contains some direct erotic motivation in the male's wish to gratify these desires and whims of the female.

In any event, Freudian derogation of the sexual patterns of *Homo Economicus* is hilariously ironic. Some of the more glaring examples of what various schools of psychiatric thought term 'psychosexual complications' are to be found among sworn enemies of the capitalist spirit. *Vide* this trio chosen at random.

Friedrich Engels (Karl Marx's colleague) was obsessed with the idea that his many mistresses must be proletarian, working-class women. Yet he proved to be an insecure, sexual status-seeking snob after all. When Engels became the lover of Mary Burns (upon Mary's death, her sister Lizzie moved into his bed), he went to preposterous lengths in efforts to establish that Mary (and later Lizzie) were related to the poet, Robert Burns.

Thorstein Veblen, that relentless foe of businessmen and industrialists, was a compulsive and obsessive womanizer. Left-leaning economist Joseph Schumpeter declared that he had three ambitions in life: 'to be a great lover, a great horseman and a great economist.'

My guess is that if Friedrich Engels had been an industrialist instead of a revolutionary theoretician, Freudians would berate him as 'demonstrating deepseated fears of sexual inferiority and inadequacy.' A capitalist Veblen would undoubtedly be labelled a latent homosexual seeking to prove his masculinity through promiscuous womanizing. I hesitate to think what the headshrinkers would give as their verdict on a capitalist Ford, Rockefeller or Getty who—like economist Schumpeter—declared his foremost ambition to be a great lover.

But I leave the guardians of the psychiatric couch to their hypotheses. None bears much relation to the real problems and obstacles I have found success to create in a businessman's sex and marital life.

Day-to-day business stresses *do* encroach on a businessman's private and home life and often take their toll. Women, most particularly wives, want to be important to their men and resent being relegated to a secondary position by anyone or anything. Women married to successful businessmen have great difficulty satisfying their emotional hunger for being needed. Their husbands appear self-sufficient, independent and they often give the impression of functioning in a world of their own. Incompatibility and conjugal discord take root quickly in such ground.

I am aware of the risks I take when I advance the proposition that women tend to stick longer to failure than to success. In some ways the trait is to their credit. Part of it, I hazard to guess, is a manifestation of the maternal instinct. Another part stems from the fact that a woman can much more readily consider herself a fully participating partner under straitened circumstances. She knows that she is sharing, and by sharing, making a worthwhile contribution. When married to—or involved with—a successful man, she is often likely to fear that she is no more than an ornamental adjunct.

My years and experiences in and out of marriage have taught many—for me, alas, belated—lessons. I have, I believe, learned much that can prevent success from being a disruptive and destructive force in a businessman's married life or, if he is a bachelor, in his relationships with members of the opposite sex. The formula is two-way, and while not difficult to comprehend in principle, does require honest intent and conscious effort by both businessman-husband and his mate.

Here are what I consider the seven key points every entrepreneur and man in business should keep in mind—and implement:

1. Women, no matter how enlightened or liberated they think themselves, are still women. They respond to—indeed, thrive on—warmth and affection, and there are very few who do not appreciate at least an occasional show of old-fashioned gallantry. Curtness, shouts and snarls may appeal to females who are mental masochists; in others, they engender only resentment.

2. A woman should never be allowed to feel she is only an ornament; merely another possession. It bears repeating that women need to be needed and to make positive contributions to a mutual effort. A man whose head is crammed with business facts, figures and problems may overlook all this,

but if he does, he makes a mistake that may well prove fatal to his marriage.

3. Many businessmen—myself very much included—frequently complain that there aren't enough hours in a day to take care of the work at hand. It's true enough. The active businessman seldom has all the time to do everything that should or could be done in his business. However, no matter how busy and successful he may be, he should make time to spend with his wife and family. This not only helps to insure the success of his marriage and enables him to understand and guide his children, it adds depth and dimension to his own nature and personality.

4. It is not my intent to discuss topics that are the province of the intimate marriage manuals. However, sex should be a mutually enjoyed and mutually gratifying experience. The physically and mentally tired businessman who comes home and then brusquely demands to 'enjoy' sexual relations is a fool. Women require attention, affection, patience and imagination from their sexual partners—and are fully entitled to receive them. The businessman should bear this in mind, even if a million-dollar contract fell through that afternoon or if all-important merger papers are to be signed the next morning.

5. A man who heads a business enterprise is accustomed to having subordinates accept and accede to his varying moods. To expect the same docile reactions in his private life is to court disaster. A wife is not a subordinate, but she is her own grievance committee. When treated as an underling, she may well decide to engage in a little moonlighting—or walk out for good.

6. Generally speaking, most women seem to prefer that the male be (at least superficially) the dominant partner in a relationship. Even so, not even the most dynamic male can long keep the love and respect of a woman he bullies, browbeats and tries to deprive of her own individuality. Being the dominant partner is one thing—to be domineering is quite another, and usually destructive to a relationship.

7. I suppose every man goes through a phase during which he views sex solely in quantitative terms, proudly counting his conquests, his chest swelling as the numbers increase. Eventually—it is to be hoped—the attitude is transformed by discernment and sensitivity. Then quality—in the sense of an

appreciation of emotional and intellectual gratification and not merely a desire for physical pleasure—replaces quantity as the criterion.

That is how I see one side, but I have had ample opportunity to observe the other, too. There is an old adage, no less valid for being hoary, that marriage is a 60–40 proposition, with each partner giving 60 and taking 40, the overlap providing the safety-margin. I've found this particularly true in marriages where the husband is a successful—or success-oriented—businessman. No man can make a marriage work and last by himself. He needs cooperation and help—plenty of both—from his wife. Following are what I think to be the most valuable pointers for any woman who sincerely wants to make a success of living with a successful man.

1. Women should not be misled by the successful man's outward show of self-sufficiency. It's another—but all too true—axiom that the closer a man gets to the top, the lonelier he becomes. Business associates and aides cannot supply the deeply penetrating human warmth he requires. This can come only from a woman upon whom he focuses affection and love—provided she returns both with the added ingredient of understanding.

2. Patience is indispensable when living with a successful man. There will be times when he forgets that he is at home and issues (or snaps) orders which he is accustomed to having obeyed without question at the office. He usually feels very badly about it afterwards, but may fail to make the called-for apologies or amends because he is preoccupied or because he can't easily drop the manner and mien that are musts for him ten or more hours a day.

3. A woman should not think she has no constructive role merely because she does not attend board meetings. Love, affection, understanding and patience are all vital contributions. So are quiet, constructive, common-sense suggestions. Women have remarkable intuition and are often able to see—or foresee—things that elude a man. The key is in *how* the suggestions are made; there should be no hint of nagging.

4. The 'bored and jaded businessman's wife' is a cliché. In this day and age, any intelligent woman who is unable to find some activity to occupy her time rewardingly is merely making an excuse for her own laziness. The carping complaint,

'I'm dying of boredom,' is not likely to sit well with any man whose mind and energies are constantly being used to peak capacity.

5. It's a purblind woman who frets and nags because her businessman husband isn't home for dinner on the dot or fails to spend as much time with her as she'd like. Believe me, most of those late-at-night business meetings are just that, and businessmen attend them because they have no choice. They would far rather be home, relaxing, or having dinner out with their wives. Of course, every man has his tolerance-limit. If constantly accused and berated, he cannot be blamed much for deciding that he might as well have the game as the name.

6. Women should realize that any successful businessman is, by definition, a creative person and, like all creative types, is sometimes inclined to be temperamental. In this regard, I might say it has often puzzled me why some women will adoringly accept the outrageous tantrums of some would-be painter, but will create an unholy scene at the slightest show of temperament by a banker or building contractor.

Social psychologist John K. Hemphill declares: 'To lead is to engage in an act which initiates a structure in the interaction of others as part of the process of solving a mutual problem.'

Professor W. J. H. Sprott writes: 'Each individual has his own biological needs for food, drink, protection and sexual satisfaction and the desire to satisfy these needs or to acquire the means for their satisfaction.'

It strikes me that these two statements sum up the real factors behind the success and sex drives of *Homo Economicus* who, despite any Freudian arguments, is not a breed apart but a completely human human being.

15

SIR WINSTON CHURCHILL'S son, Randolph, had the reputation of being an abrasive, unsociable person. We were friends, and I never found him so. Whenever we met, he was always pleasant and amiable. But, by his own admission, he suffered handicaps and hardships in life because he was the son of a great and famous man.

'I think Enrico Caruso had a son who was a tenor,' Randolph once gloomily remarked to me. 'Everyone agreed that Caruso had been the greatest tenor in history. And so everyone measured the son's talents against those of his father. Naturally, no matter how well he sang, it wasn't good enough. I've always been in the same boat.'

I had faced similar problems, albeit on a lesser scale. My father, George F. Getty Sr. never achieved (or sought to achieve) public fame or high office. However, he did gain great respect and an enviable reputation in the American petroleum industry. Throughout the first two decades of my own business career I was acutely aware that other oilmen measured my performance against that of my father rather than on its own merits.

True, this was added incentive. It became one of my motivations—and goals—to live up to the standards George F. Getty Sr. had set. After my mother's death, I was to write in my diary:

'What a task it is to be worthy of two wonderful parents. I have tried to be worthy, but I must try even harder.'

I have emphasized earlier that my father's influence and example were the principal forces that formed my nature and character. Unfortunately, I had no like degree of influence and control over the lives of my own sons. The reason for this was, of course, the failure of my marriages. Divorce courts are very much the same the world over. My wives were the plaintiffs and aggrieved parties in all five divorce suits. Consequently, custody of my sons was invariably awarded to their mothers. I must, however, give the four wives by whom I had children full credit. They were most liberal in granting me visiting rights. But to visit a growing child and even spend days at a time with him is a far cry from being able to exert continuing paternal influence.

Perhaps if I had managed to have the kind of relationship with my boys that my father had with me, things would have turned out much different. As it was—and is—there is much in the story of my sons and I that I find extremely painful to recall. Why then do I intend to relate the story—and the stories? Because by doing so, I might help clarify the record and perhaps correct some of the more distorted versions that have appeared in the public press. It may also be of value to parents who have had to cope with similar problems.

My eldest son, George F. Getty II, was born to my first wife, Jeanette Demont, and me a little less than a year after we were married. Our separation and eventual divorce took place while George was still an infant.

Allene Ashby, my second wife, and I had no children.

My third wife, Adolphine 'Fini' Helmle, gave birth to my second son, Ronald F.—'Ronny'.

After Fini divorced me, I married Ann Rork. Ann bore me two sons, Eugene Paul 'Pabby' and Gordon.

My fifth marriage—to Louise 'Teddy' Lynch—lasted much longer than any of the others. Seven years after we were married, my fifth son, Timothy—'Timmy'—was born. I was then 53 years old.

I dearly loved all my sons from the moment each was born.

Some might consider such a statement from a five-times-divorced, eighty-three-year-old man to be defensive, self-pleading—even unctuous. I accept that possibility as a calculated risk. It in no way diminishes the sincerity of the declaration nor lessens the force and genuineness of my feelings. This is a father speaking.

There is a Law of Compensation in Nature. Every plus is somewhere, somehow offset by a minus. I have long been able to exercise a very considerable degree of control over my display of emotions. This has been an asset to me in business and certain other areas of my activities. In the more personal spheres of my life, it has often been a distinct liability—nowhere more so than in my relationships with my first four sons. I found it extremely difficult to be openly demonstrative with my boys—partly due to the knowledge that whenever our visits together ended, they would return to the full-time care and custody of their mothers.

For some reason, I have always been much freer in recording my emotions and feelings in my diaries. The fragmentary excerpts from them that I offer below were written without the inhibiting reticence that comes with a fear of being too emotional or demonstrative. Taken as a whole, they might serve to provide insight into a father's true feelings about his sons.

1939
Los Angeles, California:
'May 20: Saw George, a remarkable boy rapidly becoming a man. He is 5' 9" tall and weighs 145 pounds.'
Geneva, Switzerland:
'July 8: Drove to Ronny's school near Coppet, some 20 kms from Geneva. Ronny is well, happy and likes his school. His teachers give him a good report. He is intelligent and has good character, they say. Took Ronny and Fini to the Bergues Hotel for lunch and then to Chamonix.'

(This visit with Ronny and his mother lasted until July 14. Some months later, after World War Two began, they left Europe, came to the United States and settled in a home in Southern California.)

Los Angeles:
'December 10: Went to Ann's house (Ann Rork, my fourth wife who divorced me in 1935) and saw Pabby and Gordon, bless them. They're both fine boys.'

'December 23: Met Ann and the children at the toy department at Robinson's. Saw a penguin dressed as Donald Duck walking around; Pabby and Gordon were delighted. Bought toys for them.'

'December 25: A lovely tree in Mother's sitting-room and heaps of presents. My four sons came to visit us. We are very proud of them.'

1940
Los Angeles:

'September 6: Call on Fini and Ronny. He is as bright and lovable as ever.'

'September 7: Call on Pabby at 6 p.m. It is his eighth birthday, and he is a dear, dear boy.'

'September 27: Dinner with Ann and my two dear sons.'

Mexico City:

'December 1: Telephoned Los Angeles. All four of my beloved sons are fine.'

1941
Los Angeles:

'May 29: Went to the California Military Academy and had dinner with Pabby and Gordon and then took them to their home. My chest expanded when Major Metzger, who heads the school, made many favourable remarks about them.'

San Francisco:

'June 27: For some reason, felt concern about Ronny. Telephoned Fini. Spoke to her and Ronny. All okay, thank heavens!'

Los Angeles:

'September 13: Took Pabby and Gordon to the circus.'

'September 15: George spent last night with me at my house. He told me he intends to be a lawyer. I approve. George is very mature and has an excellent mind and personality. He is a fine young man. I hope he will want to enter the family business.'

'December 20: I took George out to the Athens oilfield, where I brought in such large producing wells. I suppose this is a carryover from last September, when I made up my mind to try and interest him in the oil business.'

1943
Tulsa, Oklahoma:

'January 25: Met George and had a long visit with him. He has lived up to all my expectations, but it is hard for me to realize he is 20 years old. George is eager to get into the fight against the Axis. He is already in the Enlisted Reserve Corps and will be called up after February 8. He will probably have 13 weeks of basic training and then 13 more weeks in officers' school. He likes and is good in English, History and Languages. I love him and pray that he comes through safely.'

'April 16: Saw Paul and Gordon. Gordon recited a poem he wrote about the good qualities of Negroes. Paul is eleven years old and weighs 86 pounds. Gordon is ten and weighs 76 pounds. My sons—all of them—are great rewards.'

George was called up for service in February, 1943, and served overseas as an infantry officer. After V–J Day, he remained in the service for almost two years extra because he was by then assigned to a war-crimes prosecution team.

'The people who are responsible for the ghastly atrocities of the war must be tracked down and punished,' George wrote me. 'I can't consider returning to civilian life until I've done my part in bringing them to justice.'

I married Teddy Lynch, my fifth wife, in Rome during 1939. I've already related how she was arrested on suspicion of espionage by Mussolini's Fascists and not repatriated to the United States until early 1942. On June 15, 1946, Teddy gave birth to my fifth son, Timothy. She was then at our home in California. I was in Tulsa, for this was a most crucial period in the reconversion of the Spartan Aircraft Corporation to peacetime production. My diary entry for the day:

'My darling Teddy gave birth to a son yesterday at 9 a.m. He weighs 4 pounds 14 ounces—a seven months baby. I can't express my disappointment at not having been with her, but she wasn't expecting the baby until August. Exciting to talk to her. Sent masses of roses.'

I rushed to Los Angeles—by train. By then, my irrational

fear of flying was deeply engrained, triggered by a harrowing flight from St. Louis to Tulsa four years before. (I have never flown since.)

When I arrived in L.A., Teddy's doctors gave me heart-chilling news. My newborn son, Timothy, had a very frail constitution, and there were other complications, as these diary notations show.

> 'July 8: To hospital to see my son. Timothy now weighs six pounds but is anaemic; his red cell count is only 65. Poor little man, he has had a hard time.'
> 'July 10: Timothy home today. He has two nurses.'
> 'July 13: With Teddy and Timothy to hospital, where he had a blood transfusion. His red count was down to 47. Much anxiety and fear until the danger passed after his transfusion.'

When a man of 53 has a newborn son and the child is frail in health, all his paternal and protective instincts are aroused. It is no diminution of my love for my other sons when I agree with those who have said that Timmy became 'the apple of my eye.' Perhaps Teddy was right after all when she declared: 'Paul didn't really understand fatherhood until Timmy came along.' Worried and anxious as we both were over Timmy's health, neither of us could possibly foresee the tragedy that lay twelve years in the future.

I have said more than once that I learned many of my most important lessons in life belatedly. Among them were those that taught me what I should have long realized as a fundamental home-truth. A father should never overrate or make big a son just because he *is* a son. More than this, he must never assume that his sons will conform to his patterns.

It's necessary for a father to make realistic and objective evaluations of his sons and, if they do not measure up to his own criteria, then he must make the best of it. I suppose I closed—or preferred to close—my eyes to these facts of life. I hoped and desired that all my sons would enter the family business, eventually taking over from me just as I had taken it over from my father, who founded it. Call it a wish to perpetuate a dynasty if you will, but I had always visualized passing what I had built on to my sons. It was to take time, and I would experience many disappointments before learning that I could not predetermine their careers or the course of their lives.

Once again, I return to a starting-point—namely, that if I had managed to maintain closer relationships with my sons, things might have been much different.

Or would they?

I have, on occasion, thought that in some instances my wives may have succumbed to very human and understandable impulses. As I have noted previously, their resentment and jealousy over my preoccupation with business were strong elements in the frictions that led to their divorcing me. Obviously, I don't—I can't—know exactly what and how the mothers of my sons thought and felt after their divorces. Nonetheless, it isn't unreasonable to guess that perhaps their reasoning went something like this:

'I saw what Paul was like when it came to business and what his concentration on business did to him, to us and to our marriage. No child of mine is going to grow up in the same mould.'

No, I am most definitely not making any charges or accusations. It's merely that I've often observed how divorced wives set out to insure that their children from a broken marriage will be brought up and educated to be totally unlike their fathers. But such conjectures lead nowhere. I had best confine myself to facts as I know them and to contentions that I am able to support with at least some evidence.

16

THANKS TO THE acuity of my mother's foresight, my sons were well provided for, even beyond the large sums I contributed to their support. The trust fund that Mother insisted she and I establish jointly insured this. It also made it possible for my sons to follow their own bents and inclinations in choosing their careers.

At one time or another, each of my four older boys did try his hand in the family business. Two were to drop out after relatively brief periods. Ronny, a good businessman who proved his abilities as head of Getty company operations in Germany, eventually decided that he preferred the motion picture industry. He went to Hollywood some years ago and has since been actively engaged in producing films there. Gordon, after making sincere attempts to find a niche in the oil business, realized there was none that really interested him and chose to follow artistic and intellectual pursuits. He has composed music, is an accomplished pianist and is currently writing a book on economic theories. While I must confess disappointment that Ronny and Gordon are not active in the family business, their decisions did not change my feelings toward them. They have found fields of endeavour for which they are best suited and which provide them with the greatest sense of satisfaction. Having recognized that a father must judge his sons on the basis of objective, realistic evaluations, I am content to leave it at that.

It is when I turn to writing about my other three sons—

George, Timothy and Eugene Paul—that I encounter difficulty. Any discussions of them arouse deeply painful memories
and emotions. I would much prefer to avoid relating much of
what follows. But such an omission would be glaring and
only give rise to misinterpretation, baseless speculation and
bizarre rumour.

When George F. Getty II, my oldest son, came out of the
United States Army, he took a one-year crash-course at
Princeton University and—to my great joy—asked to be taken
into the family business. He started at the bottom, but quickly
demonstrated a flair for business in general and an affinity for
the oil business in particular. Soon after the Getty interests
obtained the Saudi Arabian oil concession in the Neutral
Zone, George went there as my personal representative. In
1954, when I made a visit to Saudi Arabia and the Neutral
Zone, it was with considerable pride that I recorded in my
diary:

'March 9 (Riyadh): My son George seems well liked
here.'

George, it became apparent, was a dynamic individual, one
who could and would be a positive and constructive force in
business. The concept of primogeniture being engrained in
the group unconscious, it is hardly surprising that, having
observed his abilities and further potentials, I began to view
George as the one who would naturally succeed me at the
head of the Getty Family business.

Saudi Arabian King Saud's award of the Neutral Zone concession to the Getty interests caused the most radical changes
in my business activities and personal lifestyle. Getty enterprises were now truly global in their scope. During 1951, I
made a trip to Europe and, at first, believed I would remain
there several months, perhaps a year at most. The stay has so
far lasted almost twenty-five years, nearly a quarter of a
century—nearly a third of my life.

The Getty companies are not corporate entities in the com-
monly accepted sense. Their control is not dispersed, with the
decisive influence being exerted by someone who owns only
ten—or even two—per cent of their shares, as is the case with

so many large companies. Clearcut numerical control is held
by the Getty Family interests and I, the head of the family,
have no qualms about describing myself as an entrepreneur.

Europe and the European capitals—Paris, Rome, London—
were the ideal headquarters for any entrepreneur whose business interests were rapidly expanding in both hemispheres.
American operations were being managed by crack, veteran
executives in whom I could have total confidence. It was in
Europe and the Middle East that pipelines, tankers, refineries
had to be built or purchased and new marketing outlets created. These and a thousand and one other projects demanded
my personal attention and supervision.

My wife Teddy and our son Timmy came with me to
London in 1951. They stayed only a short time before returning to the United States. The closing months of 1952 found
me in Paris, homesick but unable to leave France because my
associates and I were in the midst of negotiations to build a
tanker fleet in French shipyards.

'December 25, 1952: Christmas. Presents from friends.
But I wish I were home on Christmas with my sons.'

Eugene Paul—Pabby—went into the Army the next year. In
September, he was sent to Japan.

'September 7, 1953: Today is Pabby's 21st birthday,
and he is aboard a troopship en route to Japan as a
soldier. I remember my own 21st birthday on December
15, 1913. Odd coincidence that I, too, spent it at sea. I
was aboard a Rumanian ship of about 3,000 tons bound
from Athens to Alexandria. A terrific storm raged, and
I wondered if the ship could possibly last it out. But
today, my thoughts and prayers are with my son.'

Teddy and Timmy came to Europe in 1955. They were with
me in London and in Paris. I honestly believe that Teddy
and I desired to preserve our marriage, but as I have mentioned earlier, she wanted me to return to the United States,
and I could not afford to leave Europe for business reasons.
She and Timmy left. Two years later, having resigned herself
to the fact that we could not re-establish a home-life in

America within the foreseeable future, Teddy filed suit for divorce.

George F. Getty II was moving rapidly up the ladder in the family business—not because he was my son, but by virtue of his demonstrated abilities. Transferred back to the United States from the Neutral Zone, he held progressively higher executive positions in the Spartan Aircraft Corporation, the Skelly Oil Company and finally in the Tidewater Oil Company. At last he reached a point where the directors of Tidewater considered him fully capable and qualified to become president of the company.

George was no puppet or rubber-stamp president. Although he and I generally saw eye to eye, he never hesitated to speak and make his case when he disagreed with me or had views that differed from mine. As often as not, his logic and arguments prevailed. Something of the nature of our relationship is reflected by these diary entries I made in Paris.

'Feb. 24, 1958: George arrives to discuss business matters.'

My entries for the next three days are identical: 'With George all day talking business.' These conversations lasted twelve and fourteen hours daily.

'Feb. 28: Most of day with George. I stressed featuring Tidewater's leadership and advised him to lead the octane race. He left for New York by air in the evening.'

Note my phrasing. I *'advised* him.' I went no further than to give him advice. It was for George to make the final decisions. I knew he would make them wisely and carry them out efficiently. A superb administrator, he had inherited many of his grandfather George F. Getty Sr.'s priceless X-factor qualities. Executives and employees liked and respected him. He inspired and held the strong personal loyalty of the organization.

My third son, Eugene Paul—Pabby—was approaching his twenty-sixth birthday in 1958. After completing his stint in the army, he served a variety of apprenticeships in the family

business. He was married to Gail Harris, daughter of San
Francisco U.S. District Judge George B. Harris. Pabby and
Gail had an infant son, Paul, my first grandson (but not my
first grandchild; George and his wife Gloria already had a
daughter).

Pabby, Gail and the baby were in Europe and went with me
to see the Brussels World's Fair. It was at about this time that
the quantities of crude oil flowing from Neutral Zone fields
made it advisable to acquire additional refining capacity on
the European Continent. I learned that a company owned by
Italian and Swiss interests had recently built a large new
refinery at Gaeta, south of Naples, but had been unable to
operate it at a profit. The company—'Golfo'—and its refinery
were available for purchase. I opened preliminary negotiations.

Early in June, Eugene Paul made a request.

'June 6: Pabby greatly pleased me the other day by
asking my permission to change Eugene to Jean, thus
becoming J. Paul Getty Jr.'

He made the name-change official, and hereafter I will
refer to him as Paul Getty Jr. and his son as Paul Getty III.

Paul Jr. and Gail said they liked living in Italy, and he
indicated he would like to work on the 'Golfo' project,
especially if the company was finally purchased by the Getty
interests. I approved, and they and the baby moved to Milan,
where Golfo's administrative headquarters were located, and
rented an apartment there.

By late July, I was shuttling between Milan and Lugano,
Switzerland, carrying the complex Golfo negotiations forward
to conclusion.

'August 1 (Milano): To 1 Piazza Duse to see Paul and
Gail's apartment and my loved ones. Gail welcomed us.
I saw little Paul asleep in his crib, lying on his stomach.
Paul arrived from the office at 8. I am proud of my little
family. Milan newspapers are featuring stories about the
unbearable heat of the last few days, but although their
apartment is not air conditioned, Paul and Gail were
cheerful and uncomplaining.'

'August 3: Played with baby Paul . . .'

*   *   *

Business required me to go to Lugano, where I stayed at the Hotel Splendide. There was much work to be done. On Sunday, August 10, I noted:

'In my room all day. At 7 p.m. my desk is clear at last. Although I am seven years older than this century, I'm still hard at work.'

There was no let up during the next six days. Then—but I must backtrack. My youngest son, Timothy, had undergone a number of operations for removal of a brain tumour. He accepted the need for these bravely and without complaint. Dr. T. I. Hoen of New York, an outstanding American specialist in the field of brain surgery, had pronounced Timmy cured a few months before. However, some scars and a sunken spot remained on Timmy's forehead. Dr. Hoen and several consultants recommended that these be removed by plastic surgery. They told Teddy—who was, of course, with Timmy in New York—and me (by transatlantic telephone) that it would be a minor operation posing little danger. Neither Teddy nor I thought the operation would be a serious one.

Timmy, whose courage throughout the ordeals of his previous operations had been remarkable, went into the hospital on August 14. Three days later, a very large part of my personal world suddenly started to disintegrate.

'August 17: Teddy telephoned from New York at about 3 a.m. Our darling Timmy had the plastic operation on his forehead Thursday. He was very well, bright and cheerful up to Saturday morning when he suddenly collapsed. He is still very ill. I am distraught. Asked Teddy to call me if there was any change. Said a prayer. Couldn't go back to sleep. Worked on reports and correspondence in an effort to occupy my mind.'

'August 18: At 4 a.m., Teddy phoned. A severe thunderstorm here made slight difficulty in understanding a few words and Teddy was nearly incoherent with grief. Darling Timmy died two hours ago, my best and bravest son, a truly noble human being. Words are useless. Had I not been assured the operation was a slight one I would have gone to New York to be present as there was no urgency about the operation. Dear Teddy! How brave she is! Darling Timmy, the world is poorer for your loss and I am desolate.'

Timmy was twelve when he died. Always an extremely warm and affectionate child, he had a very high level of intelligence and an amazingly keen interest in everything around him. His very frequent letters to me displayed a depth of feeling and a maturity far beyond what one might expect of a child his age—and, he had developed a strong belief in God. I still treasure a touching little poem he wrote and sent me in July, 1957:

> God protects me through the night,
> God will help me win each fight,
> I know that God is ever here,
> I know in God I cannot fear,
> God will show me day by day,
> If I follow in his way.

I rail against neither God nor gods that Timmy was not helped to win his last brave fight, but his death left a void that has never been—and can never be—filled in my life.

Paul Jr., Gail and Paul III provided much solace when I returned to Milan. Still grief-stricken over Timmy, I derived comfort from identifying with their family life.

'August 27: Taxi with Paul to his apartment for lunch. Baby Paul came running into the parlour to greet us. He was most cheerful and cute. He can't talk yet. Gail made a nice lunch for us.'
'September 14: Gail brought baby Paul to see me. He was very cute, active and cheerful.'
'September 17: Baby Paul has fever. Worried. Telephoned to pediatric specialist in London for advice.'
'September 18: Baby is better . . .'
'September 19: Baby Paul is well . . .'

The loss of Timmy and the proximity of Paul III had turned me into a prototype of the overly-doting, near-hysterical grandfather.

*   *   *

Golfo's offices were soon relocated in Rome and the company's name changed to Getty Oil Italiana, SpA.

Having observed Paul Jr.'s performance over the months, I considered him capable of assuming major business responsibilities and, since he and Gail were delighted at the thought of living in Rome, I had a long talk with him.

'I'm going to leave you here on your own,' I told Paul. 'Think you can handle things?'

'I'll try my best,' he said.

It was good enough for me.

17

I SAW MUCH of Paul Jr. and Gail over the next few years. They had three more children. Paul was not setting the world on fire as a businessman, but all things taken into consideration, he was doing a creditable job in Rome and he and Gail appeared to be most happily married.

Then, almost overnight it seemed, everything started to go wrong. Paul Jr. lost interest in Getty Oil Italiana and in business. Thanks to the provisions of the Sarah Getty trust, he did not need his salary. Distributions from the trust had made him—and his brothers—independently wealthy.

There is no need for me to go into the details. What with J. Paul Getty Jr. being known to the press as 'the son and namesake of the world's richest man,' they received worldwide publicity. Rome's *paparazzi* took, and scandal magazines across the globe published, photographs of Paul Jr. with long hair, a full beard and wearing—according to one U.P.I. photo caption: 'A tie-dyed velvet outfit that would make any genuine hippie green with envy.'

Paul Jr. dropped out of the family business. He and Gail separated and, in 1966, were divorced, with Gail obtaining custody of the children. I do not know the reasons behind the breakup. I have never asked either of them. It would hardly be appropriate for me, with five divorces of my own, to pry, and in any event both Paul Jr. and Gail were adults, old enough to know their own minds and entitled to keep their personal motivations to themselves.

I can only surmise and speculate, and when I do, a suspicion that the fault was partly mine arises in my mind. Paul Jr. and Gail were both young and unsophisticated when they married—and, so far as I could see, remained so many years after. Rome is one of the world's more decadent cities. This is not a factor likely to have any notable effect on the life-styles of either tourists or the more worldly and not easily impressionable among the people who live there for protracted periods. But the effect can be pernicious on relatively inexperienced and sheltered individuals such as Paul Jr. and Gail. If this is, indeed, what happened, then I may have made a serious mistake in giving Paul Jr. the Rome assignment.

Soon after their divorce, Paul remarried and, a little later, Gail did too. Paul Jr.'s second wife was the Dutch-born actress Talitha Pol. She was the daughter of Dutch artist William Pol and step-granddaughter of the famed British painter Augustus John. In July, 1971, Talitha died after allegedly taking an overdose of drugs. Gail's second marriage was to an American actor residing in Rome, but it, too, ended in separation. Gail and her four children continued to live in Rome afterward.

In 1967, Tidewater Oil Company was merged into the Getty Oil Company. Only those who have been actually involved in the merger of two large corporations, each having thousands of stockholders, can appreciate the magnitude of the task. A great many executives and employees of both companies contributed to the success of the merger. Here, I would like to make special mention of two men who were prime movers.

David S. Hecht had been my attorney, close friend and good right arm for decades. When he died in 1959, I wrote in my diary: 'Dave can never be replaced.' It does not alter that opinion when I express my appreciation to C. Lansing Hays, Jr. By 1967, Lansing Hays headed (and still heads) the law firm Dave Hecht had founded. Hays, an equally fine attorney and loyal friend, was the brilliant legal brain behind the merger.

And it was my son, George F. Getty II, who made and implemented the merger plans, followed them through, guiding and coordinating, never losing sight of the big picture while paying minute attention to every detail. With this, George won his final business spurs. He earned the new position he received, that of executive vice-president and chief operating officer of the Getty Oil Company.

Getty Oil expanded its operations and made significant strides during the years that George was its chief operating officer. I took great pride in his accomplishments and derived confidence from them. I felt certain that the business founded by my father and built further by me would eventually pass into the strongest and most capable hands.

Then, in 1973, another portion of my personal world collapsed.

On the evening of June 6, I attended a dinner party given by my dear and longtime friend, Margaret, Duchess of Argyll. I was unexpectedly called away from the table and informed that my administrative assistant, Mrs. Barbara Wallace and her husband, Alan, who looks after the Getty interests in North Sea drilling operations—had arrived and wished to see me alone. Completely baffled, I went to a small reception room where they were waiting. I saw their faces were drawn, grim.

'Stuart Evey has been trying to reach you from Los Angeles,' Barbara said.

Evey is a vice-president of Getty Oil. It was unusual that he should be telephoning me at that hour, even more unusual that Barbara and Al Wallace would drive into London from their home in Cobham to tell me about it personally.

'Barbara's arranged to have the call put through here immediately—she only needs to dial the operator,' Al said—and then added softly, 'I think you'd better brace yourself, Mr. Getty.'

I cannot remember what thoughts flashed through my mind during the minutes it took for the connection to be made and I heard Stuart Evey's voice. It was strained, shaky. I can only remember the key phrases:

'. . . George has had a stroke . . . he's unconscious in a hospital . . .'

I managed no more than to ask that Evey stay in constant touch with me. Less than two hours later, he spoke to me again.

'George died a few minutes ago . . .'

It is impossible for me to recall much about my emotions or reactions. I am aware that very soon after, my staunch friend and attorney, Lansing Hays, telephoned from New York. Hardly less affected by the news than I—for he and

George were close friends and worked magnificently together in business dealings—Lansing took the great load of immediately imperative actions on his own shoulders. He remained in constant contact throughout the night—but again my memories are vague and confused. I am told by Margaret Argyll, Penelope Kitson and her daughter Jessica, Barbara and Al Wallace and other friends who came and stayed to comfort me that I sat for hours, staring into space, saying nothing. I was shattered and can remember only one thought—that it was untrue, impossible. I had always believed that my first son, George, would outlive me at least by 35 years. I shall be eternally grateful to Lansing Hays and the other friends I have named for the limitless help and solace they gave me.

The next day, I learned from newspapers, television and radio what Stuart Evey had refrained from telling me. George had not died from a stroke, but from the effects of a lethal combination of alcohol and barbiturates. No, he was not drunk, not by any means.

Los Angeles County Coroner Thomas Noguchi reported that a blood test 'showed an alcoholic content of ·06 per cent, and a person is not legally considered intoxicated until the alcoholic content of the blood reaches ·10 per cent,' almost twice the amount shown by the test. But George had also taken some barbiturates. Sometimes these, when taken with even modest quantities of alcohol, can have a deadly effect. As Coroner Noguchi told the press: 'Such a combination is the worst imaginable. More and more people die from this mixture.'

Barbiturates are prescribed freely by physicians in the United States and many other countries as tranquillizers and 'tension-relievers.' Pharmaceuticals manufacturers warn doctors about the dangers of using them when a person has had even a drink or two. Presumably, prescribing physicians pass these warnings on to their patients, many of whom are likely to forget them, especially when tired and under pressure.

Norris Bramlett, my chief accountant and among the closest and most trusted of my associates, was in Los Angeles and, at my request, made an independent investigation of the circumstances.

'I am convinced beyond any doubt that it was an accident,' Norris declared after making exhaustive inquiries. I accept his word on that just as I have accepted his word on whatever he has told me during more than thirty years.

My diary entry for June 9, 1973:

> 'George's funeral was held in Malibu at 10 a.m.—6 p.m., English time. At 6, I walked to the church and said a prayer for my dearest son . . .'

One question will continue to gnaw at me to the end of my own days. I remember the conversations I had with Randolph Churchill, and I know that all too many businessmen and executives rely on a few evening drinks—and barbiturates—as a means of easing the tensions and pressures created by their work. Is it possible that these were unduly greater for George because he strove too hard to live up to the images of his grandfather and me?

Barely more than a month after George died, the Getty Family received another heavy blow.

> 'July 12: Message from Paul Jr. via Gordon that Paul III has been kidnapped.'
> 'July 13: Headlines in papers on Paul III. I hope there is no truth to the kidnapping story, that he has only gone away from home without telling his mother and will soon return.'

I'd had only sporadic direct contact with Gail—Paul III's mother—since her divorce from Paul Jr. During that time Paul Getty III, my first grandson, had grown from the adorable red-haired child with whom I had played during 1958 into a youth of seventeen with his own distinctive lifestyle. Italian—and other—newspapers described him as 'The Golden Hippie' and 'the darling of Rome's hippie colony.' I had no right to interfere or even criticize—even if I had wished to do so. Gail had full custody of Paul III and the other three children by her marriage to my son, Paul Jr., and she had remarried. None the less, Paul III *was* my grandchild.

Several days passed without any definite developments. Then:

> 'July 26: Guildford police had a message for me from the Rome police asking if I would pay ransom for Paul III's return . . .

My answer was negative and based on two considerations. First and foremost, I had fourteen other grandchildren. Were I to announce instant willingness to pay ransom for one, I would be automatically placing all others in jeopardy of being kidnapped. I was particularly concerned for Gail's other children who lived with her in Rome. Between 1960 and 1973, there had been 320 *known* kidnappings for ransom in Italy. Some sources claimed there were twice as many more that had not been reported to police, with the victims' families dealing with—and paying—the kidnappers secretly. Each payment of ransom invariably encouraged more kidnappings. The second reason for my refusal was much broader-based. I contend that acceding to the demands of criminals and terrorists merely guarantees the continuing increase and spread of lawlessness, violence and such outrages as terror-bombings, 'skyjackings' and the slaughter of hostages that plague our present-day world.

The fears for my other grandchildren in Rome were later indirectly confirmed by my friend, Gianni Agnelli, head of the giant Italian Fiat company, in a *Newsweek* Magazine interview:

Interviewer's Question: 'We hear a lot about the breakdown in law and order in Italy—the kidnappings and so forth. How serious is this really?'

Gianni's Answer: 'It's quite serious, and the situation has been deteriorating.'

My initial refusal to pay ransom was widely—and, for the most part adversely—publicized. Curiously, almost no publicity was given to proposals made at about the same time by *Signor* Luigi Gui, the Italian Minister of the Interior. *Signor* Gui advocated a law to prevent kidnappers from collecting ransoms. He said the Italian Government should have the power to freeze the finances of kidnap victims' families and thereby prevent them from raising the money to meet kidnappers' demands.

There is much I would like to say about Paul III's kidnapping, but unfortunately, I cannot. Several people have since been arrested and are awaiting trial on charges of having been parties to the crime. At this writing, the entire matter is consequently *sub judice*. Were I to divulge certain information, I could be guilty of trying to influence or interfere with judicial processes. It would be the ultimate bitter irony if some guilty person were to be released on the technicality that words written by me had prejudiced a jury or prevented him from having a fair trial.

I can, however, cite published facts. After holding Paul III for nearly four months, his abductors amputated the boy's right ear and mailed it to a Rome newspaper. With that, it became apparent there was no hope of outwaiting—or outbluffing—the kidnappers. Criminals who would savagely mutilate a victim would not hesitate to kill him.

My sons—Paul Jr., Ronny and Gordon—and I held a family council. The amount of ransom demanded was huge (but most estimates published by the news media were wide of the true mark). The Getty Family closed ranks. The kidnappers were informed that the ransom would be paid.

More time was needed to establish direct contact with the kidnappers and arrange for actual payment. Finally, after what seemed an endless period, and was one of awful torment for every member of the Getty Family—the payment was made. The kidnappers released Paul III on December 15, 1973—which by coincidence happened to be my eighty-first birthday. It was the finest and most wonderful birthday present of my life.

Some postscripts are in order.

Not long after being freed by his kidnappers, Paul III married Miss Martine Zacher and moved to California. They now have a son, Paul Getty IV. But Paul III suffered severe traumatic shocks during the months he was held for ransom and, of course, from the horror of having his ear severed. His maternal grandfather, U.S. District Judge George B. Harris, considered it wise to take certain legal steps that would protect Paul III's interests until he was fully recovered from the after-effects of his ordeal. I naturally deferred to Judge Harris's recommendations.

Paul III is now attending Pepperdine College in California. I am pleased to learn that he has begun to show considerable talent as a painter. Some of his canvases have been exhibited and a number of critics have expressed the opinion that his work displays promise.

Gail and the three other children she had with my son Paul Jr. are living in England. During the summer of 1975, the youngsters—Aileen, 15; Mark, 14; and Ariadne, 13—spent several weeks with me at Sutton Place. I was delighted to have them—just as I was delighted by the visits during that same summer of my other grandchildren. My sons Ronny and Gordon and their wives and children came, as did George's former wife, Gloria, who brought their three daughters.

It was a most reassuring summer for Grandfather J. Paul Getty. It proved that despite anything and everything—be it wealth, divorce, tragedy or any of the other myriad conditions and tribulations of life—the Getty Family *is* a family and will continue to be one. That is not a boast. It is a statement of fact made with no little pride.

18

THE KIDNAPPING AND mutilation of my grandson are symptoms of a disease eating away at the foundations of our Western civilization. I have watched the rising trend of crime and violence with a sourly apprehensive eye ever since the late 1930s. It was then that the process of destroying respect for the basic principles of law and order began.

The erosion was slow and subtle at first, a form of spontaneous subversion that operated under the guise of correcting abuses and injustices. I do not deny that there were many—far too many—of those and they most certainly required correcting. But instead of seeking the highest possible level of flaw-free justice, the process became one of plumbing for the lowest possible level of laxity and permissiveness.

Gradually, concepts and principles that had been tested and proven over the millennia were thrown on the discard pile. Woolly-headed social theoreticians and dewy-eyed do-gooders encroached on the preserves of law-enforcement agencies and judicial systems. The trend steadily gained momentum, tying the hands of police and rendering judges and law-courts virtually impotent in many countries, most notably the United States.

By the mid-1960s, I was witnessing an almost total metamorphosis in the interpretation and application of laws that decreed punishment for those who committed crimes. The criminal—even if he was a constant recidivist—became an object of sympathy and pity and a subject of the exonerating rationalizations gushed out by fiercely Utopian psychologists, psychiatrists and social workers. The victim, one might be led to think, was the culpable party for having, by his very existence, incited the criminal to rob, attack or even murder him.

The liberal, 'enlightened,' view was (and is) that a criminal—regardless of his personal history, previous record or the gravity of his offense—should be re-educated, rehabilitated, given psychotherapeutic treatment. In short, society should do anything but punish him.

'Punishment is not a deterrent,' is the slogan of the do-good fraternity (and sorority).

The slogan has had a mesmerizing effect. The theory has gathered enormous numbers of adherents. As a consequence, there has been progressively less punishment meted out—and there has been progressively more crime.

In the United States, the homicide rate per 100,000 population soared 34.8 per cent between 1968 and 1973. During 1973—the last year for which official figures are available to me—there were 19,510 murders in the U.S., more than fifty murders per day. This is only a fragment of the dismal picture, as the following table shows:

Offence	Number for 1973
Murder	19,510
Forcible rape	51,000
Robbery	382,680
Assault	416,270
Burglary	2,540,000
Larceny	4,304,000
Auto theft	923,600
TOTAL	8,638,400

Great Britain has the reputation of being much more law-abiding than the United States—and 'so it is. However, in August, 1973, Britain's Police Federation issued this chilling statement:

'The number of crimes recorded has increased from 250,000 annually immediately before the war (World War Two) to well over two million last year.'

The problem in other Western countries does not seem any

less acute. The term 'law and order' is derisively rendered as 'lawnorder' and has become a dirty phrase.

I fear that I do not look very kindly on the 'liberal' whose heart bleeds for the killer, rapist, holdup man or mugger. I find it impossible to endorse the tea-and-therapy approach to a multiple-murderer or maniacal rapist. I've noted that there is considerable correlation between taking a permissive and all-forgiving attitude toward criminals and holding Left-leaning political views. This provides sardonic amusement for the objective observer.

Liberals in the Western democracies who look Left often have a very distorted view of what life is like on that left side of the fence. The courts in the People's Democracies are still very much aware that—strangely enough—people don't like to be punished and will go to great lengths—even unto obeying the letter of the law—to avoid punishment.

Courts in the People's Democracies do not hesitate to hand down severe penalties to those who violate the laws—and, as a result, People's Democracies have proportionately far fewer law-violators. In lands ruled by commissars, it is still known that the fear of punishment is the most effective deterrent to crime. I am yet to hear of a People's Court where a pedantic psychiatrist or a soulful social-worker tells a judge what type of sentence he should pass on a convicted criminal.

When Vice President Nelson Rockefeller came to visit me at Sutton Place in July, 1975, he was accompanied by a platoon of American Secret Servicemen.

'I have thirty-six assigned to me so that nine can be with me at all times,' Vice President Rockefeller told me.

In addition, British law-enforcement authorities sent two police cars plus four men with guard dogs to supplement Nelson's security force. He had no say over any of this. The 36-man American detail is the minimum considered necessary to safeguard the life of the Vice President—and the British weren't taking any chances.

The need for such a security force speaks volumes—and it should be remembered that Vice President Rockefeller's visit took place before the two assassination attempts against President Ford in the United States. The political leaders of many Western democracies must be constantly guarded against those political extremists or plain lunatics who may try to murder them.

Political assassins, terror-bombers, skyjackers, extremists who take—and often slaughter—hostages have all become familiar figures on our landscape of violence. Still, there is no apparent inclination in the Western countries to fight fire with fire.

During World War Two, when faced with the menace of the Axis, the greatest criminal conspiracy of all time, President Franklin D. Roosevelt did not hesitate to take a hard stand.

'We will meet force with greater force, violence with greater violence,' he declared.

This is the only kind of language some people understand—and the only kind of action they fear (or even take seriously). There will—and can—be no downturn in the crime and violence trend until those who wield authority are once again willing to accept the fact and act accordingly.

Much has been written and rumoured about my own security precautions, most particularly those in force at Sutton Place. According to some versions, the estate and manor house are virtually a fortress-complex—which is absurd.

Much of the estate is ringed by the same fence that was there when the property was owned by the Duke of Sutherland—and even before, when it belonged to Lord Northcliffe. There are two main entrances to the estate. They are barred—if that is the word—by openwork gates. Those near the Woking road are made of wood. Those on the Guildford side are of ornamental iron. Neither set is a very formidable barrier.

In any case, the gates are open during much of the day. Several dozen English employees work for Liberian Operations Ltd., which has an office building near the main house. They drive their cars in and out regularly, coming to work in the morning, going to lunch and returning, leaving at the end of the working day. At other times on weekdays, the gates are opened electrically by the gate-keepers—without formalities or delays. On Sundays and other days of religious observance, the gates remain wide open to provide worshippers access to the church located within the boundaries of the estate.

Yes, of course there is a security staff at Sutton Place and there are elaborate fire and burglar-alarm systems. The security men are not, however, a Praetorian Guard. They are not there solely—nor even mainly—for my personal protection, although that is part of their unarmed task. The manor house contains art treasures—paintings, tapestries, Oriental rugs, antique furniture, silver—worth millions. These must be protected. A considerable part of the security men's salaries is offset by savings in insurance premiums, which are much lower because of their presence.

Then, journalists who write of my 'personal bodyguards' are evidently unaware that industrial espionage is a very big and lucrative business. The filing cabinets at Sutton Place contain reports, documents, oilfield survey maps and other material for which unscrupulous competitors would willingly pay very large sums.

The security force is augmented by Alsatian guard dogs. There is even a pride of lions at Sutton (but anyone trying to intrude on their privacy would have to bring along an acetylene torch to cut through the steel-wire fence that forms the enclosure around their home).

If opinion polls are to be believed, what I am to say next will arouse a storm of wrath in 47.8 per cent of those who read it. This is said to be the overall percentage of those who are opposed to capital punishment under any circumstances. (I am inclined to doubt the validity of the figure. I rather suspect that there are far more people who favour the return of capital punishment—at least in certain types of murder-cases—than the polls indicate. However, that is neither here nor there. I am too far along in life to withhold an opinion merely because it fails to agree with any overwhelming consensus.)

I am old-fashioned—or, if you prefer, arch-reactionary—enough to believe that the death penalty is the one even partially effective deterrent to murder and some other particularly heinous crimes. I'm aware that fierce pro-and-con debates have raged on this subject for many, many years and that there is no conclusive proof to sustain either side of the argument. The only evidence I find convincing is, I'm sorry to say, negative evidence. Wherever the death penalty has been abolished—or, if not wiped off the statute books, simply not carried out—the homicide rate has risen sharply, often skyrocketing. For example, in New York City, the annual number of murders has more than trebled since the days when 'getting the chair' was a fear that hung over every potential killer's head.

George Bernard Shaw was once asked to sign a petition demanding an end to the death penalty. His reply:

'I'll be delighted to sign—if you'll get the murderers to sign first.'

Capital punishment for murder has now been abolished—*de jure* or *de facto*—in most Western countries. The maximum penalty is now generally a life sentence—which, in most instances, is a travesty. In the United States, the average 'lifer' is paroled or has his sentence commuted after eight to ten years in the penitentiary. True, it does not always automatically follow that he leaves prison and kills again.

But let us look at the problem realistically. The fear of execution undoubtedly kept many potential murderers from killing. (Again, the negative evidence—when the fear no longer existed, homicide rates zoomed.) The prospect of a maximum eight to ten year prison stretch does not—and cannot possibly—have the same effect.

In my opinion, the Western World would be a better and safer place for its law-abiding citizens if capital punishment were reintroduced and made mandatory in the following categories of homicide:

1. The killing of a law-enforcement or prison officer while he or she is performing duties.

2. Any killing committed by a person or persons who are perpetrating a robbery or other felony.

3. The murder of a woman by a rapist.

4. Multiple murders—unless the killer is adjudged insane.

5. Causing death to a person during a kidnapping, skyjacking or during the course of politically motivated terrorist activities.

6. Causing death through *any* terrorist acts such as bombings, indiscriminate shootings and machine-gunnings and similar outrages.

Even as these words were being written, I happened across another public opinion poll, this one taken by a leading London daily newspaper. It indicated that no less than 75 per cent of Britain's teen-agers favour the return of capital punishment for certain crimes, particularly for murders committed by political terrorists. There is comfort in the thought that perhaps I am not so hopelessly old-fashioned and out of step with modern times and attitudes after all.

I fear for the safety and security—and the future—of our society. During little more than a decade, the United States has seen the assassination of President John F. Kennedy, Black Nationalist leader Malcolm X, the Reverend Martin Luther King, Senator Robert F. Kennedy, and an assassin's bullet permanently crippled Alabama Governor George C. Wallace. In the period 1964–1973, 858 American law enforcement officers were slain in line of duty. There have been numberless mass-murders: six such cases in the State of California alone in a four-year period, these including the Charles Manson 'family' slaughters and the massacre of nine persons in the home of Walter Parkin near Lodi. In Texas, two youths confessed to participation in the torture murders of 27 people over a three-year period ending with their arrest in 1973—the year during which the United States had 19,510 murders overall.

In England, according to recently published reports, there have been twenty murders in a single section of London alone during the year preceding September, 1975. Bomb-outrages in England have taken a toll of more than fifty lives. The British Police Federation says that during 1974, one police officer in every ten was assaulted while performing his duty, and has issued this statement:

'It is now an everyday occurrence for criminals to use guns to murder, to wound, assault and to rob. The threat to public order continues unabated.

'The average law-abiding citizen must make his voice heard in telling those in authority and other leaders within the community, some of whom are prepared to tolerate and even condone law-breaking, that the time for change is now upon us.'

American President Theodore Roosevelt is said to have remarked: 'There is more law in a policeman's nightstick than there is in all the statute books of the State of New York.'

Sad though it may be, there are indications all around us that Teddy Roosevelt was right. Unless authority and respect are once again given to the policeman—the law-enforcement officer—the tide of crime and violence will continue to rise.

It will continue to rise even higher and more swiftly unless the men who administer our judicial system once more awaken to the simple fact that soft words do not discourage hard criminals. Only hard punishment—and fear of it—will serve as an effective deterrent.

Unless present trends are reversed in the United States, we Americans may have to take a page from the Communist book as a last, desperate resort. This will involve the drafting and implementation of a harsh—even draconian—criminal code. We may even have to adopt the repressive and repugnant Communist system of block captains. I would hate to see this, but I have seen respect for law and order lessen and crime and violence increase to the point where there are more than 8·6 million crimes—and over 19,500 murders—annually in the United States. If we permit the trend to continue, you and I will be the all-out losers in the final breakdown, in the chaos and anarchy that must inevitably follow. It is tragically true that our Western civilization is rapidly approaching such a point of no return—beyond which the only remaining question will be one of individual survival.

The case was summed up in October, 1975, by the prestigious Paris newspaper *Le Figaro*. France is one of the few Western countries that still metes out capital punishment. When a savage young murderer was recently sentenced to death by guillotine, the French public raised no outcry, for—as *Le Figaro* commented in a lead editorial:

'We are entering the age of violence on the part of individuals and clans because we have entered the era of the weakness of the parents and the state. We are entering the age of execution again because we are already in the age of assassins.'

I have certainly had ample opportunity to observe the process and progression of the democratic countries' entering into the era of the weakness of the state. Paradoxically, the State has grown weaker and less effective even as it has appeared to grow more powerful and wield a greater and ever-more pervasive influence on our lives and activities. The phenomenon bears closer examination.

19

THE YEARS SINCE World War Two have been marked by grave deterioration in the social structure of the Western democracies. People have become almost ungovernable. I—for one—fear there is a question whether the democratic form of government can be ultimately successful unless there are major changes—even complete reversals—in the established behaviour patterns of both the governed and those who govern.

A democratic government may be loosely defined as one that exists by consent of the majority. Consent is not enough to guarantee the survival of democracy. A democratic government can only work if the people cooperate with it. Conversely, people will cooperate with their governments only if those provide leadership and demonstrate strength and courage.

Today, we are in the Age of Big Government. Size may be awesome, but it alone does not automatically imply courage, strength or the ability to lead. On the contrary, the growth of government has very often implied a disastrous sapping of these qualities. Bluster and bombast are no substitutes for courage. Indiscriminate—and inconsistent—exercises of power are not demonstrations of strength (more often, they are evidences of fundamental weakness). Government interference and meddling at every level and in every sector of human life and endeavour hardly constitute leadership.

Nancy, Lady Astor, who served in Parliament from 1919 until 1945, was noted for her trenchant wit. In the very early

1950s, we had a chat during which she told me she was very glad to be out of the political mainstream.

'I've never been good at parlour tricks,' Lady Astor said. 'Politics have passed into the hands of prestidigitators who gull the public with the illusion that movement is action.'

Nancy Astor's observation has proven true—with a vengeance.

In the United States, the Federal Government has almost three million civilian employees on its payrolls. New York City alone has 320,000 municipal employees—and one million more or less permanent welfare clients. In Britain, almost sixty per cent of the total national income goes on public spending.

That is movement.

But the United States is floundering in recession. New York City teeters on the thinnest imaginable edge of bankruptcy. Britain is experiencing the highest inflation rate in the Western World.

That is action—or rather, the lack of it.

Arpad Plesch once went to great lengths telling me about a science-fiction horror film he had seen. It had to do with a mysterious blob of organic matter that reached Earth from Outer Space. At first tiny, the blob began to grow. Defying all human efforts to destroy it, the blob spread in all directions until it engulfed entire cities, suffocating every living thing in them.

'Stock science fiction,' I commented, unimpressed.

'But no!' Arpad countered. 'It was a magnificent allegory. Look at the political bureaucracies oozing in from all sides to stifle us!'

The ooze has since turned into torrents.

Being an octogenarian, I can actually remember the days when the terms 'Civil Service' and 'civil servant' still retained their original meanings. The Civil Service and its employees existed to serve the citizen and taxpayer. In more recent decades, even lower-rung civil servants have come to wield as much power as medieval barons or Persian satraps. Taxpaying citizens (their employers) must appear before modern-day civil servants obsequiously, hat-in-hand. In Big Government, it is the civil servant who decides whether a citizen may build a home on a certain piece of property, open a

corner grocery store or grow leeks instead of soy beans on his
own land.

Cattle batten on grass. Many species of birds live on a diet of
worms. In democratic countries, the sustenance of politicians
is provided by votes. Once upon a time, unscrupulous politicians faced with vote-shortages would pass out dollar bills
from their own pockets as bribes to those who would cast
their ballots for them. That crass—and, to the politician,
personally costly—practice is largely out of fashion. The
astute modern candidate buys his votes wholesale, but with
the taxpayer's money, not his own.

A pledged Aye for a measure to dredge a harbour in a
seacoast town that has no particular need for it may cost the
Federal Government $50 million. But it buys several thou-
sand votes for the campaigning congressman who makes the
pledge. A senatorial candidate's solemn vow that he will push
for a billion-dollar increase in welfare benefits has immense
purchasing power. It insures that 100,000—or 500,000—professional welfare clients will put their 'X' next to his name on
the upcoming voting-paper.

But then, who doesn't love a bargain?

It is less than fair to blame the decay of our social fabric
entirely on politicians. As Theodore Roosevelt remarked: 'The
most successful politician is he who says what everybody is
thinking most often and in the loudest voice.'

A candidate for public office naturally plays to the gallery,
seeking to derive the greatest good (for himself) from what
the greatest number are thinking. Thundering out his plat-
form, he gives the illusion of leading. More often than not, he
is merely following. Shrewd instinct tells him what the crowd
wants—not only to hear, but to have.

The law and order issue is a case in point. I do not believe
that the *original* blame for the growing disregard for the
principles of law and order can be ascribed to politicians. The
most convincing evidence available indicates it probably began with the family in the home and stemmed from entirely
understandable human emotional responses.

During the Depression years, many millions of people
knew hardship and want. They resolved that their children
would 'have it better.' The resolve manifested itself in giving

children more freedom and privileges. Next came the advocates of progressive education who argued that schools and teaching methods were too rigid, strict, harsh. Children, they maintained, should play their way to knowledge. If the children failed to gain knowledge or a sense of values—well, hell, at least they enjoyed themselves in the non-process.

This line of reasoning—if it can be dignified by the word—was greatly reinforced by Spockian doctrines of permissiveness. Not only the rod but even mild remonstrances had to be spared. Let Johnnie break his toys—or the windows or the family's best china. Better that than to have him 'repress his normal, healthy aggressions.'

Discipline became one of the most obscene words in the language.

The 'Liberal Approach' oozed—as my friend Arpad Plesch might have put it—down from the ivory towers and into homes, schools and even law courts. Sensing the mood of the pack, the politicians vied with each other to say what everybody was thinking most often and in the loudest voice—and poured oceans of enlightenment into the legislative mills.

Suddenly, by what seemed Instant Common Consent, there were no more bad boys or bad girls. All sneak-thieves, street thugs and sadistic killers less than eighteen years of age became maladjusted juveniles. Kindly counselling, courses in basketweaving and leathercraft and drama lessons were decreed to be the surefire re-adjustment cure-alls.

As might be expected, those in over-18 age-groups were quick in protesting that they were the victims of discrimination and to demand equal rights to be considered maladjusted rather than malefactors.

The United States is a country that can boast of 8·6 million serious crimes a year. Cynics might be inclined to contend it follows that the criminal (or potentially criminal) population represents a significant reservoir of votes. Going a step further, the ultra-cynical might even advance the argument that this could explain why ultra-liberal politicians have so assiduously pressed for further relaxation of laws. The theory is doubtless without basis. None the less, by one means or another, laws have grown lax and the courts have shown ever-increasing reticence to enforce them.

University students riot and injure faculty members and destroy entire buildings; university administrators sit down with their ring-leaders and meekly accede to their demands. Federal, State and City governments appoint social workers to act as liaison agents and mediators between vicious street-gangs whose members are known to have committed murder, mayhem and innumerable other crimes. Convicted criminals assault guards and set fire to prison buildings; august panels are formed to hear (and act upon) the prisoners' grievances.

When an F.B.I. sharpshooter kills a heavily armed sky-jacker who is threatening to blow up an airliner and its passengers, he—and law-enforcement agencies in general—are accused of 'overreacting'. When, as Governor of New York State, Nelson Rockefeller refused to exceed his consti-tutional authority and intervene in the Attica Prison riot—a matter for authorities on the scene to handle—he was lam-basted by the liberal press and lunatic-fringe do-gooders. Police officers grappling with robbers or killers they have caught after chasing them along crowded sidewalks risk being pelted with garbage—or being physically assaulted—by sup-posedly law-abiding passers-by.

For the benefit of visitors from another planet, a short glossary. In our enlightened American society, a law enforce-ment official is a pig. A criminal is a victim of social injus-tice. The average citizen is a cipher producing revenue for Government until election time when he becomes part of the political prestidigitators' captive audience. The business-man . . .

Ah, yes. The businessman.

The Getty interests are associated with Dr. Armand Ham-mer's Occidental Petroleum, Lord Thomson of Fleet's Thom-son Scottish Associates and Allied Chemical in a large North Sea oil exploration and drilling project. Not long ago, Dr. Hammer, Lord Thomson and I attended a conference held in London. Among the others present was a prominent Ameri-can businessman whose name I shall refrain from using for reasons that will be obvious. This man, an entrepreneur with people by the tens of thousands on his payrolls, had spent two weeks in Washington before coming to London for the con-ference. Asked by someone how he gauged current political climates for business in the United States, he scowled and his face became flushed.

'Gentlemen, I can only describe it like this. God help us if any businessman comes out publicly against spitting in the streets. If he does, a week later Congress will pass a law making it a felony to expectorate anywhere else.'

There were laughs—but they were nervous and sour. The graphic hyperbole was too close to the truth for comfort.

Some weeks later, an enterprising young journalist came to interview me at Sutton Place.

'You are richer than John D. Rockefeller Sr. or Sir Basil Zaharoff ever were,' he said—then asked: 'How do you feel about having so much power?'

'Power?' I repeated. 'What kind of power do you mean?'

'Why, political power, of course.'

I forced a smile. 'Let me think,' I said. 'I have one twelve-thousandth the power of the employees who work for the companies I own or control. I have one one-millionth the power of New York City's welfare recipients. I have . . .'

'You're pulling my leg, Mr. Getty.'

'Am I?' I retorted and went on to say that I cast my absentee ballot in every Federal election and in every State election in California, where I am legally resident. In other words, I pointed out, I had exactly ONE vote. The companies I own or control have about 12,000 employees; they have a total of 12,000 votes. The million people on New York City's welfare rolls have a presumable total of a million votes.

'But you can use your money in campaign contributions . . .'

'You should bone up on the laws about *that*,' I suggested. 'In any event, businessmen who make campaign contributions very frequently find their money being used against them.'

'I don't understand.'

'The candidates to whom they make the contributions often get into office and push through legislation that raises taxes on business or otherwise makes it more difficult for legitimate businessmen to operate their enterprises profitably.'

I think my interviewer went away unconvinced—but, being British, he had never been asked to contribute to an American campaign fund or to vote in an American election (and, he had never been a businessman).

20

MIGUEL ALEMAN AND I became friends in 1940 when he was a minister in Mexican President Manuel Camacho's government. (Miguel himself served as President of Mexico from 1946 until 1952.) In 1941, Aleman came to Los Angeles and we spent much time together. A great attorney and jurist—he had been a justice of the Mexican Court of Appeals—Miguel Aleman was also a man of culture and refinement.

'July 12 (1941): Met Miguel Aleman at 12:30. We lunched at Vista del Arroyo, then went to see the Huntington Collection. His knowledge and appreciation of fine art surprised me and the curator, who escorted us. We later had dinner at Mocambo.'

I mention this here because I remember our dinner-table discussion. Aleman revealed that he and President Camacho had recently thrown a prominent Mexican politician out of office and insured that he would have no political future. The man's offence: he had exceeded the budget set for his department by almost fifty per cent.

'Did he embezzle the money or use it for his own personal purposes?' I asked.

'No, the money was spent on departmental operations,' Aleman replied.

'Then what made you take such drastic action?' I inquired.

146

Miguel Aleman answered by quoting the line from Voltaire about the hanging of Admiral John Byng:

'Pour encourager les autres.'

Possibly the ruthless expulsion of one government department head *is* the only effective means to encourage others to keep their spending of public funds within the limits set by the budget. A taxpayer long painfully aware of habitual overspending by government agencies, I have never heard of any other methods that succeeded in serving the purpose.

As Government has grown bigger, its spending—and its giveaway programmes—have grown even faster and larger. A realist readily comprehends the dynamics involved.

Incumbents are lavish with the taxpayers' money because they want to remain incumbents. Their challengers are familiar with the rules of the vote-getting game and promise that once they're in office they'll up the ante. Where the spiral will stop, no one knows—or seems to care.

U.S. Federal expenditures in 1900 were less than $500 million; fifty years later, they were closer to $50 billion*—a hundredfold increase. By 1974, they topped $300 billion, SIX HUNDRED TIMES what they had been at the turn of the century.

It should be noted that during the same period, the population of the United States increased less than threefold, from 76 million in 1900 to an estimated 212 million in 1974. Thus, Federal spending rose over two hundred times more than the population.

Among the early flags used by American colonists when they rose against King George III's Britain was one designed by Colonel Christopher Gadsden, a member of the Continental Congress. It had a rattlesnake poised to strike emblazoned on its field; under it were the words: 'Don't Tread On Me.' Had that flag been finally adopted instead of the Stars and Stripes, in our present time it would be highly fitting to have the rattlesnake in a hoop, tail in mouth, eating itself.

It would be an apt symbol of what our American Big

* *Editor's note:* Here, as elsewhere in this book, Mr. Getty uses the 'American billion', which is 1,000 million.

Government is doing—and, worse, what we Americans are not only permitting, but insisting, that it do. The insane over-spending by Federal, State and Local governments is literally devouring the future of our society.

My great, good friend, the late Captain Ian Constable-Maxwell, was an authority on gaming (he was one of the founders of London's exclusive Clermont Club). As Ian frequently remarked, 'There has never been a gaming casino in the world that wouldn't go bankrupt if it weren't for the house-limit on stakes.'

Obviously, without a house-limit, gamblers would simply keep doubling their stakes until they won—which they would eventually do, no matter how bad a losing streak they were having.

Governments could learn from gaming casinos—but they won't. They continue to double and re-double their expenditures—and close their eyes to soaring deficits. (The United States Federal Debt was over $475 billion at the end of Fiscal Year 1974. Debts owed by the various States totalled another $60 billion.) True, Congress does periodically set a 'house-limit' in the form of a National Debt ceiling, but this is virtually meaningless. The ceiling is invariably raised.

The astronomical figures are most frightening because so much of the money is used to implement programmes that penalize the productive and encourage (and subsidize) the indolent and the malingerer. A staggering amount of Government—of the taxpayers'—money has been spent on buying a loss of initiative, self-reliance and, worst of all, self-respect for countless Americans. During the post-war decades, millions of them have been conditioned to expect—to demand—that whatever they need or want, it should be provided by Government largesse.

Two years ago, a writer I know was commissioned to prepare a major magazine article about the psychological impact that Welfare payments had on recipients and their families. The writer was given a list of names and addresses by the editors. He started with the first name and went to the address. He was greeted at the door by a robust white woman of forty or so. She said she had been living on welfare for twelve years. No, she had not worked nor sought work. She had a 19-year-old son, a daughter 18—neither of whom worked either—and another son, aged 13. The boy was home. The writer asked him:

'What would you like to do when you grow up?'

'Get my own welfare cheque,' the youngster replied.

Some ultimate of absurdity was reached a few years ago when—if newspaper accounts are to be believed—Welfare clients in a large American city went on strike. Demanding immediate supplemental benefits, they announced they would not leave their homes to cash their welfare cheques. An *ad hoc* committee representing the strikers called it a 'starve-in'. Men, women and children would simply stay in their homes until their demands were met.

City officials are said to have knuckled under within 48 hours. According to published reports, social workers in armoured cars made the rounds, bringing cash to the strikers— together with copies of an emergency City Council Resolution guaranteeing they would receive the supplements for which they were 'striking'.

Days now almost beyond recall used to produce 'underprivileged' individuals like my close friend, Melville 'Jack' Forrester. Born in the Hell's Kitchen slums of New York City, Jack became a half-orphan before he was ten, when his father deserted him and his mother. Mrs. Forrester went to work. Jack augmented her slender income by tap-dancing for pennies on street corners. He worked his way through high school, and there his formal education ended.

Jack Forrester's tap-dancing talent got him jobs in Prohibition era night clubs. Making a visit to the United States, Maurice Chevalier saw Forrester's act and invited the American—who was barely twenty—to come to France and stage his Casino de Paris Revue. Jack spoke no French, but grabbed at the chance, and was a success until the Revue closed during the Depression.

Jack next teamed up with the famous French boxer, Georges Carpentier,* and the two men toured Europe and South America doing a song-and-dance *cum* boxing-exhibition routine in nightclubs. In the mid-1930s, they returned to France. Forrester started his own motion picture production company. Among

*Editor's note: World Light Heavyweight Champion, 1920–22. He died in 1975.

the notable films he produced was *J'Accuse,* starring Harry Bauer, and at one time he had Marlene Dietrich under contract.

Jack lost everything when the Nazis conquered France. He went back to the United States penniless, and for a time did odd—indeed menial—jobs. When America entered the war, he was one of the first to join the O.S.S. and was sent to the Nazi-dominated European Continent. Operating from a base in the Pyrenees Mountains, he organized and led a Resistance unit with great bravery and distinction.

At war's end, Forrester again found himself back to Square One. For a time, he worked for the Ryan brothers—grandsons of Thomas Fortune Ryan—scouring Europe and Asia for promising investment opportunities. Accumulating a modest amount of capital, Jack went into business for himself. Soon, he was the president of the World Commerce Corporation, France. Long before his untimely death in 1963, he could count himself a millionaire.

'Georges Carpentier claimed he never minded being knocked flat because he knew he'd get up again sooner or later,' Jack told me. 'That's how I always figured.'

Jack Forrester and his mother made the grade without turning to Family Counselling Services, social workers, relief cheques or unemployment compensation. Jack himself never considered it demeaning, degrading or ego-annihilating to take 'low-status' jobs when there was nothing else available.

The resilient, self-starting—and self re-starting—breed is, I fear, being rapidly thinned out by prevailing social and political forces.

At the opposite (and to ever-increasing extent, today's standard) end of the pole is a man I choose to call by the pseudonym, Warren Blair. He is of another generation, born 25 years after Jack Forrester, and light years removed in outlook and attitude.

Until two years ago, Warren Blair was an executive earning—if one counts his perks—about $50,000 a year. The company failed. Although he has a wife and two children, a heavily mortgaged house and a load of other debts, Warren Blair has not worked a day since. Yes, he could have had a job from the very day his old company went out of business, but not with the same title and salary. Offered a $30,000-per-year job, he refused it.

'I had my reputation and status to consider,' Blair ex-

Sarah Getty, J. Paul Getty's mother,
to whom he was devoted.

This photograph, taken in 1894,
already has the Getty features.

Boyhood. J. Paul Getty in San Diego, California (about 1900).

(Left to right) George F. Getty, Snr, with his niece, June Hamilton, J. Paul Getty and Sarah Getty at Kingsley Drive in 1908.

J. Paul Getty with his fourth wife, Ann Rork, high in the Alps, 1931.

This picture, taken in 1942, reveals the typical Getty stance.

(Left to right) J. Paul Getty with Dorothy Spreckels, Mrs. Peck and Gregory Peck at L'Eléphant Blanc in Paris.

J. Paul Getty and King Saud, (Mina Saud, 1956).
King Saud's yacht is in the background.

With King Saud and the Sheikh of Kuwait
on board the *Aminoil* (1954).

Theodora (Teddy) Lynch, J. Paul Getty's fifth wife.

This is 'Timmy' (aged three), J. Paul Getty's youngest son
who died tragically.

The North Front of Sutton Place provides the background
for this picture taken in 1964.

J. Paul Getty and Nubar Gulbenkian at a
Foyles Luncheon, 4th May, 1961.

J. Paul Getty enjoys the fun at one of his famous
children's parties at Sutton Place.

Getty presents the trophy to Miss Britain of 1964 at the
National Amateur Bodybuilders' Association Awards.

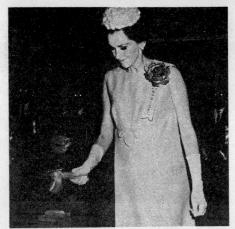

Ann Getty launching the
S.S. 'Washington Getty' at Nagasaki
Shipyard, 9th July, 1965.

Men of power: J. Paul Getty with Richard Nixon.

J. Paul Getty with Victor Lownes and Ringo Starr
at a Playboy Lunch.

J. Paul Getty with Hugh Hefner.

J. Paul Getty with the Duke and Duchess of Bedford.

J. Paul Getty with Sheikh Ahmed Zaki Yamani,
Saudi Arabian Minister of Petroleum
and Mineral Resources.

J. Paul Getty greets H.M. Queen Elizabeth, the Queen Mother, during a visit to Sutton Place, July 1969.

A front elevation of the Getty Museum, Malibu, California.

Some treasures in the Regency Room of the Getty Museum.

plained later, when he asked me if I had a 'suitable position' open for him.

No, I told him, I was sorry but there was nothing. I refrained from adding that I was not accustomed to hiring spoiled, prestige-happy types at any price.

There are more than a few Warren Blairs everywhere around us and at all levels of our society. They have been created by a system that seems hellbent on producing a race of spoiled, pampered people devoid of self-discipline and unwilling to assume responsibility for their own lives.

The unemployment rate in the United States is above seven per cent. The most recent statistics I have seen suggest there are 1·5 million people out of work in the British Isles.

The loudest political voices heard in either country view the situation with customary alarm and demand that Government take action—by spending more. They urge public works programmes and other pump-priming projects.

Trade Union leaders on both sides of the Atlantic make their customary statements damning Business—and demand that Government take action by spending more. They call for Government to conjure up jobs—even make-work jobs.

Many businessmen—American and British—let loose their customary barrages at Labour and demand that Government take action. They want massive Federal loans or subsidies for their companies.

Some years ago, H.R.H. Prince Philip, the Duke of Edinburgh, was subjected to a storm of criticism by press and public for having suggested that the answer to Britain's economic ills could be largely solved if Britons 'got their finger out.' I would most certainly give my own countrymen—politicians, labour leaders and businessmen—the same advice. Rather than lining up at the Government handout counter, they should get their fingers out—fast and without asking Uncle Sam to tug at their wrists.

Without doubt, there are serious unemployment problems in the United States, Great Britain and many other Western countries. But, I am willing to wager that those who cry doom the loudest have not tried to hire domestic help or someone who will paint a fence or clean up an empty lot. Nor have they sought to count up how many—how very many—jobs are open and going begging for lack of applicants.

The New York *Sunday Times* classified advertising section each week carries page after page of ads listing jobs that are available. Employment agencies from one end of the country to the other report they have vacancies they cannot fill. Surveys show that many people who are unemployed do not want work at all, or they will accept only jobs that satisfy their terms (and whims).

'I'm in no hurry to take a job until my unemployment compensation runs out.'

'Either the position is as good as the one I had before, or I won't consider it.'

'What? Travel half an hour each way every day to get to work? I'm looking for something that pays well—and is near my home.'

I have before me a London daily newspaper published on Friday, October 17, 1975. The issue carries no less than 1,375 column inches of display and classified advertising placed by employers who need workers. The jobs offered range from £35—about $70—a week junior clerk posts to executive positions paying upwards of £8,000—more than $16,000 a year.

I read this particular newspaper regularly. I have noted that many advertisements run week after week. I find it exceedingly difficult to believe that with 1·5 million unemployed in Britain, there aren't sufficient people qualified to fill every vacancy. The paradox would be completely baffling—were it not for glimmers of explanation that occasionally come to the surface.

Consider this item that appeared in the London *Daily Telegraph* in early Summer, 1975:

'Because unemployment benefit and other short-term National Insurance benefits are tax-free, the point has now been reached at which a married man earning £55 ($112) a week would have more disposable income for anything up to 14 weeks, if he lost his job.

'A single man earning up to £40 ($82) a week would be better off unemployed. So far as married men with dependent children are concerned, the discrepancy in favour of short-term unemployment prevails even when normal earnings are as high as £60 ($123) a week.

'These facts emerge from a detailed Parliamentary answer . . .'

I do not know President Gerald Ford personally, but I know Vice President Nelson Rockefeller, and I have no doubt in my mind about the present U.S. Administration's desire to end recession and bring back a high level of employment.

In England, I have had the honour and pleasure to meet Mr. Harold Wilson, when Prime Minister, and Mr. Denis Healey, the Chancellor of the Exchequer. As I am a guest in England, I show my hosts the common courtesy of expressing no opinion—good, bad or indifferent—about their political system or the merits of their political parties and programmes.

However, it is no breach of this courtesy when I say that Prime Minister Wilson impressed me greatly, as a man of charm, intelligence and ability. Mr. Healey is also a highly personable individual with a fine intellect. These key British political leaders are clearly intent on building and strengthening their nation and its economy.

President Ford, Vice President Rockefeller, Prime Minister Wilson and Chancellor of the Exchequer Healey cannot work overnight miracles, though. Nor can they be blamed or held responsible for the social and economic problems their respective countries are burdened with today. The roots of these lie in the past, and their identification may provide indicators as to means for resolving the problems.

21

LIKE MANY PEOPLE, I am periodically subject to gloomy spells, as these excerpts from my 1952 diary illustrate:

'April 11: I ponder on capitalism. Many say it is disappearing, and I tend to agree. Capitalists don't control anything today, not even their own businesses.'

'April 12: I don't know why I continue to be active in business. Force of habit, I suppose. I'd be much better off to sell out and go into tax-exempt bonds.'

Such moods have always passed quickly. At least, they have until the last few years. I must confess that it now becomes progressively more difficult to get over them. This has nothing whatsoever to do with my chronological age.

According to the dictionary I have at immediate hand, 'existentialism' is defined as:

'Any doctrine which maintains that the purpose of philosophy is the analysis and description of concrete existence, considered as the act of a freedom which constitutes itself by asserting itself.'

Accepting that as a definition, entrepreneurs are true existentialists—and I classify myself as an entrepreneur.

Therein lies the rub.

Any analysis and description of concrete existence around us shows there is steadily decreasing elbow room for the entrepreneur. His contributions to the economic health and strength of society are denigrated by those who believe that capitalism should be eliminated. His freedom of action is being gradually straitjacketed into non-existence by punitive taxation and governmental taxation and governmental regulation and restriction. He is widely considered to be expendable— but no one has yet come forward with a viable substitute to take his place.

I have been friends and have had dealings with a great many entrepreneurs during my business career. All were men who devoted their minds and energies to building productive enterprises. They concentrated on expanding them and making them more efficient to produce more and better goods and services for more people. In the process, they created more and more jobs and wealth for all because it is the mark of the entrepreneur that he re-invests much (usually most) of his profits in his business ventures. And, he is always personally involved.

Aristotle Onassis was an outstanding example. He was a very good friend, and it was always a fascinating experience to see him operate. I discussed business with him many times. Very often, I had a retinue of assistants, executives, attorneys and engineers with me. Ari would come to such meetings alone. Yet he easily held his own on all points that were discussed. Every enterprise he owned or controlled was his *personal* business; *he* was the business, and the business was Aristotle Onassis and no one else.

I remember a remark Ari's first wife, Tina Onassis, made about him to me before they were separated and divorced.

'Ari can't think on any but a huge scale,' Tina said. 'If he had been an artist instead of a businessman, he would paint nothing but immense murals.'

The innate capacity to think on a large scale is one of several characteristics that all entrepreneurs have in common. Among those I have known and feel I can call friends are: Dr. Armand Hammer, Paul Louis Weiller, David Rockefeller, Lord Beaverbrook, Lord Thomson of Fleet, Jules Stein, Charles Hayden, Sir Charles Clore, Emil Bustani, Sir Isaac Wolfton— and I could list numbers of others if space permitted.

These men not only thought on a large scale from the time they went into business, they possessed imagination and enterprise. Another common trait is the courage to take huge risks and gambles—to stake enormous sums on ventures that lesser businessmen shun.

A perfect example is provided by Lord Thomson of Fleet. In 1955, he learned that the programme contract for Scottish Independent Television was going begging.

'No one else would touch it with a barge-pole, I was told,' Lord Thomson has said.

The venture required a very big capital investment. Lord Thomson invited several score others to subscribe funds (no, he didn't ask me—if he had, I would have gone along, for I have limitless respect for his business acumen). Only a tiny percentage responded favourably. Most thought the risk too great. In 1957, Lord Thomson obtained the contract, providing 80 per cent of the capital himself. He has publicly related how every £100 subscribed came to be worth £22,000. Entrepreneur Roy Thomson's profits could be counted in the many millions.

Those profits were legitimate reward for readiness to accept risk, for foresight, courage and hard work. It should also be borne in mind that the company he formed provided thousands of people with jobs—and millions of people with entertainment.

One evening a few years ago, I received an overseas telephone call. A breathless operator asked if I was *the* J. Paul Getty and, if I was, would I speak to the representative of a radio station in an Iron Curtain country (which, for my own reasons, I do not wish to identify further). I asked the operator to put through the call. In a few moments, a voice speaking perfect—although ever-so-slightly-accented—English came on the line. I was asked if I would answer a few questions for listeners in the People's Democracy from which the call originated. I said yes.

'Mr. Getty, here is our first question. Do you believe that millionaires are good for a country?'

I answered that I know that good business is good for any country, and that I never saw a good business that didn't produce millionaires.

The next question: 'Do you think that fifty years from now there will still be millionaires?'

Tongue only partially in cheek, I replied: 'Considering the rate at which taxes are going up and government interference in business is increasing, I doubt whether *anyone* anywhere will have any money fifty years from now.'

There was a dead silence at the other end of the line. After some seconds, the voice somewhat shakily said, 'Thank you, Mr. Getty.'

The interview ended then and there. Obviously, the replies I gave were not what the interviewer—or Commissar of Broadcasting—had hoped to hear.

No one in his right mind believes that taxes can be abolished. But anyone with a grain of common sense should be able to see that the Western World's systems and structures of taxation and tax-policies are in desperate, long-overdue need of drastic overhaul.

The overhaul must begin with an about-face change in basic Government philosophies regarding taxation and the uses to which tax money is put.

Governments—as they are represented by the politicians who form them—like to overestimate the strength and financial resources of private business. They seem to feel that business is a bottomless cornucopia that can be tapped and drained indefinitely.

Human beings require incentive in order to function productively. The salaried worker has his pay, hopes of promotion and raises as incentives. The businessman and entrepreneur are moved to invest—to risk—their capital by the incentive of a reasonable expectation that they might make profits.

Tax away profits, and there is no incentive—and then there are no investments. Without investment, business and industry wither—and, sooner or later, die. Of course, business and industry can be taken over by Government. There is only one trouble with this formula. It fails to resuscitate. By and large, governments do notably less than a spectacular job of managing and operating business firms and industries they nationalize. Instead of making even slender profits, the government usually manages to run up whopping losses. These have to be made up out of further taxation—and tax increases hit no one harder than the worker who is trying frantically to keep his head above water.

Governments have forgotten that the purpose of taxation is to obtain revenue required for carrying out normal governmental functions as prescribed by the Constitution. The United States Government has long since broken loose of the Constitutional frame, rushing pellmell in all directions to get its hand into sectors and areas of human endeavour that no Founding Father ever considered to be the Government's business.

In recent decades, more and more Federal (and State and Local) expenditures have gone to support non-productive (and very frequently counter-productive) socialistic schemes. As an example, Welfare payments are made regularly to millions of people—whether they need (never mind whether they deserve)—them or not. A whole sub-species of American has been created. Its members take it as their inalienable right to collect welfare cheques indefinitely, without making the slightest effort to work—or even seek work. There is apparently no requirement for them to do anything but make an initial application. Once it has gone through the mazes of bureaucratic application-approving, it is stamped, sealed and becomes a lifetime licence to live off the taxpayer.

Unless I'm mistaken, some Welfare Department social workers' manuals strictly prohibit the social worker from inquiring how or why it is that the Welfare recipient is not working after he or she has once been certified as being eligible. Such questions—according to the manuals—are held to be 'demeaning' to the recipient. Needless to say, those same manuals say absolutely nothing about the rights and prerogatives of the working man and woman whose taxes subsidize the 57—or 557—varieties of 'social welfare' services Government not only offers but flings around with profligate abandon.

Tax and tax—and then tax even more . . .

Unfortunately, the machinery has long since lurched out of any semblance of balance. No matter how much present-day governments tax, they cannot keep up with their own giveaway spending manias. Staggering amounts are poured out on Welfare. vocational training for poodle-groomers, psychotherapy for chronic recidivists and a myriad other socialistic projects and programmes.

The tax shortfall is further aggravated by the spendthrift habits of government agencies carrying out normal government functions. For example, in sixty-some years as a businessman, I have always considered a contract binding. If I entered into one and lost money on it, that was my headache. It was up to me to swallow the loss—and try to recoup it in other transactions. Today, many government contractors ritually file claims for fifty, a hundred, two hundred per cent 'cost-overruns'. One wonders if the bureaucrats who handle such matters even glance at the contracts before reaching for the voucher-pads and approving the extra payments.

I have already cited the staggering U.S. National debt: over $475 billion. I read that according to current estimates, the U.S. Federal deficit for 1975 will range between $80 and $100 billion—increasing the National Debt just that much more. Even a nine-year-old Hottentot would realize that something is very wrong, that there must be fantastic waste—and certainly there are mountains of fat that could and should be carved out of federal budgets.

But—I'm sorry to say—the United States Government is not run by nine-year-old Hottentots. It is managed by vote-hungry politicians and don't-give-a-damn bureaucrats. They know that Government—unlike business or the working man and woman—does not have to worry about income exceeding (or at very minimum, equalling) expenditure. Government has the unique power of control over the printing presses that churn out Himalayas of 'new money' in the form of banknotes. These have no backing save other banknotes, and they decrease in buying power as their quantity increases.

It never ceases to amaze me that there are still those who are baffled for explanations whenever someone brings up the subject of 'runaway inflation'. While they see inflation shrivelling the value of their paychecks and weakening entire national economies, they can't understand WHY. They stammer that probably the phenomenon is caused by the excessive demands of Labour or the excessive spending of consumers.

This is patent nonsense. Dr. Milton Friedman recently tried to inject a note of reason by declaring that neither Labour nor the Housewife can be blamed for inflation. What we are experiencing, Dr. Friedman pointed out, is Printing Press Inflation. Whenever Uncle Sam's legions of open-handed spenders run out of ready cash, someone on the banks of the Potomac simply flicks a switch. Instantly, the presses begin to spin at top speed, spewing out a few more billions.

There was once a time when the American dollar was backed by gold. If the citizen disapproved of what the incumbent Government was doing, he had a fiscal power over and above his vote. He could go into any bank and demand that his paper-money be redeemed in gold. This power—or threat—made Federal Governments exercise caution in their spending. They were acutely aware that the citizenry could express its disapproval by trading paper for gold and thus lowering the Government's gold reserves and thus its international credit. When gold—and silver—backing of American money ceased, the U.S. citizen lost his ability to exercise any control over Government spending. If he takes a $20—or any other denomination—banknote to the U.S. Treasury for redemption, all he will get is another banknote.

Theoretically, the Federal Government borrows the money it creates out of thin air on its printing presses. And, in actual practice, it does pay interest on it. But the theory is never-never accounting fiction. No rational person can honestly believe that Uncle Sam will ever be able to repay a National Debt that already approaches—and will soon exceed—the half-*trillion*-dollar mark.*

A song popular a few years ago was titled 'Where Have All the Flowers Gone?'

Fittingly, it was an anti-Vietnamese War song. One might change the title to 'Where Has All the Money Gone?' and reply that it went down uncounted ratholes, the Vietnamese War being one of them. But the war is over and the wild over-spending goes on and on.

I do not glow with optimism. I believe things will continue to grow worse for some years yet—perhaps for as much as a decade or two—until even the most myopic Government public-money spender sees that D—for Disaster—Day has been reached.

I freely, very seriously (but by no means happily) predict that the action taken then will shatter all democratic precedents—and the term 'draconian' will be a mild adjective to describe it. Quite probably, one of the first steps will involve forced redistribution of population—mainly a dispersal of

---

* *Editor's note:* Here again, Mr. Getty uses the U.S. method of numeration, a trillion being one thousand times a thousand million.

non-productive urban masses. Professional public-assistance recipients will be moved from cities to communities established for them in low-population-density rural areas. They will be provided with shelter, a plot of ground, basic tools, seeds and fertilizers. From then on, each able-bodied individual will be on his or her own. Graduation up the ladder from this level of enforced agricultural labour and home-industry craftsmanship will be allowed only to those who prove themselves willing and able to work and be self-supporting.

The next—possibly concurrent—step will be the passage of strong legislation to insure ZPG: Zero Population Growth. Although it may not come in my own lifetime, I do foresee the day when people will be required to obtain permission—a government licence—before they can have children. No doubt, permission will be granted only to those who meet certain criteria, chief among them is certain to be a satisfactory track-record of productive work on the part of both parents. Anyone who has been—or may be considered likely to become—a Welfare client or public charge will be refused. Corollary legislation is almost certain to prescribe mandatory abortion for any woman who becomes pregnant without official sanction.

These are not Apocalyptic visions from some murky recess of my brain. Although nothing has been said publicly, considerable research has already been done at official levels toward drawing up preliminary contingency plans along these lines. I recently spoke with a prominent scientist who is on the staff of a leading American think-tank organization. He glumly disclosed that if present trends continue, computer-projections indicate that our great cities—the centres of our commerce and industry—will be dead shells within ten or twenty years. Our metropolises will be peopled by the indolent, the parasites and criminal elements. The cost of containing the resulting anarchy will alone be two to three times the total of the entire present National Budget.

Perhaps the capitalist democracies can head off total collapse by borrowing from the system that prevails in the Communist Soviet Union. There, able-bodied persons who refuse to work are denied housing and food instead of being given lavish handouts by the State. The more a Soviet worker produces, the higher pay and honours he receives. Those were the principles that once made the democratic capitalistic system strong. They could well be the only principles that can once again endow it with strength and vigour.

22

BECAUSE I HAVE lived abroad for almost twenty-five years, people (almost all Americans) are constantly asking me if I still consider myself an American.

Of course I do.

I am an American citizen by birth. I have retained my American citizenship. The thought of renouncing it has never once crossed my mind. My permanent residence is in the State of California and, as I mentioned in a previous chapter, I vote regularly—by absentee ballot—in all U.S. elections.

But I think of myself as an *objective* American. I do not allow my love and loyalty for my native country to make me a blind chauvinist. I try to see my country's flaws and weaknesses no less clearly than its perfections and strengths. This—unless I have totally misunderstood every lesson I ever had in Civics—is not only a right but a duty of citizenship.

Being an objective observer, it strikes me that the amount of pure prune juice in American politics is unbelievable. For instance, the United States Congress has long found it all but impossible to realize that its jurisdiction is not world-wide. Aided and abetted (or misled) by the Executive Branch during some Presidential Administrations, Congress has come to believe that the United States should be both alms-giver and policeman to the world. Little wonder that we Americans have somehow gotten the idea that we are the Good Lord's anointed, superior to all other nations and peoples in our wisdom and righteousness.

Our national *idée fixe* is that the American system and form of democracy can be crated up and shipped anywhere on the face of the earth in the same manner as an automobile manufactured in Detroit or a bedroom suite made in Grand Rapids. When—to our disbelief—this particular export item is not received with joyous shouts and instantly embraced, we bridle. The recipients are obviously ingrates—but we will give them a few more chances. We try to buy, bribe, bulldoze—or, I regret to say—blackmail other nations into 'being like us.'

It is here that we have made some of our worst and costliest mistakes.

America should not persist in trying to change the governments or the forms of governments in other countries. All nations are indigenous. All are not Switzerland or Sweden—or the United States of America—nor do they all want to be. Each nation is entitled to develop its own form of government without outside interference. Some can stand only a little bit of democracy; each should be permitted to find its own level—in its own way.

I expressed my personal opinions about President Woodrow Wilson in an earlier chapter. Strong on idealistic theories, but weak in his ability to give them practical application, his domestic policies were muddled and contradictory. His conduct of foreign affairs after the 1918 Armistice was disastrous. Wilson did his share—and more—to lose the peace that was patched together at Paris and Versailles.

There is not much that anyone can say for his successor, Warren Gamaliel Harding—save, perhaps, that being so wholly inept, he was more victim than villain. Calvin Coolidge was shrewder than most historians credit him with being, but he was out of step with the times and lacked lustre and touch. It must be remembered that Silent Cal was the last U.S. President who made any real effort to reverse the one-way flow of American money to foreign countries. When his advisers urged Coolidge to cancel European war debts, he gave this historic one-line reply:

'They hired the money, didn't they?'

I knew President Herbert Hoover personally. I think he was a good man and a careful President, but a poor politician. He is also one of the more unfairly maligned Presidents in modern

American history. It is the conventional wisdom that the great depression which began in 1929 was Herbert Hoover's fault. This makes about as much sense as blaming President Gerald Ford for the economic conditions that prevail throughout most of the world today.

The roots of the depression had taken firm hold long before Herbert Hoover assumed office. They were visible to anyone who cared to look beyond the stock market reports that appeared daily in the popular press of the 1920s. The Federal Government then had very little power to control developments—and after the Stock Market Crash, Herbert Hoover followed a principle that has much to recommend it. He believed that Government should avoid excessive meddling in historical economic movements. The principle stems from the theory—never disproven in recent times because it has not been given a fair trial—that a sick economy is self-healing. Eventually, it recovers, and Government interference only aggravates the malady and retards the cure.

Franklin Delano Roosevelt held different views. He wanted Instant Action—and, for the most part, he got it. A man of limitless charm and ability, F.D.R. was also a master politician. He was the perfect man for the times—and I will always feel honoured to have known him and to have enjoyed some small degree of his confidence. (I might add that I was one of his staunchest supporters, voting for him in each of the four elections in which he was a Presidential candidate.)

My support for F.D.R. reached—and remained at a—high peak after Europe went to war in 1939. A few random diary entries from 1941:

'May 10: Met —— who tried to get a contribution from me for the America First Committee.* I was polite but did not promise a penny. Personally, I am a follower of our F.D.R. and the America First Committee will get nothing from me.'

Roosevelt knew and trusted me. It was at his direction that I was telephoned by Wayne Johnson:

* *Editor's note:* The America First Committee was a notorious isolationist group dedicated to trying to prevent the United States from entering the war. Many of its members were later exposed as pro-Nazi sympathizers. It is to prevent possible embarrassment to an individual that Mr. Getty omits the man's name.

'May 26: Wayne Johnson called from N.Y. and asked
if I would accept an appointment in Washington.'

In the event, the matter came to naught. The special board
on which I was asked to serve was not formed.

On September 11, 1941, President Roosevelt made a radio
address in which he declared America's determination to
protect U.S. shipping on the high seas. I sent him the following telegram:

'Your speech tonight is a great document in American
history. If Axis raiders and submarines were permitted to
continue their present activities, war would seem inevitable
. . . If their aggression continues you will have a united
nation should you ask for a declaration of war. May God
bless and strengthen you in your great responsibility.'

Naturally, I could not be sure that F.D.R. would even see
the telegram; he must have gotten tens of thousands after his
speech. I was therefore stunned a few days later. I received
telephone calls from J. F. T. 'Jefty' O'Connor—a mutual
close friend of F.D.R. and me—and from Ed Flynn, Chairman of the Democratic National Committee. The President
had asked each of them to convey his personal thanks to me. I
saw President Roosevelt personally only twice during the war
years, and both times he was his cordial buoyant self. When
he died, I was one of the uncounted millions throughout the
world who grieved and felt that he had lost a beloved and
wonderful friend.

I never met Harry S. Truman personally, but I had great
respect for him. I remember Jefty O'Connor showing me a
letter that Truman wrote him on the day F.D.R. died. Truman
did not mail the letter until the next morning. At the bottom,
he hurriedly scrawled this poignant postscript:

'Last night, the world fell on my shoulders.'

I hold that Harry Truman was a good president. Feisty,
courageous, he had a large measure of personal integrity.
Many historians forget that while politicians opposed to Truman accused him of being 'soft' on Communism, he was a
leader who took a firm stand against the Reds. Truman's
resolute action broke the Berlin Blockade, and he did not
hesitate to meet Communist aggression in Korea with force.

Unfortunately, the Korean War did not have popular support in the United States. Men fought and died; the public assumed a detached attitude. The American news media made many errors in their coverage of the war. Not the least among these was their failure to give credit to the many United Nations contingents that fought alongside American troops. Few Americans were aware that the British Commonwealth Division numbered upwards of 25,000 men—or that one of the great sagas of military history was provided by the fantastic heroism and sacrifice of the Gloucestershire regiment. Nor was due credit given to the French, Greek, Turkish and other contingents that fought with exceptional valour and suffered such heavy casualties.

In my opinion, Harry S. Truman's most serious mistake during the Korean conflict was that he ignored the advice of General Douglas A. MacArthur. I came to know General MacArthur very well in Southern California after he had completed his tours of duty as Army Chief of Staff and before he was sent to the Philippines prior to World War Two. MacArthur not only epitomized leadership, but was one of those rare military men who had the breadth of vision to be a superb statesman (as he proved later in Japan). I believe Douglas MacArthur would have made a very great American President.

Regretfully, I cannot say as much for another General who succeeded Harry Truman in office. Dwight D. Eisenhower and his Colonel House-like *eminence grise*, John Foster Dulles, took appalling risks with world peace by following their policy of 'brinkmanship'. It was during the Eisenhower–Dulles years that the American practice of endless interference in the internal affairs of other countries came into full flower. There was something abysmally depressing about Dulles's eternal scuttlings around the globe, wrapped in his self-righteous evangelist's mantle, hard-selling the 'American Way'.

I have met and known various members of the Kennedy Family. Some have impressed me favourably, others have not. John F. Kennedy had dazzle—he made 'charisma' part of everyday idiom—and he had mastered the art of playing to the gallery as few others have, before or after. But I have always harboured reservations as to whether the White House—

modelled after the Duke of Leinster's house in Dublin—was architecturally suited for transformation into Camelot.

It strikes me that President Lyndon B. Johnson will long be remembered as an American Chief Executive who excelled in the exercise of poor judgement. His 'Great Society' giveaway programmes—most of them transparent popularity-buying expedients—did much to undermine the American economy. They also set even more pernicious precedents, for any marked increase in Government spending is invariably followed by even greater increases as appetites for public money, once whetted, grow more and more ravenous.

But Johnson's worst judgement by far was in getting the United States so deeply involved in Vietnam. I say now what I said then—not only in private conversations, but in talks with legislators I knew and who, I thought, were intelligent and reasonable men.

The United States should never have gone into Vietnam in the first place. American intervention in Vietnam was a terrible—a ghastly—blunder. However, once the insane commitment had been made, there should have been no vacillation, no backing and filling. Subsequent prolongation of the 'war' led only to the waste of countless additional lives and diminution of American prestige and credibility.

The world may not like a *fait accompli*, but does understand and respect it. The world has only contempt for any country—especially one that prides itself as being a great world power—that fails to live up to its announced commitments and fails to achieve its stated goals.

Richard M. Nixon is the American President I have known best. I am well aware that it is the current rage to damn and deride Dick Nixon. I refuse to go along with the game—and not merely because I consider him a personal friend. I contend that he was a good President.

Paradoxical as it may sound, I rank Richard Nixon with Franklin Delano Roosevelt. Although worlds apart in fundamental political philosophies and the policies they pursued, each was the right man for his time. It is my firm conviction that history will vindicate Nixon. His alleged transgressions will be forgotten when his real and lasting accomplishments are seen in proper perspective and without the fog of accusations, invective and rumour that now obscure them.

Of course, I suspect that much of the Richard Nixon known to the public was created by a largely hostile press. The Dick Nixon I have known for several years was always a cheerful, convivial person who enjoyed trading jokes, playing the piano and chatting with friends. Not once did I observe in him the heavy, brooding quality that so many accounts claim to be among his more prominent attributes. Whenever I talked with Nixon, he demonstrated that he had a quick and crystal-clear mind and a thorough grounding in the intricacies of international affairs.

Richard Nixon regained much of the respect for the United States that had been lost by his predecessors. Foreign Heads of State listened when he spoke. His contributions to the cause of world peace were many and significant.

Watergate?

Europeans were unable to believe the U.S. reaction over this molehill affair. They laughed at our naïveté—and were baffled by our willingness to tear our country apart over what, when all is said and done, was just another minor political scandal. Such scandals have blown up—and usually blown over—during every Presidential Administration. And, more specifically, the Nixon Administration was hardly the first to employ wiretaps or electronic eavesdropping devices.

Those who wish to demand that I be tarred and feathered are free to do so. But I retain my respect and liking for Richard M. Nixon. He would be a warmly welcomed guest in my home at any time.

The future course of American political developments is difficult to foresee. The nation is still convalescing from the effects of the Vietnamese War and the Watergate scandals. Domestic and international economic conditions are a powerful factor—and, at the moment, largely unpredictable.

There are faint early-warning signals that the nation's economy may be taking an upward turn again. This will solve many immediate problems. Restructuring a nation that has lost many of its value-standards and discarded many of its fundamental principles will take much longer and involve processes that require strong and courageous leadership.

Being an objective American—and a realist—I expect no

overnight miracles. I recognize that President Gerald Ford has inherited innumerable enormous burdens in addition to those which any President must normally expect to assume. But the 1976 national elections will be crucial—perhaps more crucial than any ever held in the United States during times of peace.

As yet, at the time of this writing, I have not seen a strong Democratic candidate emerge on the scene. This does not mean that one—or more—might not appear long before this book is published.

It is not even certain whom the Republicans will choose as their candidate. I do know this. If they choose Gerald Ford or Nelson Rockefeller, either will have *my* one, absentee-ballot vote. Both are wise and dynamic leaders versed in the art of government and governing and figures of more than sufficient stature to receive respect at home and abroad. These are salient—even indispensable—qualities for any man who takes office as President on January 20, 1977. The four years that will follow are certain to be decisive in making—or breaking—the social, economic and political future of the United States of America.

23

MY CLAIM TO being an *objective* American must be, I realize, qualified and amended. I cannot pretend to objectivity when I look back on my years and experiences in the United States. There are too many feelings and emotions involved in recalling my personal life. For by far the most part, these recollections are warm and pleasant and, naturally, the passage of years adds an even rosier glow to memories of people and incidents.

This is particularly true of the between-wars years when I spent much of my time in Southern California. It was then—from 1919 to 1939—that the world of the California oilman and that of the Hollywood motion picture industry touched, met and often overlapped.

There were many reasons for this. First and foremost, oil and motion pictures were then Southern California's two principal non-agricultural industries. As a normal consequence, they were among the area's chief producers of wealth. Successful oilmen and movie-people could afford to build their homes in the more exclusive residential areas, belong to the best clubs and dine in the more expensive restaurants. Thus, it was not surprising that the circles of acquaintance and friendship so frequently interlocked and merged. Then, oilmen and people prominent in the motion picture industry shared an important trait. When at work, they concentrated on their work and worked very hard. Whenever they had the opportunity to play, they played with equal concentration and energy.

There was yet another key bond of commonality. The fate of people in both industries was decided by wild and unpredictable swings of fortune.

An oilman down to his last dollar one day could (and not infrequently did) finds himself a millionaire the next morning when one of the wells he was drilling came in a gusher. Or, being a millionaire on Wednesday, he could (and not infrequently did) find himself down to his last dollar on Thursday when some grandiose drilling project proved a failure and had to be abandoned.

By much the same token, anonymous and stony-broke film extras became highly-paid stars overnight. Shoestring producers on Poverty Row needed only one lucky-hit sleeper to catapult them into the mogul-class. Conversely, established stars knew that a box-office flop might banish them to the ranks of unemployed—and unwanted—actors. Producers and directors were aware that adverse criticism of their latest film in the trade-papers could bring a sudden end to their careers.

It was a camaraderie of high-risk takers—of people who were willing to gamble much (even everything) on the next thousand feet of drilling or the next thousand feet of film.

Nita Naldi summed it up one afternoon when she and a group of other film people were sunning themselves on the sand at my beach home.

'For all of us, it's either *paf*! we're up, or *pouf*! we're down and then there aren't any *pouffes* to keep us from breaking our bones.'

John Gilbert was no less conscious of the unpredictability of filmland fortunes.

'Never—but never—be rude to a doorman, any doorman,' he counselled wryly. 'You may get thrown out, and who else will help pick you up off the sidewalk?'

Rudolph Valentino's tragically brief career (he died at the age of 31) epitomized the capriciousness of the fates governing the motion picture industry and the luck and progress of all who worked in it.

I became friends with Valentino early on, when he was still a dancer in night club floorshows and earned somewhere in the neighbourhood of fifty dollars a week. He was a good friend, an excellent companion, and we got along very well together, going to innumerable parties. However, surprising (or disillusioning) as it may be to the generation of females who idolized Rudolph Valentino, his real-life personality was entirely unlike what it appeared to be on the screen later.

Rudy was shy—even bashful—with women. His male friends—I among them—were amazed when Rudy achieved his legendary success as the screen's greatest Great Lover and Ultimate Male Sex-Symbol. We remembered how it was often necessary to prod—sometimes all but bodily push—Rudy into actually speaking to some girl who had caught his fancy at a party.

Success did not spoil Rudolph Valentino. He remained an essentially modest and goodnatured person, loyal to his old friends and retaining a healthy sense of perspective and humour.

'You've become one of the world's most famous celebrities,' I said to him when *Blood and Sand* was smashing all box-office records. 'How does it make you feel?'

'Greasy,' Rudy replied with a grimace. He ran his hand over his hair and showed the palm. It was slick with hair-oil. 'The studio makes me use quarts of the stuff. I hate it.'

There were, of course, sharks and swindlers. Some sharp-dealing oil promoters tried to talk wealthy motion picture producers, directors and stars out of large sums as 'investments' in dubious (or wholly spurious) oil ventures. Then, there were film producers who thought successful oilmen were easy marks who could be prevailed upon to put up the money needed to make their pictures. Usually, neither species of predator got very far.

On occasion, there was a reverse-twist, and I fell afoul of one. In 1920, a group of wealthy men—movie producers among them—told me they wanted to 'cash in on the oil boom.' I demurred. While crude prices were high, I foresaw a break. They insisted. I gave in—against my better judgement— and we incorporated a company capitalized at five million dollars. The company began drilling in California and Oklahoma, and with some success. But my associates knew nothing of the oil business, and they chafed because they were not making millions weekly (or daily). My patience ran out. I bought up 99 per cent of the company's stock—and dissolved the corporation. I made a solemn oath (never since broken) that I would never again embark on oil business ventures with others who were not oilmen.

Most of the leading Hollywood producers and studio exec-utives had similar feelings about their film-making enterprises. They sought their business associates among other experienced cinema people. Certainly, this was true of men like Joseph Schenck, who was not only my friend but a nearby neighbour—for his luxurious home was located not far from mine. Joe Schenck organized United Artists with Douglas Fairbanks, Mary Pickford and Charles Chaplin (all three of whom were also my friends). Later, Joe and Darryl Zanuck were to join forces and make more spectacular strides in the film industry.

Jesse L. Lasky was one of my particularly good friends during the 1920s and 1930s. We were both members of the Santa Monica Beach Club—where we first met. We took an immediate liking to each other, and I found him to be a man of wide knowledge and great—sometimes barbed—humour. One of the film industry's early pioneers, he could spin uproariously funny tales of the motion picture business, never hesitating to tell any that made him the goat.

Clara Bow was another close friend, and it was through her that I met her producer-director, Sam Rork. It was Sam Rork's daughter, Ann, who later became my fourth wife.

Clara Bow had a fey, free-wheeling sense of humour. Once, when I was acting as my own drilling superintendent on a site near Long Beach, a caravan of gleaming limousines suddenly drove onto the property. Clara had impulsively decided to have a picnic and, at the same time, give herself and several of our mutual friends an opportunity to see how oil wells were drilled.

She, Pauline Frederick, John Gilbert, Dorothy Gish, David Mdivani and a number of other Hollywood personalities alighted from the limousines. Liveried chauffeurs began unloading huge hampers of food, drink and elaborate picnic paraphernalia.

It was an excellent picnic, but none of my visitors saw any actual drilling. The men on my crews understandably brought all work to an immediate halt. At first, they just gawked. Then Clara invited them to join the party and help demolish the mountains of food that had been brought. My men ate and then collected a bumper-crop of autographs—with some sort of prize for originality going to one of my drillers, who was a particularly avid Clara Bow fan.

'Will you autograph my car, please, Miss Bow?' he asked.

'Gladly,' Clara smiled. 'But won't it wash off in the first rain?'

'No, ma'am, it won't,' the driller said—and produced a freshly-sharpened cold chisel. 'Just scratch your name right into the paint on the hood—close to the windshield on the driver's side, so I can always see it when I'm driving.'

Clara laughed, took the chisel and complied. The postscript to this story is that the driller had the autograph that Clara scratched into the paint and metal electroplated to protect it from rust.

There were many others prominent in the Hollywood colony with whom I established lasting friendships and had good times. Pola Negri, Janet Gaynor, Norma Shearer, Gloria Swanson, Joan Crawford, Vivian Leigh, Jean Harlow and Mary Pickford's sister, Lottie, were among the loveliest and most charming women I have ever known. Then there were such men as Rudy Vallee, Louis B. Mayer, Cecil B. de Mille, Sam Goldwyn, Douglas Fairbanks, Bruce Cabot, Cary Grant and Tyrone Power. Studio moguls or leading men, they were intelligent and lively, wonderful hosts and excellent guests, and I gained much from the friendships we formed.

Composer Igor Stravinsky and pianist Artur Rubinstein were very much a part of the Hollywood scene, but predictably each had a distinctive personality that was unusual even in Hollywood. Stravinsky gave lavish parties in his home, and he was a unique character—brilliant, expansive and extremely temperamental. One was never quite sure what Igor might do next. At one party, a male star who had drunk a little too much made the grave error of setting a highball glass on Igor's piano.

'Peasant!' Stravinsky roared. He disappeared into the back of the house and returned with a fire extinguisher—and doused the offending actor with its contents.

On another occasion, Igor told me it was a great pity that no one had ever written a piece of music that tried to capture the drama of oil exploration and discovery.

'It is very difficult to find the right kind of paper to compose oil music on,' he said, eyes twinkling. 'Not even Beethoven would be properly inspired unless he could use thousand-dollar bills on which to write the score.'

Few married couples were more hospitable and enjoyed such close rapport with each other as Artur and Nella Rubinstein. Artur once told some of us what had evidently been something of a secret until then. It seems that he went to Warsaw and gave a concert there before the war. He met and fell in love with the daughter of the director of the Warsaw Opera House.

'I asked her to marry me—and she said yes. All the preparations were made for a very big wedding to be held in the Warsaw Opera House. On the appointed day, everyone was there—but me. I was on a train—leaving Poland. I had gotten feet that were not just cold, they were ice. The Director of the Warsaw Opera House was ready to kill me if he ever saw me again.'

The rest of the story is, I am sure, familiar to most. The Warsaw Opera House Director's daughter—Nella—and Artur met again a few years later, and this time they were married.

'My feet had finally thawed,' Rubinstein concluded his story.

Nella, who had listened silently throughout the narrative, laughed.

'Not altogether,' she said. 'On our wedding night, they were cold. *I* remember, even if Artur doesn't.'

Barging in on people at unexpected—better still, impossible—hours was a form of practical joke that had wide currency in Hollywood during the 1920s and 1930s. Around three or four a.m., the guests at a Hollywood party would suddenly decide to descend on some other member of the movie colony whom they knew was at home and fast asleep. All would pile into their automobiles, drive to the victim's house and ring the doorbell until someone—servant or master—answered. Then the entire mob would troop into the house.

'Thought we'd drop over for a drink,' somebody or other would blithely inform the sleep-befuddled—and coerced—host and/or hostess.

There were many popular variations on the basic barge-in theme. One of the most frequently used involved hiring an entire band—preferably a brass one. The band would be taken along to the victim's house. Once the door opened, the band—instruments ready—rushed in. The band then paraded through the rooms blaring and banging out renditions of 'The Stars and Stripes Forever,' 'Twelfth Street Rag' or some equally ear-shattering melody.

Needless to say, one was expected to react to these nocturnal invasions with aplomb. It was not always possible to do so. For example—although I was not personally present—there was an instance when a 15-piece band and some forty people poured into the home of a married female star whose husband was in New York. A male star (also married) broke his ankle jumping from her upstairs bedroom window when he heard the pranksters come marching in.

My friends Phil Connors and David Mdivani once organized such an invasion of my Malibu Beach home. It was past four in the morning. Luckily, I was alone in my bedroom and Mac, my houseman, was shrewd enough to delay answering the incessant sound of the door-buzzer. This gave me the few minutes I needed to dress—all but necktie, which I took with me to tie outside—and slip out through a back door. The milling crowd poured into the house, the hired band heading for my bedroom, to which it had been directed by Phil Connors.

I tied my tie, waited five or ten minutes—ample time for the invaders to taste their disappointment in having failed to wreck my sleep—and then sauntered up to the door, whistling.

I entered, stopped dead and stared at the faces turned toward me.

'Good God!' I exclaimed, screwing up my face in what I hoped was a convincing expression of surprise. 'I must have got my dates mixed—I thought the party was tomorrow night!'

Phil Connors later opined that on a sliding scale of ten, I rated about five for my performance, neither good nor bad. Top scores went to men like the famous European director who came downstairs to meet an invading throng stark naked, nonchalantly smoking a huge Havana cigar, and the Warner Brothers executive who sat through an hour-long melee playing solitaire, never once glancing up from his cards. The next day, he sent identical telegrams to each of the interlopers:

> LONG TIME NO SEE WHEN CAN WE
> GET TOGETHER FOR BREAKFAST

My relationship with Charlie Chaplin has been the subject of considerable gossip-column rumour, and I might as well try to set the record straight—or at least, give my version.

Charlie and I first met in 1918 or 1919. I liked him immensely, and he was excellent company. But Charlie had reason—or, at minimum, suspected that he had reason—to be perturbed about me *vis-à-vis* some of his lady friends. It all began with Edna Purviance who was Chaplin's leading lady in his early comedies. Charlie suspected that she was more interested in me than in him. It was pretty much the same story in the 1930s with a girl whom I remember only as 'Lorraine,' and with Joan Barry and Paulette Goddard.

Now, Paulette and I were very good friends—and still are. I received a letter from her only a few weeks before writing these lines. Of course, I was also a good friend of her late husband, the great German-born novelist, Erich Maria Remarque. But it was over Joan Barry that my friendship with Charles Chaplin foundered and remained sunken for almost three decades.

Miss Barry, an aspiring actress, had been one of my girlfriends for a brief (and, I must confess, quite hectic) period. She later transferred her attentions to Charlie. He gives a graphic and detailed account of his difficulties with Joan Barry in his autobiography,* and it is not for me to rehash what he has to say.

It is, however, a matter of widely-trumpeted public record that Miss Barry became pregnant, had a child, and claimed that Charles Chaplin was the father. She brought a paternity suit against him, which was settled out of court. Next, a nasty (and, in my opinion, wholly unwarranted) Federal criminal action was brought against Charlie—it was an outgrowth of *l'affaire* Barry. I was subpoena'd and required to testify. There was nothing I could do but answer the questions put to me while I was on the witness stand. These dealt with matters of fact which were so trivial that I was hard put to understand why I had been called as a witness in the first place.

I was greatly pleased and believed that justice had been done when the jury cleared Charles Chaplin of all charges brought against him. I was very sorry—and could not understand the reasons—when it became apparent that the trial had caused a final rupture of my relationship with Charlie. And, like so many others, I was dumbfounded when the Barry paternity case was reopened and, although blood tests proved

* *Editor's note: My Autobiography*, by Charles Chaplin, published in the U.K. in 1964 by The Bodley Head.

he could not possibly have fathered Miss Barry's child, the jury ruled against him.

The breach between Charlie and me was not healed until 1971, when he and I were both invited to—and attended—the same party in London. We greeted each other cordially and, when we had the chance, went off into a corner by ourselves. There is no need to recount our conversation. Its gist will suffice.

Charlie was then 83; I was 79. We agreed that it was the height of absurdity for men our age to bear grudges over jealousies or differences concerning women we had known thirty and more years before. We shook hands, Charlie beaming his famous smile. I felt—and feel—very happy. I only hope that Sir Charles Chaplin fully realizes this and that he, too, has been gladdened by our meeting and reconciliation.

24

I HAVE ALREADY mentioned the travel-pattern I established in 1927 and maintained each year until 1939. I spent seven months in the United States and five in Europe during those years. The pattern was broken in 1940 and not resumed until 1949 when, in the late Spring, I sailed from New York. After spending a few weeks in London, I went to France. One of my diary entries notes:

'I visited the site of my old *petit meuble* at 12 rue St. Didier. Countless memories tumble through my mind. Those were wonderful days (in 1927–28). How much Paris—and the entire world—have changed since then!'

Charles and Elsie Mendl divided their time between their homes in Hollywood and Versailles. They were two of my dearest friends—and two of my favourite people. They were in France during the summer of· 1949, and I spent considerable time with them. Somehow, whenever I was in the company of the Mendls, odd things would happen to me. (Or I would find myself doing odd things or in the midst of odd situations.)

There were several good examples during the summer of 1949, but before I recite some of them, I must recount two stories that Elsie told me about her marriage to Sir Charles. The first had to do with the manner in which they became engaged.

Elsie de Wolfe was, of course, very rich and successful. Sir Charles Mendl was a British Foreign Service News Department official. Both lived in Paris during the 1920s, and they were good friends. Elsie being several years older than Charles, he often went to her for advice. In 1926, they were both in a party of people that went to Deauville for a weekend.

On the first evening, Charles asked Elsie if he could have a long, heart-to-heart talk with her. They walked along the beach.

'I'm thinking of getting married—it's about time I do, I suppose,' Charles said. He mentioned the name of the young woman to whom he intended to propose.

'Impossible!' Elsie exclaimed. 'She's not at all suitable for you.'

Mendl, very much taken aback, stammered: 'Why—that is, you're an excellent judge of women, Elsie. But who do you think might be more suited?'

'Me,' Elsie de Wolfe replied casually.

That stopped Charles dead in his tracks. He stared at her. 'I—I never thought of you, Elsie.'

'Why not?'

'Because you're wealthy—and you know I have very little.' (Charles Mendl's annual income was around $11,000.)

'If it doesn't disturb me, it shouldn't disturb you, Charles.'

With that, Elsie told me, they were engaged—and this led to her second tale.

The engagement received an enormous amount of publicity. The date of the wedding was set, the invitations were sent out. About a week before the wedding, Charles came to Elsie.

'There's something I have to tell you.'

'Yes, Charles?'

'Umm—well, to be frank, it so happens that I have several mistresses and I don't want to give them up.'

When Elsie told me this I laughed and asked, 'What did you say, Elsie?'

'What could I say? After all, the invitations *had* been sent. One can't just suddenly call off a wedding because of a few mistresses!' She gave an airy wave of her hand. 'Besides, one or two of them were quite nice girls. I approved of them for Charles.'

But back to 1949, France—and my visits with the Mendls.

One evening I took two girls to dinner at the Mendls' villa,

Petit Trianon, at Versailles. After dinner, Elsie and Charles showed a film in their private projection room. I had already seen the picture and I felt very tired, for I had been up late the three previous nights.

Elsie had designated a room in the villa that I could use whenever I wished. I thought the filming was a marvellous opportunity to sneak off and get a couple of hours' sleep. I slipped out of the projection room and went upstairs to what I thought was the right bedroom, lay down on the bed and promptly fell sound asleep. I did not awaken until morning.

Elsie gave me a thorough scolding.

'After the film ended, we noticed you were gone,' she said. 'No one knew where you were. The girls you brought were furious—and so was I, to say nothing of Ian Campbell.'

The girls had to be taken home. Elsie singled out another male guest, Ian Campbell—later the Duke of Argyll—whom she knew was a friend of mine.

'Ian, you take Paul's girls home,' she ordered in the that's-settled manner she had.

I cringed when she told me about dragooning Ian into the task. One girl lived about twenty miles north of Paris and the other even farther to the *south* of the city. Ian must have had to drive for two hours to get them both to their homes. I hardly imagine it's necessary for me to add that the girls treated me icily for a long time after—and that Ian never missed a chance to needle me mercilessly about the incident.

Two weeks later, I was again staying with the Mendls at Versailles. Greta Garbo—whom I had come to know very well in Hollywood—was another guest. Now, whenever Greta was with friends, she showed none of the elusive shyness that was ascribed to her by newspapers and motion picture fan-magazines. On the contrary, she was warm, amusing—and greatly enjoyed being amused—and quite outgoing.

One morning, Greta and I were sprawled in deck chairs beside the Mendls' swimming pool. I was unshaven and haggard—quite disreputable in my appearance, I'm afraid—but Greta and I chattered away. Then Elsie suddenly appeared at the poolside.

'Paul!' she snapped. 'I'm ashamed of you! How can you sit there with Greta looking the way you do?'

I flushed with embarrassment. Greta merely arched an eyebrow.

'Elsie, what a horrible colour you're wearing this morning,' she murmured. It was probably one of the very few times in her life that Elsie de Wolfe Mendl had ever been outpointed. She didn't even glance at me, but beat a hasty retreat. By noon, both Greta and I were forgiven.

There is an addendum.

Some days later, Greta announced that she was going back to New York. She asked if I could have a suite reserved for her at the Hotel Pierre, which was then owned by the Getty interests. I assured her I would take care of the matter. I sent a cable to Frank Paget, the manager of the Pierre, requesting that he hold a suite for Greta Garbo on the dates when she would be in New York City. I saw no need to confirm the cable by letter.

I spent a few weeks touring the Continent and then went to England for a brief visit. One poignant incident remains sharp in my mind:

'October 2: Dined as the guest of Lord and Lady Portarlington at their home. He is the brother of George Dawson-Damer, who was with me at Oxford and was killed in World War One.'

We spoke of George. The conversation brought back memories of our close friendship and the wonderful times we had together in 1912 and 1913.

When I returned to New York, I stayed at the Pierre. Naturally, I talked with Frank Paget, the manager and, *en passant*, asked if Greta Garbo had seemed to enjoy her stay.

Frank blinked. 'Funny you should ask that, Mr. Getty. Miss Garbo arrived—oh, I guess it must have been in late July—and said she had a reservation. We couldn't find any record of it, and we were booked full, not a room in the hotel. She was miffed—and went to the *Plaza*.'

I was mortified. Evidently my cable had been lost in transit—as cables sometimes are. I consoled myself with the thought that I would have plenty of time to plan some way of making proper amends to Greta—as I automatically assumed she had gone on to Hollywood.

As luck would have it, I walked down Fifth Avenue the very next morning—and there, coming directly toward me on the sidewalk was none other than Greta Garbo. I panicked and to avoid meeting her ducked into a lingerie shop.

'Good moming, Paul!'

I froze. Greta walked in right behind me. I was trapped, doubtless the only person who had ever purposely tried to elude Greta Garbo, who was famous for her own elusiveness in public. I made—or, more accurately, babbled—my profuse apologies and after a few moments, Greta relented, smiled and said she forgave me.

It was my 1951 'annual visit' to Europe that became the prolonged stay extending twenty-four years into the present.

The reasons behind this protracted stay stem, as I have already said, from business considerations. Europe and England are the most strategically advantageous places for an entrepreneur to be if he has large-scale business interests on every continent. I had long thought this, even as far back as 1938, when the Getty interests had made only a few and relatively minor forays into international operations. This is shown by a diary entry made while I was in France that year:

'October 16: Spent the day looking at a magnificent country house near Chantilly. It is for sale at a most reasonable price and would make a fine European head-quarters for the overseas operations of Getty companies.'

No, I did not buy. The political situation was worsening daily in Europe. I felt that war was inevitable—and imminent. True, the Getty interests had gained a toehold in some Continental countries with their Veedol lubricants marketing organization. But the best I could hope for: that it would not be totally swept away by war. Any plans for further expansion in Europe had to be shelved.

The picture was much different in 1951. By then, Getty companies and enterprises were active—or being rapidly established—in numerous countries on both hemispheres. I was convinced that I should remain in Europe. This would enable me to supervise the expansion there personally. It also gave me a central location in so far as global operations were concerned.

For the next nine years, I led an anomalous, nomadic existence. Little wonder that there were those who labelled me an eccentric. I owned lovely homes in California, Oklahoma and New York City. I could have easily afforded to buy others. Yet I moved from one eastern hemisphere city to another, living in hotels, my personal effects and working papers packed in suitcases. My office was wherever my secretary—or I—opened the battered brown overnight bag that contained the URGENT PENDING cables, letters and other papers.

Each stop was to be the last—or the next to last ('I have to go on to Munich from here—but that's going to be it')—and then I would return home to the United States. But there were always new developments, new opportunities—or new crises.

Twelve-hour workdays were anything but uncommon and many stretched to fourteen or more. Even so, the brown overnight bag was seldom empty. Steady streams of telexes, cables, written reports and letters of all kinds poured in from—it seemed—every conceivable corner of the globe. Then there were the telephone calls—local, international and transoceanic—and executives of Getty companies and engineers, accountants, attorneys and other businessmen who had to be seen personally. What astounds me is that, despite it all, I still managed to have time for my private life every now and then.

Random excerpts from my 1952 diary provide a quick-skim montage of my work and life patterns and styles and some of the thoughts and reflections that occupied my mind.

Rome:
'February 14: I visit the room where Teddy and I were married in 1939. Memories flood over me.'
'April 12: I don't know why I continue to be active in business. Force of habit, I suppose. I'd be much better off to sell out and go into tax-exempt bonds.'
'April 13: All day in hotel suite studying reports and working on correspondence. Telephone calls re: Tidewater from New York and re: exploration problems from Jeddah. Had to make three appointments for tomorrow. Still a mountain of correspondence left. Haven't even opened today's pile of incoming mail.'
Athens:
'May 19: All day discussing Greek oil with U.S. commercial attache and Greek government ministers.'

'May 20: Yesterday all over again—until nine p.m. Then read mail and reports until three in morning.'

Cote d'Azur:

'August 20: André Dubonnet is a good friend and companion. Lunched at his villa. It is a dream—modern, luxurious, directly on the water. I must try and complete my business over here so that I can return and once more enjoy my own house.'

Paris:

'November 6: Dinner at the Duke and Duchess of Windsor's. David looks extremely fit and is the same as ever. Wallis is the perfect hostess—but then she is a perfectionist in all things.'

'December 15: I am sixty today and apparently in good health. I feel sad at leaving the fifties, for sixty seems old, while the fifties seemed so much younger.'

On December 25, 1952, I made myself a solemn promise:

'This is my last Christmas away from home. I am resolved to return to the United States before the next holiday season comes around.'

But on January 9, 1953, I was writing:

'I hope to get commercial quantities of oil or gas out of the Neutral Zone this year.'

The January 9 hope was not fulfilled, and this made it impossible for me to keep my promise to myself in 1953. Soon after 1953 ended, I was making preparations to go to Saudi Arabia and the Neutral Zone and take personal charge of those operations which I considered needed a boost from The Boss himself.

25

I HAVE MADE more than a few business mistakes during my career. Some were whoppers. High on the list is the opportunity I allowed to slip by in 1932. I then had representatives in Bagdad conducting negotiations for an Iraqi oil concession. They were close to reaching an agreement that would have given my companies the right to explore and drill for oil over a vast area. The initial cost would have been minimal, a matter of some tens of thousands of dollars.

But there was an abrupt and disastrous break in U.S. crude oil prices. The great East Texas oilfields had been opened up. Crude was selling for ten cents a barrel—and even less in some instances. The American oil producing industry was consequently thrown into panic, and I was not immune to its contagion. I was reluctant to expand into the Middle East under these conditions and ordered my agents to break off the concession negotiations. It is impossible to estimate how much revenue the Getty interests lost because of my precipitate decision.

By the end of World War Two, I realized it was imperative that my companies obtain a foothold in the oil-rich Middle East. I knew the task would be anything but easy. Oil companies of all nations were engaged in a frenzied scramble to obtain Mid-East concessions, most of which were acquired by giant corporations with many times the financial resources of the Getty interests. Much of the dust churned up by the scramble had settled when 1948 rolled around. For some reason that remains a mystery to me, one very significant area had been passed over by the oil business behemoths.

This was the Neutral Zone, a 2,400-square-mile wasteland lying between the Kingdom of Saudi Arabia and the Sheikdom of Kuwait which, by treaty, had joint ownership of the Neutral Zone's mineral rights. Kuwait granted its undivided half-interest in the Zone's oil and gas rights to the American Independent Oil Company—AMINOIL—a consortium of ten U.S. oil companies. That left the Saudi-Arabian half-interest still open and unallotted.

I sensed an opportunity to make up for my 1932 mistake and sent Dr. Paul Walton to make a survey of the Neutral Zone. Undoubtedly one of the best geologists I have ever known, Dr. Walton made aerial surveys of the Zone and sent me this terse cable:

STRUCTURES INDICATE OIL SIGNED   WALTON

Paul Walton's verdicts were very seldom wrong. His opinion was sufficient to justify opening negotiations with the Saudi Arabian Government. They moved along rapidly, but the days of bargain-basement oil concessions were long past. On February 20, 1949, attorney Barnabas Hadfield—a senior partner in the law firm representing the Getty interests—signed a long and complex agreement in Riyadh. Pacific Western Oil (later Getty Oil) obtained the concession on Saudi Arabia's undivided half-interest in Neutral Zone oil and gas rights. The agreement provided that PacWest would pay the Saudi Arabian Government an immediate cash consideration of $10,500,000. Some of the additional terms specified that Pacific Western would, among other things:

. . . Pay a yearly $1 million advance on agreed 55-cent-per-barrel royalties on all oil produced.

. . . Pay 25 per cent of net profits to the Saudi Arabian Government.

. . . Build a 12,000-barrel-a-day capacity refinery and storage facilities for 150,000 barrels of refined products in Saudi Arabia.

. . . Deliver 100,000 gallons of gasoline and 50,000 gallons of kerosene annually to the Saudi Arabian Government.

. . . Pay the salaries of Saudi Government inspectors and

other personnel (such as police, Customs and Quarantine inspectors) who would be concerned with Company affairs.

. . . Provide pension, retirement, insurance and other benefits for Saudi Arabian employees of the Company (who were also to receive free medical care and hospital facilities).

. . . Provide educational, vocational training and other facilities for the children of Saudi Arabian employees.

. . . Build and maintain housing and office accommodations for personnel—along with telephone and telegraph facilities, a mosque, roads, a post office and an adequate water-supply system.

And there were other considerations. By the standards of some oil companies operating in the Middle East, the terms were viewed as being much too liberal—even 'outrageous.' It was widely predicted that 'Paul Getty has finally overreached himself—and he'll lose his shirt in the Middle East.' Ignoring such prophesies, I felt the agreement was just and equitable, with Getty interests giving no more than Saudi Arabia was entitled to receive in return for granting a concession on one of its major national-resources assets. (In the next chapter, I will seek to demonstrate why this stand was right and to show where so many Western oil companies and governments went wrong in their dealings with Middle Eastern and other oil-producing countries.)

Once the agreement had been signed, exploration and drilling operations could begin. However, AMINOIL argued it was the senior company in the Zone by virtue of having obtained the Kuwaiti concession first. The argument went further. AMINOIL executives maintained it would be foolish for their company and Pacific Western to conduct separate exploration and drilling operations. These would be duplications of effort and result in greatly increased costs for both companies.

Unfortunately, I permitted myself to be talked out of launching an independent PacWest exploration and drilling operation. Only a small, skeleton PacWest staff went to the Middle East. AMINOIL conducted the field operations (with PacWest paying half the costs and expenses).

No oil was found in 1949—nor during 1950, 1951 or 1952. The initial strike was not made until 1953. The discovery well came in at 3,500 feet. Gratified as we were by *any* discovery, Getty company executives, geologists—and I—were convinced that the truly important pay-zones lay in other parts of the Neutral Zone and at other levels below ground.

My eldest son, George F. Getty II, had gone to the Zone as early as 1949. His was one of the strongest voices calling for a change of policy—and, above all, for a complete revision of exploration and drilling procedures. Some of the genes that had endowed his grandfather—my father—with remarkable instincts for drilling in exactly the right places must have been transmitted to George.

'The area is practically floating on oil,' George insisted. 'But the people running things are spudding their wells wide of the mark. I've argued myself hoarse. It does no good.'

On one occasion, George showed me a map of the Zone. The sites where some dry-hole wells had been drilled were marked by small red circles. About a mile to the west of the most westerly duster, George had made a blue 'X.'

'There's oil there—I'll bet on it,' he declared.

Later, when the Getty interests began conducting their own exploration and drilling operations, a well was drilled on the spot George had indicated. It came in a record producer. But before that happened, I was determined to see for myself just what the hell was going on in the Neutral Zone.

I made only one extraordinary preparation for my trip to the Middle East. My travels and stays in various countries had enabled me to speak French, German, Spanish, Russian and fair Italian. I now locked myself into my hotel suite and took an intensified course in Arabic. While this by no means qualified me as an Arabist, I did learn enough of the language to get by in most ordinary conversations. On February 18, 1954, I left Venice on the Orient Express for Istanbul. The rest of the journey was made in easy stages as I took advantage of the chance to see places of historical interest and view the countryside. It was not until March 2 that I reached Kuwait. After making a quick once-over inspection of the Neutral Zone, I went on to Riyadh.

When I had called on Saudi Arabian Government officials—as prescribed by protocol—I was invited to call on Crown Prince Faisal, the half-brother of His Majesty King Saud (and himself later King of Saudi Arabia). The reception I received from His Royal Highness exceeded all my expectations. An honour-guard escorted me into the courtyard of his palace.

Thirty of his retainers were ranged there in symbolic greeting, each with a falcon on his arm. Prince Faisal's personal welcome was warm and most gracious. We talked for almost an hour. It was evident that he possessed a keen brain and much wisdom, even then—and these qualities were to make him an outstanding ruler of his people in later years.

Dinner with His Majesty, King Saud, was another memorable experience. I recorded in my diary:

> 'March 6: His Majesty is a tall, dignified and pleasant man. After a short conversation, we go into dinner. The dining room is vast. There are about 60 at table. I am seated second from the King's right, with the Turkish Ambassador being placed between us. Dinner is European style. Forks, spoons and knives are used. The waiters wear white gloves. His Majesty is a most pleasant host. After an eight course dinner, we proceed to a large salon where coffee is served.'

I conversed with His Majesty in Arabic, which pleased him. He had an excellent sense of humour and, at one point, remarked in English—which he spoke quite well—that he would test my knowledge of Arabic.

'Wain zait, wain fluss?' he asked me. ('Where is the oil, where is the money?')

I replied that I was determined we would very soon find and produce oil in large quantities—and that the revenue would then begin to pour into Saudi Arabia.

His Majesty chuckled.

'You are to be congratulated,' he said. 'You have learned the business words in Arabic very well.' He gave me a long—and friendly—look. 'You know of course what your President Franklin Roosevelt said to my father?'

I nodded and repeated F.D.R.'s words—which are, of course, a matter of history. He told His Majesty King Ibn Saud: 'I am essentially a businessman, and as a businessman I am very much interested in Saudi Arabia.'

'You, too, are a businessman,' King Saud said. His manner made it clear that he was paying me a great compliment.

He asked me what I thought of the Neutral Zone's potentials. I replied that I believed them to be immense and explained why.

'You are praising the Neutral Zone so highly, I feel I should pay it a visit myself,' His Majesty declared. He added that he tried to keep travel to a minimum because people 'made such a fuss' over him wherever he went.

I was greatly impressed by the apparent sincerity of this remark. Although custom and protocol made it necessary for him to live in truly regal style, King Saud was, at heart, a remarkably human human being.

We met again in 1956, when I again visited the Neutral Zone and spent four months there. By then, the Getty interests had taken over control of their own Neutral Zone destinies, making their own discoveries on the basis of their own exploration and drilling programmes. There was no longer any question of *'Wain zait, wain fluss?'*

An Arabian Nights party was given for His Majesty, King Saud, His Royal Highness, the Sheikh of Kuwait—and me. It was held aboard an ocean-going vessel that had been converted into King Saud's royal yacht. I attended—with aides who brought along Neutral Zone maps. These were spread out on the priceless oriental carpets that covered the decks. It was left to me to describe the progress being made and explain the geology of the region.

'See,' King Saud said to the Emir of Kuwait. 'He is able to tell us where the oil is in Arabic.'

The Getty Oil Company's Neutral Zone operations have been a success. In 1974, crude production in the Zone levelled off at around 82,000 barrels daily. This success is due in no small part to the fact that Getty Oil has sought to operate fairly and in a friendly manner. The company and all its executives and American personnel have a very high regard for the people of Saudi Arabia and Kuwait and all have tried to insure that Getty Oil would be a welcome guest.

And this leads me to a number of observations I believe must be made about Middle Eastern and other countries which belong to OPEC—the Organization of Petroleum Exporting Countries. Much bitter criticism has been directed at OPEC and its member-nations lately. Although I am an oilman, I am forced to admit the OPEC countries have their side of the story—and I believe it deserves a hearing and an objective assessment.

26

THE OIL-PRICE RISES instituted by the OPEC countries came as a shock to the highly industrialized nations which are net importers of oil. But the people raising the loudest hue and cry about OPEC policies have generally managed to overlook some basic facts of life, economics and history.

OPEC countries raised their oil prices to meet levels already established by competing energy-sources. Take coal as an example. One ton of coal provides about the same amount of energy as four barrels of crude oil. With coal selling for $40 per ton at the pithead, crude oil selling for ten dollars at the wellhead works out to about the same price for the same amount of energy.

That, however, barely scratches the surface of the story—and the reasons—behind OPEC actions.

It is regrettable, but the world petroleum industry and the highly industrialized nations are sometimes their own worst enemies. Until very recently, they were always in an invincible position from which they could call the tune, and they kept the prices they paid OPEC countries at artificially low levels. At the same time, the prices industrialized nations charged for their manufactured products rose—steadily and steeply.

For most OPEC countries oil is the chief—in some cases, virtually the sole—revenue-producing export-item. It was inevitable that these countries should realize that their oil reserves are not inexhaustible. Those reserves are depleted by each barrel of oil drawn from the ground.

Now, not being industrialized themselves, the OPEC countries have always had to buy practically everything from automobiles to zip-fasteners abroad. Naturally, they thought of the price of imported goods in terms of barrels of oil.

The price they received for each barrel of crude remained more or less constant—and low. The prices of whatever they bought went up and up. Faced with these conditions, it is not overly surprising that the OPEC countries should seek to restore the buying-power of their oil.

Whereupon much of the world roared in protest.

It was—and is—a curious paradox.

Consider what has been happening in the United States, Britain, France, West Germany, Italy and other industrialized nations during the last fifteen years or so.

—Whenever Labour found that rising prices diminished the buying power of their wages, Labour demanded (and usually received) higher pay.

—Whenever business firms saw costs spiralling higher and higher and reducing their profits below the danger-line, they increased the prices they charged for goods and services.

—Whenever governments—national or local—felt the need for more revenue, they did not hesitate to hike existing taxes or impose new ones.

Everyone—or almost everyone—in the industrialized countries went along with round after round of Labour–Price–Tax increases. There was only a moderate amount of complaint and grumbling. After all, everyone 'at home' was sharing in the affluence and enjoying the good things that more money could buy—even at higher prices.

And then the OPEC countries boosted their posted prices of crude oil. THAT was different. OPEC countries were not part of whatever geographical entity was considered 'home.' They were remote, distant, foreign. American reaction was typical. Workers demanding more pay, businessmen raising their prices and politicians calling for higher taxes felt no qualms about joining the chorus that accused OPEC of extortion, gouging, blackmail.

Some voices—at least in effect—demanded: 'Send in the gunboats!'

*   *   *

Algeria, Ecuador, Indonesia, Nigeria, Saudi Arabia, Venezuela . . .

The worldly cynic does not have to read very far down the list of OPEC countries before an ugly suspicion begins to form in his mind. He wonders how much of the resentment and rage directed at OPEC member-nations arises from remnants of imperialist attitudes lodged somewhere deep in the Western group unconscious. Could it possibly be that the good citizens of highly industrialized democracies still harbour notions of exploiting small, faraway countries?

True, there was once a time when Algeria was a French colony, Indonesia belonged to the Dutch, Lawrence was the uncrowned King of Arabia, and Uncle Sam looked down at Latin American countries as 'banana republics.' Those days—for the benefit of Rip Van Winkles and Colonel Blimps—are long gone.

The people of the OPEC countries are proud and independent—and, in fact, they still smart from the days when they were colonials and treated as inferiors. The educated Saudi Arabian or Nigerian is the equal of the educated American or Briton or Frenchman (perhaps even a bit more than equal in some respects thanks to a higher degree of motivation). Societies in the OPEC countries are making huge and rapid strides. In Kuwait, for example, the government provides free education even through university and postgraduate studies for all who qualify academically.

The Arab oil-producing countries are usually cast as the chief villains in the OPEC-versus-the oil importing countries drama. The West became particularly incensed when the Arab countries imposed an embargo on oil shipments.

According to reputedly reliable stories emanating out of Washington, there were actually contingency plans for employing classic gunboat diplomacy to break the embargo. If this was true, we should all be grateful that cool heads prevailed. Any military action would have—in my considered opinion—resulted in a disaster of incalculable proportions.

It is a sad commentary on the state of Western civilization that there are still those who believe military intervention to be a solution. Sadder still—for it is more widespread—is the double-standard by which Americans and other westerners assess and pass judgement on the use of economic pressure to obtain political ends in international affairs. When 'our side' puts the economic squeeze on another country or countries, we applaud the statesmanship of our leaders. Let some 'other side' take economic action that has a negative effect on us, and we scream 'Foul!'

The Arab nations do not feel in an apologetic mood over having imposed an oil embargo. Why should they? Having discovered that they possessed a powerful economic weapon, they used it—just as the United States and most other Western countries have used (and still use) a vast array of economic weapons when it suited their purposes.

Centuries of tradition have produced a very highly-developed sense of *sharaf*—honour—in Arabs. They feel that the State of Israel was carved out of their lands—and, rightly or wrongly, they fear that Israel may seek to implement an expansionist policy and take more of their territory.

But when it comes to oil itself, their feelings are those of any person of any race, religion or nationality who sees that he has been gulled, bilked—in a word, suckered. Arabs know that the Western Powers arbitrarily established unrealistically low prices for Arab oil and kept them there for decades. The Arabs also know that with the Western World's ever-increasing need for and dependence on oil, the crude being produced in their countries is easily worth the prices they are charging for it.

OPEC countries—Arab or otherwise—are not the culprits responsible for the world's energy problems. During the 'energy crisis' aggravated by Arab oil embargo, I was repeatedly interviewed by journalists who believed that because of my long experience in the industry, I had some magical formulas at hand.

'There *must* be an answer,' one reporter insisted. 'We've always had all the oil we needed before. The world didn't just suddenly run dry of oil!'

I could only sigh. The misconceptions implicit in the journalist's questions and remarks were being widely trumpeted by people who seemed to think that all the oilmen in the world had united in a sinister cabal and shut down the flow valve on every oil and gas well on earth.

There are no plots. There can't be. Oilmen are—and always have been—fiercely competitive. Take any large number of them and, while they might reach general agreements on haute cuisine or flower arrangement, they will not form any unanimous plans for action in regard to the search and production of oil. (Small numbers will, however, at times form consortiums to spread risks and share costs in ventures.)

Oil producers' natures and attitudes are formed by the basic legal concept of 'The Law of Capture.' This holds that oil is like the wild animal in the jungle—in its natural state, it belongs to whoever is the first to capture it. Permit me to explain this further.

In the United States, a subterranean reservoir of crude oil may extend under properties owned or leased by a dozen—or, conceivably, any number—of individuals and companies. Oil migrates underground. Hence, if one oilman drills on the parcel he owns or leases and brings in a producing well, there will be an immediate and frantic race as other oilmen drill on adjoining properties. All who complete producing wells will be drawing from the same reservoir or 'pool.' Each will strive to obtain the largest share of the available crude before the pool is exhausted.

Each producer is consequently engaged in a constant competitive struggle. This does not lend itself to the formation of cabals.

In any event, while it is true in a broad sense that the world has usually had all the oil it needed, in recent years demand for oil and natural gas has been rising much more rapidly than the supply could be increased. The demand for energy doubled in the United States during the last twenty years. It will practically double again by 1985.

By and large, the petroleum industry did a creditable job of meeting rising demands as long as it could reasonably do so. Since 1914, the year I first became active in the oil business, there was almost always a greater or smaller surplus of crude oil—until the beginning of World War Two, that is.

Before World War Two, it was much easier to 'find' oil, for there were great untapped pools only a few thousand feet below the surface of the earth. As time went on, these were depleted. It became necessary to search further afield and drill much deeper.

On occasion, shortages would develop. These were immediately reflected in the market. In 1920, for example, some

Oklahoma crude was bringing $5—even $5.20 and $5.50—per barrel at the well-head.

Take into consideration the buying power of the dollar in 1920. It was three, even four, times what it is today. Thus, in terms of present-day dollars, crude was then selling for $15 to $20 per barrel. Yet, I do not recall public anger over the 'high price of oil' or agitation to force producers to reduce their prices.

Stated another way, America had an oil shortage 55 years ago. But it was shortlived. Traditional marketplace dynamics became operative. High prices encouraged more drilling and resulted in higher production—and then prices dropped.

Let us take a glance at the economics of oil production. In 1914, I could drill (and complete) a producing well in Oklahoma for as little as $2,500. Today, an 'average' onshore well in the United States costs upwards of $75,000 to drill. That is petty cash—postage stamp money—compared to offshore costs. Occidental Oil, Allied Chemical, Thomson Scottish Associates and the Getty Oil Company are associated in a U.K. sector North Sea exploration and drilling venture. It costs $50,000 *a day* merely to operate a deepsea rig (the rig itself now costs about $50 million).

There has been much in the press lately about the 'excessive' profits earned by oil companies. I fear that the legends of Coal Oil Johnnie and the long-ago scandals of Harry Sinclair and Teapot Dome are colouring financial writers' views. Yes, some oilmen do make money—but only after taking very great risks with immense amounts of capital. Out of every 100 exploration wells drilled in unproved areas, only nine find pay sand—and of these, only TWO prove to be of commercial value. In effect, the oilman is betting his capital against 50-to-1 odds.

In 1972, the thirty leading U.S. oil companies had a total gross revenue of $106.3 billion, but their net income was only $6.9 billion, a low 6.5 per cent return. It was in that year that the real dimensions of oil shortage and energy crunch began to show themselves. Oilmen foresaw what lay ahead and urged they be permitted to raise their prices. They wanted funds for crash expansion programmes to head off crisis. Their warnings and requests went largely unheeded.

Then what the oilmen had predicted became reality. The petroleum industry was damned for having failed to make plans and implement them in time. It was easy to hurl the charges, impossible to substantiate them. As John L. Loftis Jr., general manager of Exxon Corp.'s minerals department wryly observed: 'Industry cannot be expected to plan itself into bankruptcy. Exponential increases in costs cannot be covered by constant prices.'

Oilmen were also accused of failing to build refinery capacity at a rate sufficient to keep pace with predictably increasing demand. Yes, there is no question that refinery construction lagged in the United States—but why?

For one thing, the costs of building refineries had soared into the stratosphere. Using 1946 cost levels as a base expressed as 100, by 1972 materials costs stood at 278.2 and labour costs at 545.7. By sharp contrast, the prices refining companies could charge for their products had not advanced more than 18 or 20 per cent during the same period. Costs were not the only brake, either.

While I, personally, appreciate clean air and litter-free landscapes as much as anyone, I fear the environmentalists went too far. Due to the efforts of these well-meaning—but often misguided and overly emotional militants—refinery construction was not only slowed, but finally stopped dead. It has become virtually impossible to locate a refinery anywhere in the United States without going through years of court actions, public protests, demonstrations and the obstacles created by hastily drawn-up prohibitory laws.

There are, I am happy to say, some gleams of light in the darkness. The market is giving the first, feeble signs of curing itself. The present price of new crude oil—while not high in comparison with the purchasing power of money in the past—is encouraging many producers to increase operations. Wells that had to be shut down as unprofitable are now operating again. Locations that did not warrant drilling under the old price structure are being drilled.

Every drilling rig is active. Drilling contractors are turning away business because they can't handle more than they already have. A higher return on invested capital has enabled companies to expand their operations. Exploration budgets show increases of billions of dollars. (But inflation is eating into those budgets, reducing their real value in terms of what materials and work they can buy.)

The Getty Oil Co. made capital expenditures of $450 million in 1974 alone—and this, my associates and I know, is but the proverbial drop in the crude barrel that will be needed for maximum expansion.

Eventually, as history—and my own direct experience—have shown, the high prices brought about by shortage will make possible greatly increased exploration and production. This, in turn, will increase supply and eventually produce surpluses, which are certain to ease the price picture to some degree (how much depends mainly on the inflationary rate that prevails).

In the meantime, the question of energy and oil supply is really in the hands of governments. If governments want more oil—or energy sources of any kind—for their people, they will aid rather than hinder oilmen in achieving greater levels of production. Once the oilman sees he is receiving some consideration, being given a fair chance to profit after risking his capital at staggering odds, he will respond. He always has and always will. It's the nature of the breed.

But, if governments levy excessive taxes, pass restrictive legislation and otherwise make the petroleum industry a target and whipping boy—the future will only grow darker. It's an old saying that oilmen scare easily. They become very frightened, indeed, when after being called upon to make multimillion and even billion dollar expenditures on 50-to-1 shots, they suspect that governments will not permit them a fair return for their risk and efforts. They'd much rather put their capital into savings banks. That would at least be a safe bet, even if it failed to produce a single additional barrel of oil.

27

MY 1954 VISIT to the Middle East forced me to once again postpone any plans I might have had for returning to the United States. The Neutral Zone potential was obviously great, and development and ancillary programmes demanded that I remain on the Continent.

I went back to Paris, took my usual suite at the Hotel George V and immersed myself in business. My diary entry for July 1, 1954, gives a fair indication of how my days were spent. It also provides excellent insight into why it was so advantageous for me to be in Europe rather than anywhere else.

'Worked on tanker arrangements with Ari Onassis. Lunch with Charles Wrightsman and with Percy Ebbott, president of Chase National.'

Now, Aristotle Onassis had reputedly obtained what amounted to a monopoly on tanker-transportation of all oil produced in Saudi Arabia (including that produced from the Saudi Arabian concession in the Neutral Zone). Naturally, the oil companies were up in arms, for they had their own tanker fleets or tankers under charter.

The Getty interests were in the midst of large scale tanker construction programmes in anticipation of Neutral Zone production. An Onassis monopoly would wreak havoc with those programmes—and with much other Getty company planning. But Ari and I were friends, there was a bond of mutual trust and confidence between us. As always when the two of us sat down and talked, obstacles were quickly ironed out. Our conversation ended successfully—and with a handshake which, for Ari, constituted an ironclad agreement.

As for Charles Wrightsman, with whom I lunched that same day, we had been close friends for many, many years. Charlie had been one of America's great independent oilmen as far back as the 1920s, one of the wildcatting breed—and a man who had both a great (if sometimes Rabelaisian) sense of humour along with a deep appreciation of culture and art.

For instance, years ago Charlie was an inveterate party-giver. Being a millionaire many times over, his parties were always lavish, and generally there were numbers of beautiful women among the guests. I remember that Wrightsman used to carry elegantly engraved cards in his pocket, ceremoniously handing one to each of his lady-guests. The cards read:

'Mr. Charles Wrightsman presents his compliments and wishes to inform you that anything he says to you this evening is all in fun unless he confirms it in writing tomorrow.'

Of course, Charlie would later become most famed for his magnificent art collection.

At any rate, Charlie was in Europe in July, 1954, and our lunch led to our entering into a joint oil exploration and drilling enterprise.

Any time spent with Charlie was invariably time well spent, for his good humour, vitality and willingness to be a friend through thick and thin were inexhaustible.

As can be gathered, these meetings with Ari Onassis and Charles Wrightsman during the course of the same day had far-reaching consequences. The meetings would very probably not have taken place at all if I had been elsewhere at the time. Europe in the 1950s was where, to use the current idiom, it was all happening for the international businessman and entrepreneur.

While I'm on the subject of Paris and entrepreneurs, I must digress and pay a very special tribute to a very special friend, Paul Louis Weiller. I have long divided people into two groups—those whom I call 'life-enhancers' and those whom I think tend to detract from life and diminish the life-enjoyment of those with whom they come into contact.

It has been my great good fortune to meet, know and become friends with a very large number of life-enhancing men and women, many of whom I have already mentioned by name. But I have known few men who can equal Paul Louis Weiller in this regard. A highly (and most deservedly) successful entrepreneur, Paul Louis is at once the shrewdest of businessmen and the kindest and most considerate of human beings, a man of impeccable taste and manners, yet without the slightest trace of prejudice or snobbery.

He is also a man of immensely diplomatic generosity—as is so clearly illustrated by the acts of thoughtful kindness he showed Sir Charles and Lady Elsie Mendl. During her fantastic and flamboyant career as an interior designer, the former Elsie de Wolfe had earned—and spent—fortunes. Returning to France after the end of World War Two, she resumed the gay and expensive whirl that made her and Sir Charles leading figures of Continental society.

Then Elsie became ill; her vitality began to ebb. The Mendls' finances reached a precarious low. Elsie owned a magnificent string of oriental pearls. They had originally cost a huge sum, but the advent of cultured pearls had broken the market; her pearls were worth very little. But Elsie was in her nineties. She did not realize this and announced that she would re-establish fiscal balance by selling the pearls. Neither Sir Charles nor any of the many people in her large entourage dared tell her the truth.

Paul Louis Weiller heard of Elsie's predicament and paid her a visit. He pretended to be downcast. Elsie asked him why.

'I have been looking all over Paris for a very particular gift for a very particular lady-friend,' Paul Louis explained. 'A necklace of genuine oriental pearls. There is none of fine quality to be found.'

Elsie Mendl suspected nothing. She had her necklace brought and shown to Weiller. He opened his eyes wide.

'Perfect! Exactly what I've been trying to find. Would you possibly consider selling them, Elsie?' He named a price considerably higher than what she had paid for them—and much more than they were worth on the current market. Elsie accepted his offer, and she never did learn the truth about the transaction.

Ludwig Bemmelmans has related that later, when Elsie's health and finances deteriorated even further, it was Paul Louis Weiller who bought the Mendls' Versailles villa at an exorbitant price. The sum was more than adequate to enable Elsie to live luxuriously. And the Mendls were to remain living in the house—rent free—until her death.

Paul Louis Weiller has been a most magnanimous host to me whenever I have been in Paris. I cannot begin to count the number of times he has thrust aside his own many business responsibilities in order to suit my schedules—or to gratify some wish I may have expressed in passing. He owns several magnificent homes; all have been open to me as though they were my own. He has given splendid parties and receptions in my honour. Yet, I have been able only once to prevail upon him to be my guest at Sutton Place.

Paul Louis finds his greatest satisfaction—and, perhaps, his very *raison d'être*—in giving his time, attention, energies and friendship. There is tremendous, engaging charm in his almost boyish shyness about taking from others, asking even the slightest favour for himself or ever putting anyone else out, for whatever reason.

One of the rare few I place on a par with Paul Louis is another close and cherished friend, Heinrich 'Heinie' Thyssen. Originally, our chief common interest was fine art. The Thyssen Collection, housed near Lugano in Switzerland, is among the most famous private collections on the Continent—indeed, in the world.

As Heinie and I came to know each other better, we realized that we had many friends in common and that we held similar views on a wide range of subjects. Suave, urbane and once known as something of a playboy, Heinie is an individual of remarkable depth and dimension. The hours speed by in his company—and, on one occasion, I fear he was saddled with not only my company but that of several dozen transient visitors.

I had come to stay at Heinie's villa for what I (and, I am sure, he) thought would be two or three days. Early in my visit, a very serious crisis affecting my business interests arose. Thyssen's telephones began ringing incessantly as calls came in for me from all over Europe, the United States and the Middle East. I was, of course, greatly embarrassed.

'This is only going to get worse, Heinie,' I said. 'I'll leave and go to a hotel immediately.'

'I refuse to hear of it!' Heinie said.

'But there'll be people flying in from half a dozen countries,' I protested. 'I'll have to hold conferences—some lasting far into the night. This house will be worse than a railroad station.'

'Then let it be' was all he said.

It turned out just as I had predicted—and the chaos lasted for more than a week. Throughout it all, Heinie Thyssen was the super-perfect, always cheerful and generous host. I don't believe anyone has ever made me feel more completely at home before or since—and I shall never be able to repay Heinie for his graciousness and hospitality, which were far, far above the call of friendship. Nor shall I ever forget that when I suffered the loss of my beloved son, George, it was Heinie Thyssen who immediately offered to do 'anything—anything at all—that might help.' He stood ready and willing to give whatever I might have asked of his time and energies—and one can never forget such demonstrations of genuine friendship. If Heinie and Paul Louis Weiller read these pages, they will now know that I state publicly what I have told them personally many times. My home is theirs—just as they have made their homes mine so often and so spontaneously.

As I've mentioned, I made my second trip to the Middle East and Neutral Zone in 1956, staying there four months. After that, I began to give serious consideration to establishing a permanent liaison centre on the European Continent for use by the Getty companies.

No, I had no intentions of setting up any corporate headquarters in the conventional sense of the term. Rather, what I envisioned was a comfortable residential type of accommodation, the aim being to avoid a strictly-business kind of environment. The liaison centre would provide an easy, relaxed atmosphere and pleasant surroundings in which Getty executives and businessmen from all over the world could meet, exchange views and ideas, yet conduct no formal business.

Naturally, plans and programmes could—and probably would—grow out of such meetings. However, the actual business of firming them up, formulating agreements, signing contracts—would be conducted later, in the appropriate company headquarters. It seemed to me that a large country house with ample grounds located fairly near a European capital city would fill the bill exactly.

At first, I thought of Italy. As early as February 24, 1952, I had noted in my diary: 'I have made a study of the Italian business situation. Italy is in better shape than France and is now efficiently competitive. I rank Italy next to Germany for business prospects.'

(The Getty interests did buy an Italian oil company and refinery in 1958, but this had nothing to do with my concept of establishing a liaison centre for the Getty companies. Nor did my purchase of two houses in Italy—which I shall relate in a later chapter.)

But in 1957, my choice of location for the liaison centre was veering toward France. There were several reasons for this. Paris was better served by international airlines than Rome or Milan (and unlike me, most businessmen habitually travelled by air). The kind of properties that would have suited my purpose located within reasonable distances of Rome or Milan were either very highly priced—or, if not excessively expensive, usually in disrepair. On the other hand, there were large numbers of villas and chateaux with extensive grounds available for purchase within easy range of Paris. The prices on these were comparatively reasonable.

Good friends like Paul Louis Weiller, Jack Forrester, Mrs. Penelope Kitson and Mme. Mary Tessier volunteered their help. They made inquiries, found properties for sale and made arrangements for me to inspect them. Quite often, they accompanied me on these jaunts. More than once, one or another of them would point out some serious flaw or drawback that I might have missed.

Months passed. I made no decision, but continued window-shopping. Then, I sensed that Paris wasn't right, either. Property developers were buying up huge land parcels outside the city; before long, the city would be building outward and any peaceful retreat would be engulfed by housing projects or industrial complexes. Then, in May, 1958, the French political situation came close to disintegration. France was balanced on the thin edge of civil war—a catastrophe only barely averted when General Charles de Gaulle became Premier. In September, the de Gaulle constitution, increasing executive powers, was adopted by an overwhelming majority of the French electorate. Wise and experienced observers felt the climate was changing in France and foreign businessmen might no longer be quite as welcome as they had been in the past.

By then, I had suffered the great blow caused by the death of my youngest son, Timothy, and I was in Italy. The Getty interests took over Golfo, the Italian oil company and its refinery in Gaeta, south of Naples. The headquarters of Golfo were moved to Rome. I once more scouted the area for a liaison centre—to no avail.

My attention was drawn to England. The country was stable, its political system functioned with fewer major upheavals than those of most Continental countries. London remained the financial, commercial, insurance and shipping capital of the eastern hemisphere. I knew the country and its people well—and had, ever since 1912.

Now, it is a curious fact that in June 1951, I had been in England and made this diary notation on June 26:

'Drove alone to Sutton Place, another stately home. There are some rooms over one hundred feet long . . . there is a fine Holbein in the drawing room.'

About four years later, I again had occasion to visit Sutton Place, this time in the company of Mitchell Samuels. We had both been invited to lunch by the Duke and Duchess of Sutherland. After that, I did not give Sutton Place another thought until 1959, when I had left Rome and returned to London, where I stayed in a suite at the Ritz Hotel. As it happened, Paul Louis Weiller had business reasons for coming to London in June. One day, he dropped by to see me at the Ritz.

'We're invited to dine with the Duke and Duchess of Sutherland tomorrow evening,' Paul Louis informed me. 'I'll pick you up.'

The following diary entry is for June 27, 1959—exactly eight years and one day after I first visited Sutton Place.

'In the morning went to my shoemaker, Lobb, and then to my tailor, Kilgour, French and Stanbury. In the evening went with Paul Louis Weiller in his Rolls to Sutton Place for dinner with the Duke and Duchess of Sutherland. There were 18 for dinner. The Duke told me he had bought the estate for 120,000 pounds sterling in 1917 and declared that he would now like to sell it. After dinner, we saw a good war film in the Duke's Cinema Room. Paul Louis and I drove back to London afterwards.'

A few days later, it suddenly dawned on me that the Getty interests had found what they needed.

Further inquiries were made. Geordie Sutherland was ready to sell the stately, 72-room manor house—considered the finest example of Tudor architecture extant—for a price I conservatively estimated at less than one-twentieth its replacement value. The offer included 750 acres of grounds (later expanded by further purchases to 1,100 acres).

Sutton Place, located some 30 miles from London in the Surrey Green Belt, was not only a bargain, it was ideal in every respect for use as a liaison centre and a good investment besides.

The decision was made to buy. E. Dudley Delevigne acted as agent. Slaughter & May, one of Britain's leading law-firms, handled the manifold legal aspects involved. Miss Robina Lund, the young woman solicitor in direct charge of the detail-work, did such a superior job that she was later retained as my own legal adviser on matters involving British law.

The purchase was completed in record time. Before 1959 ended, the Getty companies took possession of what was to become their Eastern Hemisphere liaison centre. Executives and businessmen would thereafter meet there, compare notes and discuss economic problems and trends and a thousand other matters in a quiet, congenial—and luxurious—atmosphere conducive to constructive thinking.

No one—least of all I—then guessed that future developments would cause me to spend much of the next sixteen years at Sutton Place.

28

THE MANOR OF SUTTON is mentioned in the Domesday Book as Sudtone. King Edward the Confessor (1042–1066) had a hunting lodge on the lands. It was located very close to the spot where the present Church of St. Edward the Confessor now stands, about a quarter of a mile from the manor house in Sutton Park.

In 1521 the Manor of Sutton was granted by King Henry VIII to Sir Richard Weston, one of his favourite courtiers. Sir Richard promptly began having Sutton Place built, a task which took five years. The exterior and interior of the great house changed very little in the ensuing four centuries.

Sutton Place is one of the earliest English manor houses to be constructed purely as a dwelling place and without any regard to defence. Sir Richard Weston had visited the French Court on an embassy to Francis I and accompanied Henry VIII to the Field of the Cloth of Gold in 1520. It was probably during these journeys to France that he became familiar with the architecture of the Continent, especially with the Italian style which was then popular. The use of moulded terra-cotta rather than stone to embellish the brickwork of Sutton Place was doubtless a result of this influence. Such use of terra-cotta is quite unusual in English houses of the Tudor Period, and it is highly probable that Sir Richard brought Italian artisans to England to do the work.

Sir Richard Weston enjoyed a long and distinguished career in the service of Henry VIII. He was made Knight of the

Bath in 1518 and subsequently became a Gentleman of the Privy Chamber, Master of the Court of Wards, Treasurer of Calais and Under-Treasurer of England. Henry VIII himself was a frequent visitor at Sutton Place after the manor house was completed. There is reason to believe it was there that he first met Anne Boleyn, who became his second queen in 1532. Sir Richard Weston's son, Francis—then about twenty-one years old—was made Knight of the Bath at Anne Boleyn's coronation. But four years later, Francis Weston was beheaded on Tower Hill after being implicated as one of the Queen's lovers in the trial that also led to her execution.

There is no record of Sir Richard Weston's feelings about the beheading of his only son. He remained high in the King's favour, and there are records showing that he was present at many royal ceremonies including the funeral of Jane Seymour, the Baptism of Edward VI and the Reception of Anne of Cleves in 1539.

Sir Richard lived until 1542. His estates passed on to his grandson, Henry Weston, then aged seven. In 1559 Henry married Dorothy, daughter of Sir Thomas Wardour of Arundel and a cousin of Queen Elizabeth I.

The Weston family remained Roman Catholic after the Reformation and played very little part in public life. The great-grandson of the builder of Sutton Place, the third Sir Richard Weston—born in 1591—did achieve considerable note as an agriculturalist and made numerous experiments in farming on the land around Sutton Place. He published a book on husbandry which is considered a classic on the subject.

Sutton Place remained in the possession of the Weston family and their descendants until the end of the nineteenth century. It was then leased and occupied for some years by Alfred Charles William Harmsworth, Viscount Northcliffe. Lord Northcliffe was, of course, the newspaper magnate who founded the *Daily Mail* and *Daily Mirror* and later acquired *The Times*. In 1918, Sutton Place was purchased by the Duke of Sutherland, from whom I bought it for my companies in 1959.

A great deal of work and a considerable investment were required to renovate and refurbish Sutton Place so that it would suit the needs and purposes for which it had been acquired. The great manor house, set like a jewel on an expanse of lawn and formal gardens, had more than a dozen reception rooms, fourteen principal bedrooms and ten principal bathrooms. These, of course, were in addition to servants' quarters, kitchens, pantry and many other rooms used for special purposes.

The main problems were those of renovation, modernization (for example, the installation of new and up-to-date kitchen equipment and fixtures) and redecoration. These were not tasks to which I could personally devote much time. I had my own work—which I continued to do in—and from—my suite at the Ritz. The responsibility for overseeing the Sutton Place transformation project was left largely in the most competent and highly talented hands of my very dear friend, Mrs. Penelope Kitson. Penelope—or Pen, as I have called her these many years—combines a remarkable flair for design and decoration with a rare touch for supervision, for getting difficult things done. (She established an enviable reputation for herself among shipbuilders with her fine designs for the interiors of officers' and crews' quarters aboard tankers and super-tankers built for the Getty interests.)

I'm not quite sure how Pen managed to take care of her personal chores—or even eat and sleep—during the next several months. I never asked her, and if I had, I doubt if she would have had the time to pause and give me an answer.

I'm afraid that I was considerably less than a help to Penelope Kitson. For some reason that escapes me, I failed to consult her before meeting with a group of top-level Getty companies executives who unanimously agreed that a large housewarming party should be held at Sutton Place when all the work was completed. I simply asked my secretary to check contractors' commitments. These indicated that all work was to be finished between April 30 and May 15, 1960.

'Ample margin for us to hold the party on June 30,' I said. 'We can start making up the guest-list.'

The list was long, containing the names of more than 1,200 people all over the world. Only after the invitations had been printed and addressed did I think to tell Penelope—who promptly went into a state of something very closely approaching shock.

'Oh, no!' she groaned.

Some contractors undertaking certain phases of the work at

Sutton Place had fallen behind schedule despite Pen's best efforts to hold them to their promises. Many items that had been ordered were—according to advice from suppliers—'subject to indeterminate delay.'

'Pen—are you saying we can't meet the deadline for the party?' I asked.

For a moment, Penelope seemed to ignore the question. 'I could strangle you, Paul—literally and with my own hands,' she said through gritted teeth, then broke into a smile. 'But we have to make the deadline now, don't we?'

Penelope Kitson and all the others who pitched in somehow succeeded in working miracles. Although not every last detail was perfect by the set date, Sutton Place was certainly ready and entirely presentable by June 30—and the party was a complete success. Twelve hundred guests had been invited. More than 2,500 people came (many brought by friends who had invitations, but many others were gate-crashers). They consumed almost as many bottles of champagne and other wines and liquors; ate nearly an equal number of portions of caviar, lobster and giant English strawberries with Devonshire cream and danced to the music of three orchestras until after dawn the next day.

My diary entry for Thursday, June 30:

'At the house all day. Everyone is working like mad to get ready for the party. At 8:20 I am in white tie and downstairs. So are Ian Constable-Maxwell and Jack Forrester. While dressing I noticed a handsome couple in full evening dress walking across the lawn toward the main entrance to the house. They turned out to be Alan Mead and his wife. At 8:50 we went into the dining and drawing rooms for dinner. I had 54 at the table in the dining room and Ian had about the same number at small round tables in the drawing room.

'My table and the side tables sparkled with plate. I had no tablecloth in order to show off the beauty of refectory table's elm top. It was very effective. The dinner menu included caviar, consomme, roast veal, fraise des bois. (The lobster was served later as part of a late supper.)

'I had the wife of the Venezuelan Ambassador on my right; Mary, Duchess of Roxburgh, on my left. Pamela

Mountbatten Hicks and her husband David were at my table. So were Lloyd and Margery Gilmour who had flown over from the U.S. for the party and are turning right around to fly back in the morning, for they are themselves giving a party in New York tomorrow night.

'At 10:30 we finished dinner and I joined Ian Constable-Maxwell and his daughter Jeanette in the Great Hall to greet the guests for the ball. We three stood in line for one and a half hours shaking hundreds of hands and saying "How do you do?" or "Good evening" many hundreds of times. By 11:30 p.m. there must have been well over 2,000 people in the house.

'It was so jammed in the Great Hall and on the staircase that I couldn't get up to the Long Gallery at the first try. Later I managed it and enjoyed dancing with Robina Lund and then Madelle Hegeler. Later I had a dance with Ethel Le Vane. Then I went outside with Madelle to the swimming pool to see and enjoy the gay scene there. The dance floor at the swimming pool was packed with swaying couples. There was a milk bar and a beautiful, gentle cow wandered about, happily making the rounds of the poolside. Later the friendly animal even made an exploratory excursion into the Great Hall, much to everyone's amusement.

'Going back to the house, I went into the drawing room. It, too, was filled with dancing couples. At 6:15 in the morning, a fourteen piece orchestra was still playing, and a crooner was still singing, in the Long Gallery, but the crowd had thinned out. There were only a few guests still dancing. Pen—who had done so very much to help make the evening a success—and I had a dance, and the memorable party was over.'

There is one more line for the day's entry:

'Just as I was in bed, Pen phoned up from downstairs that one of the Lamerie sugar casters was missing from the dining room!'

That bit of news was most disturbing. The casters were superb examples of Paul Lamerie's work. I had paid £14,000 for the pair. Luckily, it was later recovered. A guest had taken it as a souvenir, thinking it was merely an inexpensive bit of tableware supplied by the catering firm that had taken care of the dinner. Upon learning its true value from newspaper accounts, he anonymously telephoned the police, admitted his mistake and said he would leave the caster in a certain telephone kiosk. And, he did. Police found it there, unharmed save for a tiny dent which was later repaired.

Two days after the party—on July 2—I made this diary notation:

'We had received requests from 210 reporters who asked they be allowed to cover the ball. We accepted 31, plus about ten photographers. Yesterday and today the newspapers are full of stories and photos of the party and ball. The press has been very complimentary in its articles and comments.'

The July 13, 1960, issue of the *Tatler* was especially gratifying. It published photographs of many of my friends—all of whom seemed to be enjoying themselves very much—at the dinner and ball. They included (in the left-to-right order in which the many photos appeared): Sir Victor and Lady Sassoon, Prince William of Gloucester, Baron Elie de Rothschild, the Duke of Rutland, Mr. Duncan Sandys (then Minister of Aviation in the British Cabinet), Mr. Brian Sweeney (son of Margaret, Duchess of Argyll and Mr. Charles Sweeney—both my close and longtime friends), Huntington Hartford and Earl and Countess Beatty.

Admittedly, the cost of the 'housewarming' was high (and, I should make clear, borne by me personally), but the great amount of worldwide publicity that resulted proved highly beneficial to all the Getty companies and their stockholders. As Jack Forrester—who was very wise in such matters—remarked:

'You got a fantastic bargain, Paul. It would have cost your companies fifty million dollars at the very least to buy the same amount of advertising space.'

None the less, by Sunday July 3, I felt somewhat like Cinderella after the ball.

'Am starting to unpack my papers,' I wrote in my

diary. 'Correspondence has really piled up over the last few days, and I also have several business meetings scheduled for this coming week. Have to stop thinking about parties and go back to work.'

29

READING NEWSPAPER AND magazine articles that have appeared about me, I realize there are widespread misconceptions regarding Sutton Place, its ownership and just where and how I fit into the scheme.

Sutton Place does not belong to me personally. It was—as I have said—purchased to serve as a liaison centre for use by Getty company executives and other businessmen. The estate is owned by a subsidiary of the Getty Oil Company. I pay—and at a liberal rate—for my pro-rated share of the costs and expenses involved in or incident to the operation and upkeep of house and grounds. In effect, I am merely a paying tenant.

Actually, I don't think I would be stretching the point very far if I described myself as a double or treble-paying tenant. In addition to the basic, pro-rated share I pay, I have made considerable personal investments in the improvements and furnishing of the house.

This aspect aside, the Getty Oil Company has been most fortunate in its investment in Sutton Place. The value of the property has increased greatly over the years since its purchase. The company receives the full benefit of this value-appreciation—and so, it follows, do all the company's shareholders.

There have been—and are—innumerable fringe-benefits and advantages to Getty Oil's ownership of Sutton Place. A two-storey office building was constructed near the main house. It serves as headquarters for Liberian Operations, Ltd. (England). LibOps is another Getty Oil subsidiary concerned with tanker-schedulings and provides fulltime employment for some sixty Britons of both sexes.

No dollar or pound sterling valuation can be placed on what I consider to be one of the most significant and important fringe-benefits that accrue from Getty Oil's ownership of Sutton Place. This lies in the realm of helping to maintain good relations between the United States and Great Britain. One of England's great, historic stately homes has been completely restored and is being maintained at optimum levels by a private company, at no cost to the taxpayers of either country. Then, Sutton Place is made available to a great many organizations which raise funds for charities and other worthwhile causes.

Some of the funds are collected by opening the house and grounds to visiting groups, with the sponsoring organization setting the admission price and, needless to say, retaining all the proceeds. Latest figures furnished to me by Albert Thurgood, the Sutton Place estate manager, show that about £25,000 has been netted for charity through these openings over the past several years. Other organizations have held concerts and even fashion shows for charity at Sutton Place. These have also produced sizeable sums. Among the groups that have benefitted are:

British Red Cross
English-Speaking Union
National Society for the Prevention of Cruelty to Children
Dr. Barnardo's Homes
Distressed Gentlefolks Aid Association
OXFAM
Action for Crippled Children
Royal Lifeboat Institution

There have been many others, including local—Surrey and Guildford—charities. My own favourite event is the annual party I love giving for children from the Woking Orphanage around Christmas time. It is at these parties that I happily shed the last vestiges of a staid and sober businessman image and don Beatle wigs or ludicrous paper hats. The children and I have a marvellous time—which, I think, adds some evidence to the contention that, regardless of our chronological age, there is a bit of the child in all of us. In fact, one of the higher compliments I ever received was bestowed on me by my dear friend, Lady Ursula d'Abo, after she watched me romp through one of these parties.

'I'd never have believed it,' she laughed. 'You acted as though the children were giving the party for you.'

I suppose that in a way they were—and that they do, every year.

A memorable occasion—on a much different plane—was the concert held at Sutton Place on July 17, 1969. Given under the patronage of Her Majesty, Queen Elizabeth the Queen Mother, it marked the Golden Jubilee of the Central Council for the Disabled, of which His Grace, the Duke of Devonshire, is president. I had been greatly honoured to be chairman of the event, which was called 'Violin on a Summer Evening.'

The great violinist, Yehudi Menuhin, played, accompanied at the piano by his also immensely talented sister, Hepzibah. It almost goes without saying that their performance was magnificent.

After the concert, many of those present went into the drawing room. Her Majesty further honoured me by inviting me to sit next to her. It was a rare opportunity for me to chat with this great and wonderful woman who is the very embodiment of the qualities that anyone would consider to be the ideals for Constitutional royalty. Her Majesty had known Sutton Place during the period between the wars, and I beamed inwardly when she most graciously complimented me on the appearance of the house. Her Majesty, I also discovered, has a considerable degree of knowledge about eighteenth-century French furniture and art.

But, it seems, she wasn't quite sure about who had made the gilded *appliques candélabres* flanking the drawing room fireplace. I had been called away from her side for a moment. Her Majesty turned to Nicole, Duchess of Bedford (she and Ian, the Duke of Bedford and I have been close friends for decades).

'Do you know whose work they are?' Her Majesty asked Nicole.

'I would say Pierre Gouthière,' Nicole replied—later privately admitting to me that she wasn't completely certain they had been made by the famed French metal worker.

Her Majesty saw that I had returned and asked if the sconces were really Gouthières. I said yes, they were—and noticed the look of relief that came over Nicole Bedford's attractive face.

Speaking of the Duke and Duchess of Bedford leads me off on a tangent. Ian and Nicole are not only wonderful friends, but a most amusing and hospitable couple. We have known each other a long time and I have been their guest at Woburn Abbey, as they have been mine at Sutton Place.

We often laugh at the rumour that gained some currency a number of years ago to the effect that I once offered to buy Woburn Abbey from Ian. This is totally untrue. I would never have considered making him an offer even if I had wanted to buy it, if for no other reason than that I recognize his deep love and attachment for his ancestral home.

Ian and Nicole did wonders with Woburn Abbey. During my stays at Woburn, old Bedford family retainers have repeatedly told me that the work, money—and love—that Ian and Nicole lavished on the great house not only saved it from deterioration, but restored it to a condition far superior to any it had known in the present century.

My tangent takes me further afield—into the realm of ghost stories. Like many ancient English manor houses, Sutton Place is said to be haunted. That is, one bedroom—known as the 'Red Room'—is supposed to be haunted by the ghost of the unfortunate Anne Boleyn, who occupied it when she was the guest of Sir Richard Weston and before she married King Henry VIII. I neither believe nor disbelieve in ghosts. Probably the best way of stating my views on this and other subjects dealing with the supernatural is by saying that I know there any many things which cannot be explained naturally. On the other hand, I personally do not believe in delving into them too far on the grounds that if we humans were intended to know, we would. In short, I am a cautious fence-straddler. I don't have superstitions—but I don't go out of my way to defy them, either.

But back to ghosts and ghost stories. I have never encountered the ghost of Anne Boleyn. A few of the many guests who have stayed at Sutton Place and slept in the Red Room have claimed they 'felt a presence' or 'experienced a chill' or heard strange noises during the night. I'm inclined to discount

most of these statements because if there had been any sufficiently unnerving phenomenon, the individuals would have
doubtless left the room then and there.

On the other hand, there does seem to be something more
than mere imagination to the story about the ghost that is
supposed to haunt Woburn Abbey. A few years ago, Mrs.
Penelope Kitson and I were among a group of guests Ian and
Nicole Bedford invited to spend a weekend at Woburn.

As it happened, Penelope was assigned an East Wing bedroom that has long had the reputation of being haunted. Now,
Penelope Kitson is one of the more intelligent and level-
headed human beings I've ever known. There is no trace of
hysteria anywhere in her makeup. Pen got little or no sleep on
the first night at Woburn. There were two doors to her
bedroom. After she retired for the night, both of them opened.
A breeze—or perhaps she hadn't closed them properly—
Penelope thought. She got out of bed and not only closed, but
locked, both doors. Then she got back into bed.

She says she was just drifting off to sleep—when both
doors opened again. At that, Penelope relates, she switched
on the lights and once more closed and locked the doors. She
made doubly sure, trying the handles, tugging to make sure
the doors were firmly secured. They were—but the phenomenon repeated itself during the night.

The next morning Pen, her lovely and usually radiantly
healthy face looking a bit haggard, told the Bedfords and me
what had happened. Ian and Nicole exchanged glances—and
were profuse in their apologies. They had no explanation.

'There is supposed to be a ghost in that room,' Nicole
sighed. 'It only shows itself every now and then, though.'

The Bedfords had their servants transfer Penelope's things
to another bedroom—and the next night, she had a peaceful
and undisturbed night's sleep.

'There've been some strange specimens in my family tree,'
Ian commented wryly afterward. 'I suppose there might even
have been one who liked to pick locks—but why should he
want to keep on doing it?'

The mystery of the periodically opening doors in the East
Wing bedroom at Woburn Abbey has never been solved—
and, I am told, the phenomenon still occurs from time to
time.

*   *   *

But enough of tangents and back to the original point of departure: Sutton Place.

One direct and practical value of having Sutton Place is best illustrated by a cocktail party held there on March 6, 1975. This event clearly shows how an overseas liaison centre in a large manor house can serve as a place where thoughts and ideas may be exchanged freely and informally. The party was given for diplomats and key men in the petroleum industry and their ladies. More than 200 people attended. I shall give an only partial list of the guests to indicate the scope of the affair, allowing the reader to recognize for himself how very much understanding and goodwill it could (and did) promote:

H.E. The Kuwaiti Ambassador and Mrs. Hanan Al-Nakib; H.E. The Indonesian Ambassador and Mrs. Veronica Subono; H.E. The Iranian Ambassador; H.E. The Peruvian Ambassador and Senor de Montagne; H.E. The Saudi Arabian Ambassador and Madame Al-Helaissi; The Norwegian Commercial Attaché and Mrs. Hoegh Henrichsen; H.E. The Ambassador of Thailand and Khunying Dootsdi Suphamongkorn; H.E. The Brazilian Ambassador and Mrs. R. Campos; H.E. The Portuguese Ambassador and Senhora Alda Noguiera; H.E. The Ambassador of the Ivory Coast and Madame Marcelle Aduka; H.E. The Moroccan Ambassador and Madame Marie A. Chorfi; Lord and Lady Provost of Aberdeen; Mr. and Mrs. S. A. Atoniuk (Managing Director, AMOCO Europe, Inc.); Mr. R. R. Aune (President, AMOCO Europe, Inc.); Mr. and Mrs. Charles H. Band (President, U.K. Offshore Operators Association); Mr. and Mrs. W. Michael Brown (Financial Director, Thomson Organization); Sir David and Lady Barran (Managing Director, Shell Petroleum); Mr. and Mrs. T. E. Cottrell (Managing Director, Texaco, Ltd.); Mr. A. M. Dunnett (Managing Director, Thomson Scottish Petroleum); Mr. and Mrs. A. L. Evans (General Manager, Hone Oil of Canada); Mr. and Mrs. H. R. George (Department of Energy); Mr. and Mrs. K. R. Henshaw (Chairman, Kuwait Oil Co.); Dr. S. Iwasa (London Representative, Japan Petroleum Development); Mr. and Mrs. J. R. Kircheis (Managing Director, Mobil Oil Ltd.); Sir Peter Kent (Chairman, Natural Environment Research Council); Mr. and Mrs. M. Kaneko (Managing Director, Mitsubishi, London); Mr. and Mrs. N. A. Leslie (Chairman, Petrofina (U.K.) Ltd.); Mr. and Mrs. J. A.

Molyneux (Department of Energy); Mr. S. Nori (Manager, Nissho Iwai Co.); Dr. and Mrs. N. Pignatelli (Managing Director, Gulf Eastern Hemisphere); Mr. and Mrs. D. E. Rooke (Managing Director, British Gas Corp.); Mr. and Mrs. J. J. Reynolds (Chairman, Conoco); Sir Jack and Lady Rampton (Under Secretary, Department of Energy); Lord Strathcona (Thomson Organization); Mr. and Mrs. M. Seymour (Sunningdale Oil); Mr. and Mrs. P. A. Taylor (Manager of Exploration and Production, British Gas Corp.); Mr. and Mrs. J. M. Williams (President, Texaco (U.K.) Ltd.).

Clearly, these guests—and all the others—were people in one way or another deeply concerned with the problems of expanding the world's supply of energy sources. Sipping cocktails and nibbling on canapés, they could speak freely and easily, discuss developments, ask questions, offer suggestions.

I firmly believe that business firms and businessmen have a responsibility—indeed, an obligation—to further understanding and good relations among nations and their peoples. I do not believe it pretentious to suggest that social affairs such as this cocktail party are constructive steps in those directions and that, in the long run, they serve to improve not only world political and economic conditions but also to benefit everyone, everywhere.

30

MY STAY AT Sutton Place was intended to be temporary. Once the business matters with which I had to deal were taken care of, I would go back to my home in Southern California.

Or so I thought—and so I have kept on telling myself over and over again during the last fifteen-and-a-half years. I also made the mistake of telling this to others. Consequently, items about my imminent departure for the United States have often appeared in the press. The most recent of these were published in early 1975.

Yes, each time I made up my mind to go, I meant it. And, each time, I was prevented from carrying out my intentions by last-minute business developments.

There are reasons other than plain, ordinary homesickness that make me want to return to California—at least for the winter months. I am, after all, 83 years old, and English winters are hard. For the last three winters, I have had attacks of bronchitis. The most severe of them was the one I suffered in the winter of 1974–75. After I had recovered, I all but swore an oath that my next winter would be spent in Southern California's softer, warmer climate. It's a good thing I didn't actually raise my hand and swear, for I would now find myself a perjurer.

Bitter winter or not, I shall be staying for at least another year. Damp, chill weather or no damp, chill weather, I am still an oilman, a wildcatting operator, at heart. Getty Oil has a very large stake in a United Kingdom sector North Sea exploration and drilling operation. Although Getty Oil is not conducting the actual drilling operations, it does have hundreds of millions of dollars invested in the project. I simply cannot bring myself to walk away until the operation is completed and crude oil is flowing from the offshore wells in which the Getty Oil Company owns an approximately one-fourth interest. And so, business—the oil business—is once again preventing me from boarding the homeward-bound ship that I have been meaning to catch for so long.

But let no one think that I have disliked roaming around Europe or that I regret having made England my base of operations since 1960. I have not lost touch with the United States, nor with my American friends. What is more, there have been some compensations for being away from home. I have been lucky, being richly rewarded in experiences and in the friendships I have made and strengthened on the Continent and in Britain.

While I have had much work to do, I have also known much pleasure and enjoyment—as a miscellany of my diary-entries reflects.

During April, 1952, I was in Rome.

'April 26: Dinner with my dear friends, Lord David Beattie and his wife Adele at Alfredo's.'

I had, of course, known Adele since her California childhood, for she was the niece of my old friend, J. F. T. 'Jefty' O'Connor. Three evenings later, I dined again with the Beatties—and with Faye Emerson, whom I had known and liked greatly since California days.

There were many other friends passing through—Bobo Rockefeller, Gregory Peck, Bruce Cabot, Aly Khan, Barbara Hutton. I had known Barbara's father, E. F. Hutton, very well. He used to bring hearty chuckles from his friends by saying—rather ruefully—'I can never be sure if I'm known for having married a Woolworth heiress or for being the father of Barbara Hutton.' When Barbara was married to Cary Grant, those of us who were their friends called them 'Cash and Cary,' a bit of goodnatured japery that they enjoyed as much as we did.

I was in Italy again in 1953, and was invited to stay at the villa of Bernard Berenson.

'March 1: Am a guest of Bernard Berenson at I Tatti. Berenson is always one of the best-dressed men. About 5' 2" tall, he weighs around 120 pounds. He walks with a cane. Although he is now 88, he looks a vigorous 70 or 75. He has made his huge library on art available to me for research.'

Six years later, I would make this diary-notation:

'October 7, 1959: Bernard Berenson is dead at 94. He was a great man and a good friend.'

It was during my 1953 visit to Italy that I did most of the research for the chapters I contributed to the book, *Collector's Choice*, written by my friend Ethel 'Bunny' Le Vane. It was through this book that I was to meet the noted English publisher, Mark Goulden, and his charming wife, Jane. Mark Goulden gave Ethel—and me—much sound advice about the book, and he was unstinting with his time, advice and help. Mark and his firm undertook to publish the book, but our relationship went beyond the just-business level. Mark and Jane became good and close friends, and we have had many good times together.

On September 23, 1953, I reminisced:

'I made my first trip to Europe with my parents, that was in 1909. The second was in 1912; I crossed from New York abroad the *Minnewaska*, staying at Oxford until 1913. I then toured Germany, Denmark, Sweden, Finland, Russia, Turkey, Greece, Egypt, Austria, Spain and France. My parents met me in Paris, and we sailed home on September, 1914. My third crossing was aboard the *Berengaria* in 1920. I did not go again until 1927. From then until 1939, I was in Europe every year, travelling aboard the *Berengaria, Leviathan, Homeric, Normandie* and *Europa*.'

Just ten years later, returning to England after a lengthy trip to the Continent, I booked cross-Channel passage from Le

Havre to Southampton—a short voyage that evoked great
nostalgia, for I travelled aboard the *Liberté*, formerly the
Europa:

'October 12: Lunch on board. We sail at 2. The ship is
most friendly. *M.* Ollagnier, chef de reception, gives me
the Rouen apartment. At 3:30, I am shown around the
ship. *M.* Parouty, the Chief Engineer, shows me the
engine room. The boilers are the original German ones
but retubed. The ship can make 23 to 24 knots; the
Europa was good for 27 to 28 knots.

'The French changed the salt water baths and showers
to fresh, putting in a modern electrical system and new
wiring. The old *Normandie* murals are in the *Liberté*
—strange to see them there. I later sit at my favourite
table facing the bow and watch the beautiful sea. I think
of my many prewar trips on this ship and on the *Bremen*.
The *Bremen* is gone these 18 years. The *Europa*—now
the *Liberté*—and I have grown old. But though the ship
is 33 years old she is unbelievably beautiful and impressive. She has an elegant spaciousness that moderns simply do not match. I am sad that she has only 190 First
Class passengers for New York. A few years ago she
would have had a waiting list. I am afraid that ocean
liners are a vanishing thing.

'We arrive at the tender stop at seven o'clock. We
leave by tender at 9:15. The *Liberté* looms above us, her
lights ablaze; her name in large electric lights is visible
for miles. Now she is gone, heading west across the
ocean. This is next to her last trip. She is due to be
broken up, to be scrapped. It seems incredible. She is so
elegant, so swift, so comfortable, so perfectly maintained and served. So much has changed and is changing; so much is lost and being lost . . .'

The years after 1953 sped by. In 1954, I went to the Middle
East. On my return trip, I stopped in Beirut and met Prince
Mahmad Pahlavi, brother of the Shah of Iran. Since I had
long been very good friends with Princess Ashraf, Prince
Mahmad and I became friends very quickly.

My paths crossed with other notables, personages—and old
friends of all nationalities. The Maharajah of Baroda, Doro-

thy Spreckels, Jacqueline de Ribes, Neil Vanderbilt, Baron Eugene Rothschild. I literally bumped into the Byron Foys one day—and we dined and talked about old times.

I had known Byron well in California—and I also knew Thelma when she was single, Thelma Chrysler. She laughed about the familiar tale of how I had been interviewed by shipboard reporters when I returned to New York from Europe in 1930. The reporters wanted my opinion on the future of the Stock Market.

'It'll get worse before it gets better,' I had replied. 'You'll see Chrysler down to five dollars a share before the slump bottoms out.'

My remarks were duly reported. Two days later, I received an angry telephone call from Walter P. Chrysler.

'What do you mean by telling the press Chrysler will hit five?' he demanded.

'I told them what I think, Walter,' I said. 'There's nothing really wrong with Chrysler stock, but the market trend being what it is, all stocks will continue to fall—including Chrysler.'

Some months later Chrysler shares did reach a five-dollar-low—but certainly not because of anything I had told reporters.

Space—and the patience of my readers—do not permit a month-by-month (or even year-by-year) recital of my social (or off-duty) life. But there are some highlights I think might be interesting—and perhaps even amusing. And some are deeply saddening to me, even now, as I re-read them.

1958 (Paris)

'January 19: At last I have met Maurice Chevalier. He is still a handsome, magnetic, very manly man. I was thrilled to meet him, for I have been an avid Chevalier fan for over thirty years. He was delightfully entertaining during lunch.'

'February 15: Sir Charles Mendl is dead. I've lost a great friend. I admired him very much.'

'February 17: I attended Sir Charles Mendl's cremation services at Père le Chaise. I don't like cremation, and the service was macabre.'

'March 2: Guest at Paul Louis Weiller's magnificent home at Neuilly.'

1958 (Rome)

'July 15: Alarming news. U.S. Marines have landed in Lebanon. What will Russia do? In the evening, I walk through Rome, savoring its antiquities and then the glitter of the Via Veneto. I earnestly hope this scene will not be destroyed by another war.'

'August 2: Dine and have wonderful time with my old friend, Prince Troubetzkoy.'

1959 (Paris)

'March 28: Drinks with the Maharajah of Baroda and his second son. Dinner with Jacqueline de Ribes. She is very attractive and sentimental. A lovely, entrancing woman.'

'April 22: I am sorry I didn't appreciate the greatness of the Impressionists when I was in Paris in 1909 and 1913–14. I bought my first Impressionist painting, a Renoir Paysage de Cagnes in 1938 for $1,800. I sold it in 1946 for $14,000. I bought no further French Impressionist work until two years ago.'

1959 (England)

'July 8: Shocking news of Dave Hecht's death. He can never be replaced.'

'June 10: Dinner with my dear friends, the Arpad Plesches.'

'June 16: Dinner with Margaret, Duchess of Argyll. The Niarchoses, Elsa Maxwell and Henry Tiarks among other friends present.'

'August 31: Guest of the Duke and Duchess of Gloucester and their sons, Princes William and Richard. In the afternoon, there is shooting. Many birds are bagged, but I do not shoot. Although I am a fair shot when the targets are pieces of paper or clay pigeons, I simply cannot bring myself to kill any animal or bird. However, I hold nothing against those who do. It is entirely a matter of personal taste and inclination.'

'September 2: Lunch with Lord and Lady Lovat. They are a most attractive couple. He is 6' 2", looks every inch his role as Chief of the Frasers.'

'September 13: Woburn Abbey for lunch on the lawn. Other guests whom I know include Roger Peyrefitte, Dominic Elwes, Gina Lollobrigida and the Aga Khan. All most pleasant and entertaining.'

'October 6: Lunch with Nancy Astor and her sons David Astor and Bobby Shaw at 100 Eaton Square. Nancy is 80 and incredible. She looks 45 and is still fiercely proud of her native State of Virginia.'

'November 8: Gordon Crary is dead. He and I were at Harvard Military Academy together, and he was my principal stockbroker since I started in business. I am sad. How many, many years have passed since Gordon and I were regularly gigged for infractions of military academy rules!'

'November 10: Gala, lavish dinner given by Charles Clore. Other guests included Isaac Wolfton, Sam S. P. Eagle, Simon Marks, Gilbert Miller and many more. Charlie Clore is a munificent host.'

'November 29: I was told that my great friend and art adviser for 25 years, Mitchell Samuels, is dead. Am very sad. Mitchell would have been 80 in February.'

'November 30: Gave dinner at Mirabelle for John Ringling North, Maggie Nolan and others. John North is a marvellous companion and loyal friend. Bruce Cabot is also at the Mirabelle. He has aged surprisingly since I last saw him.'

1960 (England)

'February 7: William F. "Billy" Humphrey has passed on. This is a great loss. He was a fine, able, tremendously hardworking business leader. At 75, he was still running a mile at 6 a.m. and then taking a swim before breakfast. At 8 a.m. he started his work, keeping two or three secretaries busy until the evening. He was an able president of Tide Water.'

'April 3: Drove to Cherkley to dine with Lord Beaverbrook. He is 80 but alert, a very good conversationalist and has an excellent memory and great charm. He looks 70 at the most. He has lived at Cherkley since he bought it in 1911. The house is Victorian, ugly, but comfortable in 1,000 acres of land. It is 18 miles from the centre of London.'

'April 6: Dinner at Bindy Lambton's. Met Guy de Rothschild, Count and Countess Brandolini—she is Gianni Agnelli's sister. Then on to the 400. Met Ari Onassis there. Ari invited me to fly with him to Puerto Rico to join his yacht for a cruise. As always, he laughed at

my fear of flying. "Think of the odds in our favour if
we flew together," he said. I asked him what he meant.
"It would be billions to one against anything happening
to us," he replied. Everyone who heard him was greatly
amused (and so was I).'

'June 1: At seven to 24 Lowndes street for cocktails
with Pamela and David Hicks. They are a very attractive, pleasant young married couple and their flat is very
cheerful and smart. At 8:45, I was at the Dorchester.
Bindy Lambton had 54 at one table for dinner. I sat on
Lady Churchill's right . . . I was thrilled to have the
opportunity of asking some questions about my hero, Sir
Winston. He walks 1/4 mile each day, has a day nurse
and a night nurse, is quite deaf, eats anything he likes,
including plenty of butter and cream . . .'

During the dinner, Lady Churchill told me a story I had
never before heard about her engagement to Winston. It came
about as a result of my mentioning that I had recently visited
Burleigh-on-the-Hill. She said she had a very vivid recollection of an incident that occurred while she and Winston
Churchill were secretly engaged.

'No one knew about our engagement,' Lady Churchill
related. 'And I was spending a weekend as a guest of Lord
Portarlington at his house on the Isle of Wight. In the evening, someone brought news of a fire at Burleigh. We were
told that some of the people staying there had lost their lives.
I knew that Winston was spending his weekend at Burleigh—
and then we received a report he was among those who died.

'I didn't know what to do. If I started carrying on, people
would wonder why I was so upset, for no one knew he was
my particular friend and secret fiancé.'

And so, with typical British stiff upper lip, she went through
the evening and spent a sleepless night. Hiding her emotions,
she dressed very early the next morning and started to leave
the house to get the latest morning newspapers.

'Just as I was tiptoeing out of the house, I heard Lord
Portarlington's voice,' Lady Churchill went on. ' "Where are
you going so early, Clementine?" he asked. "Only out for a
breath of air—and to pick up the morning papers," I answered, doing my very best to keep my voice and manner
under control. He said, "Well, then, I'll go along with you."

Once more I had to use every ounce of effort to maintain control and not allow my feelings to show.'

When they bought the morning papers, Lady Churchill said, she had to force herself to look at them—and then she felt like leaping into the air and shouting with joy. The latest reports from Burleigh contradicted those of the night before. Actually, none of the guests at Burleigh had been killed in the fire. Only a few had suffered what were very minor injuries.

'Naturally, I could not show my relief and happiness that Winston was safe,' she told me. 'I was forced to pretend only normal interest—but you can well imagine how I really felt!'

I could—and I could also imagine what a great and horrible loss it would have been for the civilized world if the first reports had been true and Winston Churchill had died in the fire at Burleigh-on-the-Hill.

'June 2: Lunch with Nancy Astor at her lovely flat. Bobby Shaw and an American couple there. Nancy was her usual sprightly self.'

'June 29: Left my suite, 611–612, at the Ritz for the last time. From now on, my address will be Sutton Place—but for how long? I am hoping to get all the loose business ends tidied up within the next year at the most. I long to dive into the surf at Malibu Beach again.'

The year—and many more years—passed without my hope being realized. But my life continued to be very full—and to have its exciting moments, its surprises, good and bad, after I transferred my base of operations to Sutton Place.

31

I WAS TO make several Continental trips after establishing my headquarters at Sutton Place but, since I spent so much of my time there, the circle of my British friends naturally grew larger. Also, old friends had more of an opportunity to visit with me than they had in years past when I lived in hotel suites.

'July 13, 1960: Lady Diana Cooper came to lunch. I have been dazzled by her beauty and wit for decades and pleased that I could be her host at Sutton. I was very proud when she said she liked the improvements that had been made in the house which, of course, she knows so well.'

Four days later, Lord Beaverbrook paid me a visit (now we were practically neighbours). A fascinating man and very young for his age—then 81—he reminisced about his visits to Sutton Place when Lord Northcliffe leased and occupied the estate.

'I came here often—sometimes once a week over long periods,' Max told me. He smiled. 'Northcliffe never dreamed that I would be his successor.'

Then his expression changed, becoming very thoughtful.

'My newspapers have two-and-a-half times the circulation that Northcliffe had,' he mused aloud. 'Yet, I have nowhere near the influence because in his day, newspapers were the sole news media and the main force in shaping public opinion. Today, there is radio, television . . .'

He paused and smiled again. 'The world changes,' he

murmured. 'And I suppose we've only begun to see the changes.'

Lord Beaverbrook was an astute businessman. We shared a keen interest in the theory and practice of business and in economics and politics. A year later—in 1961—he vehemently declared that Britain should stay in Africa and out of the Common Market. He confided that Sir Winston Churchill shared his views—but, being above all a farsighted realist, Max conceded that these would sooner or later prove to be lost causes.

'More of those changes—and ever more of them,' he sighed.

In 1965, Lord Thomson of Fleet gave a huge party for Max on his 85th birthday. The affair was held at the Dorchester Hotel, and there were more than 500 guests. Max made one of his characteristically witty speeches. Roy Thomson saw me laughing heartily.

'I intend giving you the same kind of party, Paul,' he said. 'It'll be held right here—on your *ninetieth* birthday.'

As of December 15, 1975, I have only seven years to wait—Roy Thomson has never been known to break a promise.

On Saturday, February 4, 1961, Albert Thurgood, the crack Sutton Place estate manager, gave me a list of accounts on the continuing improvements being made in the house and grounds. I went over the figures and that evening made this notation in my diary: 'I'm beginning to wonder if I'm trying to rival William Randolph Hearst. I console myself with the knowledge that in terms of real money-values, I am spending present-day dimes where he spent 1930s dollars.'

I must admit that I do, on occasion, find some reason or another to compare myself with Hearst. About two years after making the diary entry I cite above, Mr. Bullimore—the nonpareil majordomo of Sutton Place—kindly told me that a film about Hearst and San Simeon was being shown on the BBC that evening. My comments on the film and my reflections—recorded in my diary—provide more than a few insights into my own nature and views.

'I saw the BBC film on Hearst. Whicker attacks Hearst as the title, *Megalo-Millionaire*, suggests. Whicker poured scorn on Hearst's sensational journalism, conveniently overlooking the fact that many other U.S. publishers among Hearst's contemporaries were no better or worse.

'There were movies of parties at San Simeon in the 1930s. I saw the familiar faces of many old friends laughing and enjoying themselves, and I was saddened to think that so many of them are gone. I suppose I have much in common with Hearst. I, however, have always spent 95 per cent or more of my money on my business, while Hearst was the opposite. He lived like a Roman emperor. San Simeon reminds me of Hadrian's villa.

'Hearst's beach house at Santa Monica cost $3 million.* I was his next door neighbour. My house cost $100,000. This is a good illustration of the differences in our attitudes toward money. I suppose that in 1935 I was one-third as rich as Hearst and by 1950, I was twice as rich.

'I guess I'm like Hearst in that I admire splendour. I like a palatial atmosphere, noble rooms, long tables, old silver, fine furniture. If San Simeon had been closer to a city, I would have offered to buy it in the 1950s. I think the house and 1,000 acres around it might have been purchasable in 1952 for one-tenth its cost. It would have been a marvellous investment, considering the appreciation of property values in the years that followed.

'When I think of San Simeon, I recognize that even Hadrian's villa was eclipsed by it. The indoor swimming pool itself was 40 feet by 80.'

I could not help comparing Sutton Place with San Simeon, writing:

'The swimming pools at Sutton Place do not compare with those at San Simeon, and the drawing room at Sutton Place is inferior to that at Hearst's. I think, however, that the Great Hall, Library and Long Gallery at Sutton Place will bear comparison with anything at the publisher's Casa Grande.'

It seems that when I summed up all the pros and cons, I came to this conclusion:

Editor's note: See Chapter 6. Other sources claim W. R. Hearst spent upwards of $8 million for the house, which he had built for Marion Davies.

'When I compare Sutton Place with San Simeon I must admit that Sutton Place is a manor house and not a palace.'

But no matter what comparisons I made between Sutton Place and San Simeon, the requirements of business did not ease. Typical diary entries:

'Received a telephone call from New York. Some Getty Oil executives recommend seeking a large bank-loan to close an important stock transaction for the company. I hate and fear borrowing.'

As I have been quoted in more than one financial journal, 'I like to keep a lot of financial fat under my belt.' There is nothing that can ever take the place of cash. The overwhelming majority of business problems (and so many recent business failures) result from businessmen extending themselves too far. There is most definitely a place—and a need—for the use of credit in business. However, I have always believed that the businessman who uses credit the most sparingly is the one who has the greatest chance for achieving success.

'Sunday, January 22: Worked with Claus Bulow and Everett Skarda on Neutral Zone matters until 1 a.m. Although they are both about half my age, they caved in. I continued on alone until 3 a.m.'

The Boss has no fixed hours. When there are important matters to be studied and weighed, he must remain with the task until he has reached the necessary decisions or conclusions, otherwise he can hardly consider himself qualified to be The Boss.

'May 29: Neutral Zone business until 4:30 a.m.'

And, even though I am wealthy and have reached and passed the age of 83, I still work until the problem at hand is solved—or at very least until I know that I have done all I can. This often involves working around the clock. I am not alone—not by a long shot. Men like Aristotle Onassis, Charlie Clore, David Rockefeller, Isaac Wolfson and so many other examples of the entrepreneur breed keep no fixed hours for themselves. They work until the task or problem at hand is done or resolved.

There are notes from the years 1961 through 1964 that provide additional glimpses and insights into the various spheres and levels of my life.

On May 6, 1961, I was the guest of honour at a luncheon given to launch a book—'The Richest American'—that had been written about me by Ralph Hewins. I made this diary notation for the day:

> 'I am not a public speaker. I have always thought that a man making a speech should be either very eloquent or very brief. Unable to lay any claim to possessing the former quality, I invariably strive to be brief. I make it a point to limit any remarks I make in public to five minutes—and that is the absolute maximum.'

Odd sidelight observations have crept into my diaries from time to time.

> 'October 18, 1962: When I was in college, I used a safety razor. Since about 1950, I have gotten into the habit of using an electric.'

Just eight days later, I was to write:

> 'Cuban war scare. Russian ships are nearing the blockade area. I am pessimistic about the next few days. It is the long dreaded showdown. Nuclear war is on people's minds. Pray God, it may not come.'

My pessimism proved unfounded. John F. Kennedy's brand of brinksmanship paid off. The Russians backed down at the last moment. Perhaps there are many who give him credit for having 'won' in this grim confrontation. I do not share the view. I cannot for a single moment accept the argument that any situation is worth risking the annihilation of people by the tens or hundreds of millions—or, for that matter, the final destruction of civilization and the world as we know it. No, it is not that I am quaking in my boots with fear for myself. I have lived more than four-score years, and it has been a very full and satisfying life. I think of my children and grand-children—and the children and grandchildren of every other human being on the face of the earth.

On November 8, 1962, I attended the Dockland Settlement Ball. Princess Margaret was there, and she recognized me and we exchanged a few words. Much has been written about Princess Margaret and her husband, Anthony Armstrong-Jones, Lord Snowdon. It seems to be a fairly common sport among gossip columnists to hint (always broadly and most obliquely) that they somehow fall short—although of what, it's never made at all clear. I must say that I have met them both frequently enough and have had the opportunity to observe them and their actions. In my opinion, most of their detrac-tors seem to have their own axes to grind when they detract.

There are various kinds of honours that a private individual enjoys in life. For me, one honour was the visit paid me by ex-King Umberto of Italy in 1962. He came for lunch, and I noted with pride:

'Bullimore used the gold plate. The menu: lobster, grouse, vegetables and raspberry pudding, with bon bons afterwards.'

I was much impressed by King Umberto. Over 6 feet tall, he is an attractive man with a regal manner. He has great knowledge of art and while he has all the polish one might expect of a man originally trained to be a ruling monarch, he is most kind and a delightful companion.

Another honour—but of a different kind—was bestowed on me toward the end of the same year.

'December 4, 1962: I am pleased and flattered that France has promoted me to *Officier* in the *Legion d'Honneur.*'

I have—and shall always have—a great, abiding love for France and a feeling of affinity for the country and its people. I have never visited any part of France without feeling the same thrill of excitement, the same joy, that I experienced

during my first visit there in 1909. It is as my friend, ex-G-
man and longtime French resident Col. Leon Turrou, says:

'France is all the contrasts that one could wish for in life.
There is the glory—and the electric thrill—of Paris at one end
of the scale and the placid beauty of the Dordogne at the
other. Between the two, there is an absolute infinity of
shading . . .'

On September 14, 1963, the *Sarah Getty*, an 80,000-ton
tanker built for the Getty interests and named for my beloved
mother, was christened in Dunkirk. I had asked my dear
friend Penelope Kitson to do *these* honours and christen the
vessel. She did, and when the ship slid down the slipways, I
was glad it had been built in a French shipyard. The event
brought back countless memories of the days that my mother,
father and I had spent together in France.

But I was forced to admit that the France of 1963 had
changed. So many of my own once-favourite haunts in Paris—
Jimmy's, the l'Eléphant Blanc, Carroll's, Big Ben, Florence,
the Cafe de Paris had gone. Vast areas of French countryside
were being (or had been) transformed into high-rise housing
developments or industrial complexes. All the same, France
remained—and still remains—France. The French spirit—the
verve and *élan*, the innumerable qualities that add up to create
La Belle France, are constants that serve as a delightful and
exhilarating reassurance in this era of ever-accelerating change.

32

THE WORLD-WIDE PUBLICITY that ensued after *Fortune* Magazine named me 'The Richest American' and my acquisition of a more or less settled address at Sutton Place put something of a strain on Her Majesty's Postal Service. During the years that followed the purchase of Sutton, there were months when I would receive as many as 3,000 letters from people who were complete strangers to me. The letters came (and, to a lesser degree, still come) from every corner of the globe. They are written by men and women in all walks of life. The vast majority of these individuals want me to send them money because they've read that I am a 'billionaire'.

Some plead. Others are insistent—or even downright demanding. Some ask for a few dollars—or a few hundred. Then there are those who request sums ranging up into the tens of thousands—or even much higher. The record request came from a person whose letter indicated that he was otherwise a sane, rational human being. But he wanted no less than $200 million from me.

Admittedly, this chap put his request in the form of a business proposition. He said he would use the money to build a canal that would compete with the Panama Canal. And, the man declared, he was ready to 'share the ship-toll profits' with me. I would, he promised, receive 'ten per cent of the net.'

Needless to say, it would require a large, separate organization merely to investigate the merits of even the most sincere-sounding appeals. Furthermore, I have my own 'favourite' charities, all of them organized and reputable. Finally, not even a trillionaire could conceivably meet the demands made by these mail-order supplicants. (The total requested by mail in a single month has run as high as $75 million—and that does not count such far-out examples as the canal-building proposal.)

What continues to amaze me is that so many writers of begging letters blandly admit that they have no actual need. They often state—quite frankly—that they are writing to me because I have 'so much to spare.' An entirely typical letter, received from the United States in early 1975, went like this:

'Dear Mr. Getty:
    'I am 35, married and without children. I have a pretty good job, earning a little over $9,000 a year net. But it's hell to work at 35—during the prime of one's life. It's a time when a man and his wife should be enjoying themselves.
    'Having had so many divorces, you probably appreciate that more than most people. That's why I'm so certain you'll lend a sympathetic ear to what I am going to ask. It's really not much by your standards—not even petty cash. I would like to take two years off work and travel lazily around the world with my wife. We've checked into this with a travel agency, and we can do it comfortably for $70,000.
    'So, if you'll send the money, you'll make two people very happy and very grateful to you. I'm sure you have accountants who can arrange it so that we will receive the money tax-free . . .'

The floods of such mail over the years have been so great there is no way to cope with them save by printed form-letters. I long ago composed two versions. One goes to individuals, the other to organizations of which I have never heard (but which none the less solicit funds). These form letters go out by the hundreds each month. It is indicative of the farflung sources from which the begging letters come that the form-replies are in five languages: English, French, German, Spanish and Italian. I think it might possibly be of some interest to the reader if I reproduced the English version of each category here. First, the letter sent to individuals:

I apologise

'I apologise for not having been able to give more time and personal attention to your letter. Like most people, I suppose, I always used to be thrilled at the thought of getting mail. It was considered a misfortune if the postman came and went without leaving any mail—but that was years ago.

'I have had a great deal of publicity in the International Press, radio and TV; most of it in connection with the reputed size of my fortune. The public seem to jump to the conclusion that my fortune, or a big part of it, is in cash. They don't stop to think that my money is invested in business since I am an active businessman, and it is generally true that active businesses are short of cash for their business requirements and even the largest business organisations are frequent borrowers of money. These large business organisations don't borrow money just to prove that they can do so but because they are in urgent need of cash. I don't mean to imply that I am short of cash to the extent that I can't pay my personal bills or buy a new car when the old one wears out. I merely mean that I don't have large sums of ready cash not required for my business.

'Like most people I contribute substantially, in accordance with my means, to various recognised charities and public welfare projects in which I am particularly interested and, in general, which I have supported or helped to support for many years. Like most active businessmen I get a large amount of business mail every day and I have to spend, on an average, several hours a day reading and answering this mail. If I didn't do this I would not be looking after my business on which so many people depend.

'In addition to my regular business mail I have received in recent years a tremendous and almost overwhelming amount of mail from the General Public. This mail from the General Public is almost entirely due to the unwanted publicity I have had regarding the alleged size of my fortune. Like most people, I suppose, I don't particularly object to a reasonable amount of publicity if it is of the right sort, but I don't like publicity which seems confined almost entirely to how much money I am supposed to have. I personally think it is vulgar, boring and generally inaccurate. There may be lots of people who have more cash than I have.

'Nevertheless, due to this publicity I am, and have been, faced with the problem of how to reply to thousands and tens of thousands of people from 75 or more countries who write me at the rate of anything from 50 letters to a thousand letters a day. How can I personally read and reply helpfully to this flood of mail? Many of the letters are from five to fifteen pages long and written in a script that is barely legible. Nearly all of them want something—gifts, loans, contributions, financial help, advice, personal interviews, offers to sell, jobs, investments—or express a wish to be "pen-pals". If I could reply to each letter personally in an average of four minutes, which would be a very short time, I still could do only 15 letters an hour. Since like most people, I have my own work to do I could not possibly answer more than a very small fraction of the letters written to me. I regret this; I like people; I like to be helpful when I can; I try to do the best I can.

'A friend of mine who has also had a lot of publicity about his supposed fortune also receives thousands of letters, nearly all of them requesting financial assistance, advice, employment or offering something for sale. He has given up trying to answer his public mail and tells me it is all thrown into the fire. It is too big a burden to answer. Nevertheless, I feel people, if at all possible, should have the courtesy of a reply. I have engaged secretaries to read and answer my mail from the General Public to the best of their ability. I regret that I am unable to aid individuals. I am sure that nearly always they are sincere and truthful in what they write. If there were only a few of them I could do something but since the requests come in by the hundreds and thousands it is just impossible to investigate and, if the cases are found worthy, to assist. No private fortune in the world would last more than a very short time under such conditions and it would take a tremendous organisation to administer the money during the short time it lasted. Again I say I apologise because I was not helpful. I just wanted you to know what some of the reasons and problems are.

J. PAUL GETTY'

Organizations that make 'blind' solicitations receive this reply:

'I am writing for Mr. J. Paul Getty to thank you for your letter of recent date on behalf of your organization.

'Although Mr. Getty is appreciative of your thought in writing, he regrets that he cannot be helpful. Please be assured that this is not based on any question of merit, but it is due to necessary limitations on what he can undertake to do in any one field. As I am sure you will realize, he receives a great number of appealing requests from churches and organizations throughout the world and it would not be possible for him to respond favourably to them all.

'Since it would not be fair to contribute to one and not others, he has had to find broader ways to express his interests in religious work and educational projects and to limit his support to those with which he is associated in the communities where he lives.

'Mr. Getty is sorry to send you this reply, and he hopes that you will understand.

Yours very truly,
Secretary'

There are no replies—form-letter or otherwise—to the marriage-proposals that come in by the scores and hundreds. No, the ladies who take pen in hand are not irresistibly attracted by the blue of my eyes. The magnetism I exert is of another colour—green, the hue of my purported wealth. I must say this for the females who write as though every year is Leap Year, they are uncommonly frank and forthright—as witness this romantic epistle sent from Canada in October, 1975:

'Dear Paul Getty:
You should not be living alone and as a bachelor—not

at your age and with your money. I am only 23, blonde and healthy and strong. I could look after you. I am willing to marry you for $100,000, cash payable at the time of the wedding, plus $100,000 a year for as long as you live. We can discuss the terms of your will after you have sent me first-class air fare to come to England. I enclose some candid photographs of myself in the nude so you can see what you'll be getting . . .'

Or this one, from the first week in November, sent by a woman in Pennsylvania:

'Dear Mr. Getty:
A magazine article I just read says you have been married and divorced five times. You should give yourself another chance and make it an even half-dozen. My daughter will be eighteen next month. She has already won three beauty contests and is a wonderful dancer. She would make you a good and very sexy wife. I'd see to that. I think $10,000 a month for her and $5,000 a month for me would be a fair arrangement. Since my brother is a lawyer, he could draw up the marriage contract at a discount . . .'

My companies and I make substantial contributions to charities, organizations and worthy causes each year. I am not about to go into the specifics about my own personal charities. The amounts I contribute are a matter between their officers and me. Suffice it to say that I am interested in two universities, several organizations—including the World Wildlife Fund—and certain other projects. And, as I stated earlier, I have long since arranged that the bulk of my personal fortune will go to charity after my death.

I have a few additional comments to make on this subject of charities and eleemosynary organizations. The dogged persistence (and the peculiar mentality) found among some who seek funds for certain groups and institutions will sometimes defy comprehension.

For example, a few years ago I was prevailed upon to make a $100,000 gift to an institution of higher learning (no, NOT one of the two universities in which I have said that I am interested). The institution is in the United States. Its heads and hard-driving fund-raisers had barely received my contribution before getting the idea that this was a marvellous opening wedge. I can imagine their ensuing conversation going something like this:

'We've got a hundred thousand from Getty—let's see if we can't parlay it.'

'Absolutely! Only we really must think BIG this time!'

They did think 'BIG', all right. About three months later, I was visited by an impressive four-man delegation. Each member was highly-placed in the institution and bore long strings of academic credential-letters after his name.

'We've long had an ambitious building programme in mind,' was the gist of their approach. 'Our present estimates are that it will cost around $10 million—we've brought the plans and reports to show you. Now, if you'll just underwrite this . . .'

I not only refused, but I deeply regretted having donated the original $100,000. It could have gone elsewhere and done much more good. I needed only to make a mental calculation of what the first-class roundtrip airfares (fund-raisers do not usually travel tourist), hotel bills and incidental expenses of the delegation's visit cost. The total could not have been less than $25,000 when the expense of preparing the 'presentation' of the plans and reports was taken into consideration. In other words, at least 25 per cent of what I had given to aid the institution had been promptly spent on trying to get more money from me.

While I find incidents such as this one and the sacks of begging-letter mail more than slightly disconcerting, there is an even more irritating sub-species of fund-hunter and favour-seeker. This is the eminent (and almost always himself very wealthy) cadger—by far the most persistent of the lot. Such men are not interested in asking anything for themselves, but they always have some favourite charity, church, hospital, cause or other project for which they are soliciting funds. I hate to think how many men—millionaires and even centi-millionaires whose names are household words—have tried to zero in on me. Their opening gambits are usually more or less like these:

'Well, now, Paul. You've probably heard that I'm the honorary chairman of a committee that's trying to raise $100 million for an organization to do research into the causes of baldness . . .'

'I'm really glad to see you, old man. I've been meaning to talk to you about an organization that's doing fantastic work in curing alcoholic ferry-boat captains . . .'

'It so happens that the chancellor of Noxious University—that's my alma mater, you know—would like to see a new library built on the campus . . .'

These men never seem to give up. And I seldom if ever fail to turn them down. I take the standpoint that I have my own charitable commitments. I have ALWAYS refrained from pushing my own pet charities and similar projects to (or on to) my friends. My stand is based on the theory that they contribute to their own causes to whatever degree they are able. And I do the same.

Not long ago, a friend of mine—a Very Important Personage in America—blandly asked me to sign a cheque for $1 million to establish a Fine Arts professorship in a Southern California university.

I pleaded poverty—which made the dilettante fund-raiser stare at me with scorn. I did not bother telling him that I was even then in the midst of a $17 million project to build an art museum for the public in Southern California. Every dollar of that came out of my own pocket—and the total involved was much, much greater than the $17 million construction bill. For a moment, I was almost tempted to break my own rule, give my multimillionaire-mendicant visitor an all-teeth smile and ask if he would like to pick up a few million dollars of *my* tab.

But, I managed to refrain, and a few minutes later, this paragon of the genteel panhandling virtues departed. If he reads these lines, he will remember the incident.

Having mentioned the Southern California museum, I shall shift the tack of my narrative and go into another—and most important and gratifying—facet of my life activities. This is the story of my art-collecting—and how the collection that is now displayed in the museum—was acquired. The story is one that covers many decades and involves the expenditure of many millions of dollars, yet it had the most modest beginnings.

33

VERY EARLY ON in this book I referred, *en passant*, to a tour I took of Japan and China in 1912. I gained much from the trip. In Japan, I was immensely impressed by the politeness, industrious nature and conscientiousness of the Japanese people. Decades later, this acquaintance with Japan was to prove invaluable at a strictly practical level when Getty companies entered into many business transactions with Japanese firms. Getty Oil acquired an approximately 49 per cent interest in the Mitsubishi Oil Company. Getty tankers were built in Japanese shipyards. And there were many other business dealings. All went with exceptional smoothness; I attribute this largely to the fact that I had got to know the Japanese—and, what is more important, learned how to let them know me, my companies and their business philosophies and aims.

Although there have been no like business dealings with China, my 1912 visit there was beneficial in providing me with insight into Chinese character. Despite the enormous disparities that then existed between rich and poor in China, I recognized and marvelled at the innate strengths and qualities of the Chinese people.

Not many years ago at a luncheon at his home, Field Marshal Lord Montgomery of Alamein and I fell to discussing China and the subject of Sino-Russian frictions. Field Marshal Montgomery compared the Chinese and Russians as he had known them and made a comment that came close to defining my own feelings about the Chinese.

'I'd go into the jungle with the Chinese, but I'd be rather more than reluctant to go into it with the Russians,' Marshal Montgomery said.

His point, of course, was that the Chinese could be trusted to keep any word they gave and remain loyal to their friends.

In retrospect the most valuable benefit I gained from my 1912 trip to the Orient was the first, faint stirring of a desire to own works of art. Much attracted by the delicacy and grace of Oriental art, I bought some pieces of carved ivory, bronzes and lacquer-work. The purchases were modest, but I still have the items and, in a sense, they can be said to have formed the basis of my art collection.

But only in a very narrow and limited sense.

Having been momentarily stirred into action, my latent art-collecting urge promptly fell into a deep sleep that lasted eighteen years. However, I suppose that once it has been nudged even a bit, one's appreciation and love of fine art awakens and grows. During my many travels abroad between 1912 and 1930, I made frequent and, in more than a few instances, often repeated, visits to the great art museums and galleries of the countries in which I found myself. While I don't believe I was consciously aware of it at the time, my love of fine art increased—possibly by some process of visual osmosis. The more of it I saw, the more of it I wanted to see—and the desire to see may well have by itself developed into the desire to own. The desire did not again manifest itself until 1930, when I bought a painting by Jan Van Goyen for $1,200. There was another hiatus—and then, within a very few years, I discovered that I had become a dedicated and serious collector.

I had no carefully prepared plan—or any plan at all, for that matter. I just took it a day at a time, buying what pleased me—what gratified my own tastes and esthetic senses. I never thought that I would one day end up with a collection so extensive that I would have to build a large public museum to house it. Nor did I make any effort to specialize—certainly not at the start.

For example, at the 1933 Thomas Fortune Ryan Collection sale held by the Anderson Gallery in New York, I bought ten paintings by the Spanish Impressionist, Joaquin Sorolla y Bastida. One could hardly imagine greater contrasts than those between a Van Goyen and a Sorolla—but, as I say, I bought what *I* liked.

Granted that I began my active collecting at an auspicious time.

During the mid and late 1920s, very few works of art of good quality were to be found on the market. The best examples of almost all forms of fine art were in museums, huge private collections or held by very strong hands.

The United States was enjoying great prosperity during the Twenties, and there were numbers of fabulously wealthy collectors in America, Great Britain and Europe. These collectors were in fierce, cost-is-no-object competition with one another. Prices on any art items that did come on the market soared beyond any rational scale of values.

Although I had achieved some business success, I was still very small fry, indeed. I had nowhere near the resources to bid against collectors like the Mellons, Rothschilds, Schiffs or Hearsts. Truth to tell, in the late 1920s, it seemed to me that the days when any individual could start acquiring a good collection were over. Men—and families and dynasties—that had amassed their tens of millions long before I went into business (or even before I was born) held what appeared to be an unbreakable shared monopoly on works of art. They had bought up just about everything available over the previous decades.

Some aristocratic British and European families still owned massive treasure-troves of art; however, they were for the most part financially very well situated. If, by chance, one of them did want to sell a piece, a staggering price would be demanded—and paid instantly by some famous super-rich collector.

The situation changed with awful suddenness. The great panic—the 'Crash'—of 1929 and the depression that followed created as much havoc in the art world as it did in financial circles. Many who possessed some of the finest examples of art were forced to unload. Choice items began to appear on the market—at prices which would have been considered beneath contempt a few years before.

Now there were opportunities for would-be collectors with limited means.

*   *   *

'To me, my works of art are all vividly alive. They are the embodiment of whoever created them—a mirror of their creator's hopes, dreams and frustrations. They have led eventful lives—pampered by the aristocracy and pillaged by revolution, courted with ardour and cold-bloodedly abandoned. They have been honoured by drawing rooms and humbled by attics. So many worlds in their life-span, yet all were transitory. Their worlds have long since disintegrated, yet they live on—and, for the most part, they are as beautiful as ever.'

These words are from the book, *Collector's Choice*, in the writing of which I collaborated with Ethel Le Vane. Mark Goulden, who edited and published the book and is a discerning collector himself, flattered me by saying that those six short sentences communicated all that many collectors and art-critics had taken whole volumes to express. One reviewer put the icing on Mark's complimentary cake with these words:

'. . . in (these) few lines, the reader is made to understand what moves and motivates the collectors of art . . .'

Banal as it may sound in this glib and brittle age, the beauty one can find in art is one of the pitifully few real and lasting products of human endeavour. The beauty endures. A work of art lives—yes, it does *live*—through the generations and centuries, providing what is perhaps the only true continuity of Man's history.

I had read books on art and art history as well as visiting (and lingering in) museums and art galleries. Yet, I did not believe this to be enough. I sought the guidance and expertise of individuals whose education, training and profession made them authoritative instructors and reliable judges. I was to be most fortunate in this respect. My own knowledge and tastes were refined with the help of men like Colin Agnew, Bernard Ashmole, Bernard Berenson, John Brealey, Gerald Brockhurst, Jean Charbonneaux, Ludwig Curtius, Edward Fowles, Cecil Gould, Julius Held, Sir Philip Hendy, Leon Lacroix, Philip Pouncey, Stephen Rees Jones, Mitchell Samuels, Alfred Scharf, W. Valentiner, Pierre Verlet, Francis Wescher and Federico Zeri.

And, I owe a special debt of gratitude to Mrs. Frederick Guest. When, in 1935, I found it necessary to establish a base of business operations in New York City, I leased Mrs. Guest's lovely penthouse apartment at One Sutton Place.

(Yes, I have thought of the coincidence that I lived on a New York street named after the estate which the Getty interests were to purchase twenty-three years later.)

Mrs. Guest had superb taste. Her apartment was furnished with a magnificent collection of eighteenth-century French and English furniture. Simply living there was sufficient to make me realize that fine furniture was no less fine art than a painting or a piece of sculpture.

Although I would make many exceptions, as my knowledge and experience in serious collecting increased, I decided to concentrate on the five categories of fine art that had the greatest appeal to me. These were (and are):

1. Ancient Greek and Roman marbles, bronzes, mosaics and murals.
2. Renaissance paintings.
3. Sixteenth-century Persian carpets.
4. Savonnerie carpets.
5. Eighteenth-century French furniture and tapestries.

(I repeat. I *have* made a sizable number of exceptions, buying fine pieces outside these categories.)

Needless to say, like any collector, I have countless anecdotes about various of my acquisitions. There is the one—familiar to many people—about my purchase of a painting, for which I paid some $200 at a Sotheby's auction and which later proved to be a Raphael (the *Madonna del Velo*) worth upwards of a million.

Then, there is the unexpected triumph of my acquiring the famed Lansdowne *Hercules*. Found in 1790 amidst the ruins of Hadrian's villa outside Rome, it was purchased by the Marquis of Lansdowne, who took the Pentelic marble statue to England. Its fame grew and it eventually became known as the finest and most valuable piece in his large collection.

Adolf Michaelis, the leading authority on ancient marbles, called the Lansdowne *Hercules* 'perhaps the most important classical statue in English collections.'

The *Hercules* remained in the hands of the Marquis's descendants. Collectors assumed it was untouchable, that the family would never sell it, at any price. The Lansdowne family had sold a lesser piece, the *Wounded Amazon*, in

1930—when art prices were already much depressed—to John
D. Rockefeller Jr. for $140,000.

One afternoon in 1938, I was browsing at Christie's. I
chatted with the manager, and we lunched together at the
Ritz. I mentioned that I was always on the lookout for
museum-quality marbles.

'Mmm,' my companion murmured. 'I prefer not to be
quoted, of course. But I've heard rumours there might be
something available from the Lansdowne Collection. The
family deals mainly through Spink and Son.'

It was all I needed to hear. I opened delicate—and, as it
turned out, protracted—negotiations with Spink's and the
Lansdowne Family. The end result was nothing less than
incredible. I acquired the *Hercules* for about $30,000, plus a
ten percent commission to Spink's.

Another fabulous coup was my acquisition of three of the
world-famous Elgin marbles. One of them, *Myttion*, a fourth-
century B.C. stele representing a young girl, is one of my
favourite pieces of sculpture in my collection. It is also the
piece that brought such an enthusiastic response from Bernard
Berenson when he saw a photograph of it. *Myttion*—as I have
related elsewhere—moved Berenson to call over one of his
associates and to exclaim: 'Now *this* is a piece I would love
to have for myself!'

Rembrandt is, in my opinion, the greatest of all the mas-
ters. To my mind, his *Night Watch* is probably the finest of
all paintings. It is certainly my favourite. I have spent countless
hours during any number of trips to Holland in the Rijksmuseum,
looking at it, losing myself in it. (When, recently, I read that
it had been mutilated by some deranged vandal, I felt as
though the knife that slashed the canvas had cut my own
flesh—and I mean that literally.)

In 1928, I attended the great Rembrandt Exposition at the
Boymann Museum in Rotterdam, a city I love—as I do all of
Holland. It was there that I first saw *Marten Looten*, Rembrandt's second commissioned portrait, which he executed in
1632, when he was twenty-six. *Marten Looten* was owned by
the wealthy and intensely patriotic Dutch collector, Anton W.
W. Mensing, who had paid over $200,000 for it so that the
painting could remain in its (and his) native country.

Ten years later—in 1938—I heard that the great Mensing
Collection was being broken up. I immediately contacted the

dealer through whom I normally made my art purchases in the Netherlands. Although the imminence of war in Europe had dropped the bottom out of art prices, I authorized the dealer to bid up to $100,000 for *Marten Looten*. I also requested the dealer to keep my identity secret and say only that he was acting for 'an anonymous American'.

The auction of the Mensing Collection must have been sorely disappointing for the sellers. Bidding was low. To my amazement, I obtained *Marten Looten* for only $65,000—and unwittingly came close to precipitating an international crisis. The Dutch press and public deeply resented the thought that a great national treasure would go to 'an anonymous American' and be taken to the United States.

A campaign to raise funds to top the bid failed. I had the painting shipped to the New York World's Fair, where it was exhibited in the Fine Arts Pavilion and seen by several hundred thousand people. But in Holland, resentment lingered—and another decade was to pass before I could make any move to dispel it.

August, 1949, once again found me in Rotterdam. I made arrangements to visit Professor Van Dillen, a Dutch art authority who had been one of the most outspoken critics of the sale of *Marten Looten* to an 'unnamed American'. I went in the guise of an art-journalist to Prof. Van Dillen's home, where I was received for tea. We talked for a long time about art in general and Rembrandt in particular. He said he was astounded that any American knew so much about the great Dutch master and his work. At last, I identified myself and told him it was I who had purchased *Marten Looten*.

'Please remember that Rembrandt will always be Dutch,' I said. 'And, while the picture is in America, it is acting as a cultural ambassador of your country, its history and heritage.'

I went on, and Prof. Van Dillen's face softened.

'You are right—I have been wrong,' he said. I had not only gained my goal of lessening Dutch resentment, but I had also gained a friend. Professor Van Dillen later spoke to his colleagues—and eventually favourable articles appeared in the Dutch art-press. Within a very short time, all hostile feelings were permanently erased.

There are two more anecdotes—both amusing—that I would like to relate. The first concerns the *Ardabil* carpet, which dates from the 16th century—and which, Moslem Persians

declared, was 'too good for Christian eyes to gaze upon.'
However, in 1890, the carpet fell into the hands of an English
dealer, who sold it to American tycoon Clarence Mackay.
Seeing it, the American painter and etcher, James M. Whistler,
wrote that it was 'worth all the pictures ever painted.'

The *Ardabil* passed through three great collections—the
Mackay, Yerkes and De la Marr. When the De la Marr
collection was put up for sale, Lord Joseph Duveen authorized
his associates to bid up to $250,000 for the magnificent
Persian carpet. The sale was poor; to his delight, Lord Duveen
bought it for $57,000. I knew Lord Duveen well and got in
touch with him. I wanted to buy the *Ardabil*. Duveen's reply:
'No one has enough money to buy the *Ardabil* from me.'

Then came the first great war-scares of 1938. Lord
Duveen—by then 69 and with only a year of life remaining—
succumbed to the contagion of fear. He offered to sell me the
carpet for a little less than $70,000. I accepted instantly. At
that price, it was practically a gift.

Somewhat later, I was approached by agents acting on
behalf of Egypt's King Farouk. His sister, Princess Fawzia,
was to marry the Shah of Iran. He wished to buy the famed
Ardabil carpet and give it to them as a regal wedding present.
King Farouk's offer: a quarter of a million dollars. I rejected
the offer—and rebuffed attempts to make me change my mind
through hints that the price might be raised, perhaps even
doubled.

I donated the *Ardabil* to the Los Angeles County Museum,
and all eyes—Moslem, Christian, or of any other faith—may
gaze upon its beauty.

In her recently published autobiographical book, *Forget
Not,* my very dear friend, Margaret, Duchess of Argyll, tells
of how the Duke once frantically hunted for me in Italy,
trying to sell me a priceless eighteenth-century French writing
desk. My version of the incident is somewhat different from
hers—but then the Duke, who was also my close friend,
might have slightly coloured the account he gave her.

The piece in question is the famous 'Husband and Wife
Desk' that Pierre Verlet, Chief Keeper of the Department of
Furniture and Objects of Art in the Louvre, described as 'the
most outstanding example of its type.' It was made by the great
craftsman of Dutch origin who signed his works only as

Bv(or u)RB. (He has been identified by art historians as Bernard van Risenburgh.)

In any case, it was in 1950 that I had dinner with Ian Campbell, the Duke of Argyll. We dined at White's. Over coffee, he casually remarked that he had inherited 'some eighteenth-century furniture' and among the items was a desk he wished to sell.

'If you're interested, you can see it at Inveraray,' he told me. Inveraray was, of course, his ancestral castle and located in Scotland.

I did not relish making the trip to Inveraray, for it was the dead of winter. I decided to consult a friend who supposedly knew every piece of good eighteenth-century French furniture in the British Isles. He assured me that the Duke could not possibly have any furniture of great importance or value. This authoritative friend, I might add, was an art dealer, which might (or might not) have a direct bearing on what followed.

Not long afterward, and unknown to me, my dealer 'friend' went to Inveraray, where he promptly identified the desk Ian Campbell had mentioned to me as the great BvRB 'Husband and Wife Desk' and worth a fortune.

A year after that, I learned that the desk had ended up in the possession of a New York art dealer. I approached him and was able to buy the magnificent double-desk—at a price many times what I would have paid had I accepted Ian Campbell's invitation to visit Inveraray and buy it directly from him.

However, as any collector learns very soon in his collecting career, every purchase cannot be a bargain—and some acquisitions are a triumph no matter what the price.

Incidentally, and as a sort of footnote, recent research suggests that the name 'Husband and Wife Desk' may be a misnomer. There is some reason to think that it was made for the twin daughters of French King Louis XV—the Princesses Marie-Louise Elizabeth and Anne-Henriette—so that the sisters could study their lessons and write their letters together at the same desk. There is no documentary proof of this, though. Whether made for husband and wife or twin princesses, the double-desk remains one of the finest pieces of eighteenth-century French furniture extant.

34

I GAVE UP smoking in the 1940s.

While I enjoy an occasional drink, alcohol has never been a problem for me.

My use of drugs doesn't go beyond the aspirin and antibiotic level.

Yet, I am an apparently incurable art-collecting addict. The habitual narcotics user is said to have a monkey on his back. I sometimes feel as though I had several dozen gorillas riding on mine.

Believe me, I've tried all the cures. Will-power and determination will conquer, I've told myself—and holding that thought, have tried staying away from dealers' galleries, auction rooms and people who had some particularly choice item they wished to sell privately. When that method didn't work, I tried shock-therapy, adding up what I had spent on art-purchases over a given period and staring with something akin to horror at the seven-figure totals. Unfortunately, the shock-effect always wore off.

Total withdrawal—the 'cold turkey treatment' in common parlance—didn't work, either. I only needed to hear that the Metropolitan Museum in New York, the Tate Gallery in London, the Louvre in Paris—or any of a dozen other galleries or museums—was having a special exhibit of some artist or category of art that interested me. If I happened to be within any reasonable distance, I went.

'Only to look,' I assured myself.

But looking invariably re-awakened the addiction. It is never more than a short taxi-ride (or walk) from an exhibition gallery or museum to the headquarters of some reputable dealer whom the incurably hooked collector knows.

It is with abashment that I riffle through my diaries and see the positive proof of my solemn promises to myself quickly cancelled out by massive relapses:

'October 5, 1958: My art buying is over, except for some unexpected temptation.'

'March 19, 1959: My agent has bought an Averkamp, a Canaletto, a Degas and a Renoir for me. I like these pictures.'

The very next day:

'March 20: My agent has obtained a Corot, a Renoir, a Vlaminck, an Utrillo and a Valadon drawing for my collection. The Renoir is wonderful.'

A few months later:

'I have acquired a fine Gainsborough portrait for £34,000 plus ten per cent commission.'

In 1960, I was once again determined to reform.

'July 15: I think I should stop buying pictures. I have enough invested in them. I am also stopping my buying of Graeco-Roman marbles and bronzes. I'm through buying French furniture. My mind is set. I am not going to change it.'

The best laid schemes . . .

Unfortunately, that was the year that the Synders-Boeckhurst *The Pantry* and Bonnard's *Woman in the Nude* were made available for sale. Set mind or not, I was unable to resist. The following year, Peter Paul Rubens' breathtakingly luminescent *Diana and Her Nymphs Departing for the Hunt* was offered to me. Again, I couldn't resist, even though the price-tag ran into a very high six figure sum. The year after that, the gorillas on my back laughed with glee when I paid more than half a million dollars for Rembrandt's magnificent *Saint Bartholomew*.

Whereupon—on August 2, 1962—J. Paul (Hopeless Case) Getty yet again made himself a solemn vow, noting in his diary:

> 'I have spent enough money on art. Enough is enough.
> I am stopping, once and for all.'

There is no need to list the purchases made, breaking this rule, until 1964. The list would, I fear, be very long. But in 1965, I switched my tack. Instead of confining my resolutions to my diaries, I made them public. In my book, *The Joys of Collecting*, published that year, I stated:

> 'I continued collecting until 1964, when I more or less stopped. I felt that I had acquired enough, that I had assembled a collection of which I could be proud—and that I should leave the field to others.'

Sorry as I am to make the admission, I am not only an addict. As the foregoing record—and the history of my art collecting activities between 1965 and 1975—prove, when it comes to collecting, I am also a chronic prevaricator. Whether it is myself—or the world at large—that I address when I say I have stopped collecting, the promise does not hold for long.

Jean Charbonneaux, Member of the *Institut de France* and Keeper of Antiquities in the Louvre, has written:

> 'Generally speaking, collectors confine themselves to a period or category of objects which is more or less strictly limited.'

I believe this is true—or so I have observed it to be in many of the private art collections with which I am familiar. I suppose once—Lord only knows when—someone laid it down as an Article of Faith that a collector should specialize. After that—with numerous notable exceptions—private collectors conformed to the rule.

Whatever else I may or may not be, I have never been a conformist, at least not in the sense that I consider conventional wisdoms infallible. Quite to the contrary, I have often found that there is nothing more flawed and unreliable than conventional wisdom. This, it has been my experience, applies in all spheres of human endeavour. While I have seldom if ever set out purposely and with malice aforethought to flout convention and demolish icons, I have never felt obligated to do this, that or another thing merely because it was what 'others' were doing.

So it has been with my art collection. It is eclectic. Although—as I've said—I channeled most of my collecting energies and funds into five general categories, I could not see why a collection that includes Rembrandt and Rubens can't also include Gauguin and Vlaminck. A Boucher tapestry is not incompatible with a 16th-century Persian carpet in a collection, nor an Attic marble with an Etruscan bronze helmet provided that all are of artistic merit and museum quality.

When I began collecting, I bought what pleased and appealed to me, and I bought for myself. That is, the paintings, sculptures, furniture and whatever were purchased out of my own pocket as things I desired to have as personal possessions. For the most part, the items were sent to my home in California. (Of course, some were lent to museums or even donated to them.) For example, the ten Impressionist paintings by Joaquin Sorolla y Bastida—to which I referred earlier—graced the Lanai Room of my Southern Californian home.

This stage of my fundamental collecting philosophy did not last very long. About a quarter of a century ago, I realized that my collection had grown important enough for the public to have an interest in viewing it.

The shift in my thinking was natural. It is a phenomenon familiar to many private collectors. After acquiring a large number of examples of fine art, one develops conscience pangs about keeping them to himself.

The difference between being a barbarian and a full-fledged member of a cultivated society is in the individual's attitude toward fine art. If he or she has a love of art, then he or she is not a barbarian. It's that simple, in my opinion.

Tragically, fifty per cent of the people walking down any street can be classed as barbarians according to this criterion. They will cut down any tree, no matter how old or lovely (and healthy), tear down beautiful old buildings, ravage any work of art or architecture. They will, of course, argue that their vandalisms and destructions are committed in the name of modernization or progress or find some other handy rationalization. None the less, they are no less barbarians than those of the Dark Ages who dressed in animal skins and wore horned helmets.

Twentieth-century barbarians cannot be transformed into cultured, civilized human beings until they acquire an appreciation and love for art. The transformation cannot take place until they have had the opportunity to be exposed to fine art—to see, begin to understand and finally to savour and marvel.

These were among the many reasons why the Getty Collection 'went public.' I established the J. Paul Getty Museum in California. A large, separate wing was built on to my Californian home to house the very large number of items from my collection that were displayed (and which thereafter were no longer mine, for I donated them to the museum). The 'Getty Museum' was rather modest compared to what it would later become. But it was open to the public without charge and gave Californians and tourists visiting the State a chance to see many works of art that had no comparable counterparts in any museum west of the Mississippi River.

Public reaction to the museum was extremely gratifying to me and to all who staffed it. The number of visitors, surprisingly large from the start, increased steadily year after year. On the other hand, the collection was growing, too, and by leaps and bounds. It soon became apparent that it was outgrowing the existing gallery-space. New galleries were constructed, but the additional display space thus created was quickly filled.

It was at this point that the Trustees of the Getty Museum had to make a difficult choice. Should there be more expansion of existing facilities—or would it be more advisable to construct an entirely new building?

Since I personally would be footing the bills, the final question was put to me. I listened to all the pros and cons.

'Draw up plans for an entirely new building,' I told the Trustees. I made one reservation. 'I refuse to pay for one of those concrete-bunker-type structures that are the fad among museum architects—nor for some tinted-glass-and-stainless-steel monstrosity.'

To my delight, the Trustees beamed. They, too, wanted the museum building itself to be unique and a work of art.

* * *

There are those who hold that I am an astute, shrewd businessman and a tough negotiator. To whatever degree I may possess these qualities ascribed to me, they certainly weren't operative when I agreed to pay for building a new museum and underwriting its operating expenses.

The collection which I have donated to the museum is valued at more than $200 million by many experts. Had I been bargain-hunting and bent on tough negotiating, I could have followed Joseph Hirshhorn's lead. When he donated his collection 'to the people of the United States' in 1964, Hirshhorn set down a number of conditions. Among them, the building to house the collection was to be built and maintained by public funds. Payrolls of curators, guides, security personnel—of everyone employed in the museum—were to be met by the U.S. Government. Otherwise, he said in effect, I will simply take my collection elsewhere.

There are at least fifty cities in the world that would have liked to obtain the Getty Collection. Had I been in a hard bargain-driving mood, it would have been a simple matter to obtain identical terms. I could have announced that I was ready to donate my collection provided one of the cities would make available a choice—at least ten-acre—plot of ground, construct a museum building to my exact specifications and guarantee to meet all costs and expenses (including those of operation and upkeep *ad infinitum*).

Such an arrangement would have been financially advantageous to me, no doubt about that. However, there were other, and for me overriding, considerations. It was my intent that the collection should be completely open to the public, free of all charges—be they for admission or even for parking automobiles. Nothing of this sort could be insured if the museum were under the control of a city, state—or even the Federal—government. Almost all such museums, even though they are heavily subsidized by public monies, charge for admission. Precious few provide parking facilities of any kind for visitors—much less free ones.

Then, I am something of an anachronism. As I learned it in my youth, a gift—whether to the public or an individual—is something given of one's own volition and without strings attached. Otherwise, it is no longer a gift but a business transaction. And, if I had wanted to do business with my collection, I would have gone all-out and sold it off. Since almost every piece had appreciated considerably (even many times) over what I had paid for it originally, I would have doubtless realized a very large profit (even after paying capital-gains taxes).

One does not construct a building to house a $200 million art collection on the cheap. It cost me almost $17 million to have the new J. Paul Getty Museum built. Since its opening, the museum has cost me over a million dollars a year for operating expenses alone. Although I have never personally seen the new museum, I feel the money was—and is being—well spent, as I hope to demonstrate in the next chapter.

35

I HAVE LONG been keenly interested in ancient Greek and Roman architecture. The beginnings of my interest can be traced back to my earliest visits to Italy and Greece, where I saw the crumbled and fragmentary remnants of the architectural marvels that these long-dead civilizations had produced. With the question of a new J. Paul Getty museum design before me, I decided to reproduce a Roman villa to house my collection.

I thought it worthwhile to create one building in the Roman tradition. The Graeco-Roman buildings that remain to us have had hard usage during the last couple of thousand years. I suppose that 99.99 per cent of the buildings of Imperial Rome have disappeared. The precious few buildings left are all more or less incomplete. They have been worn by time and, those in the area near Mount Vesuvius, suffered severe damage from volcanic eruption and earthquake.

Fortunately some of the villas around Mount Vesuvius have been excavated and while none is complete, we know after studying them how a Roman villa looked even though we can't make an accurate facsimile of any particular one.

The Villa dei Papyri at Herculaneum served as an inspiration for the new Getty Museum. The Villa has not been excavated. But, fortunately for us, during the eighteenth century many years were spent in exploring the Villa by means of tunnels. We thus have very good engineering information about the peristyle garden and much of the building. I believe that the ancient Roman proprietor would find the peristyle garden in the Museum very close to the one at Herculaneum. And, even though there are some changes, I believe that he would recognize the floor plan of the main level.

What follows is taken from the Guidebook to the new Getty Museum. It tells the story of how it came to be from the inception.

In the early 1950s, J. Paul Getty decided to form an educational trust administered by a Board of Trustees that would take charge of his art collection and open it to the public. The original Museum attracted an increasing number of visitors, and the size of the collection increased steadily. Although new galleries were added, the space was rapidly outgrown.

The Trustees did not wish to commission a modern building, numerous examples of which—both good and bad—already existed among museums. Neither were they satisfied with the usual design concept whereby the structure would be a mere backdrop for art objects. They felt that a museum building should be a statement in itself—that is, be of interest for its own sake—as well as provide a harmonious setting for the collection.

Mr. Getty was fascinated with one particular building: the Villa dei Papyri at Herculaneum which had been destroyed along with the rest of the city by the eruption of Mount Vesuvius in A.D. 79. A structure patterned after it would certainly be exciting archaeologically; it would also provide the ideal setting for the antiquities collection, one of the finest in the United States . . .

The site of Herculaneum (which was buried under volcanic mud that later turned to stone and then by later lava-flows) was not re-discovered until 1709. Many excavations were undertaken, mainly for the purpose of looting the buried city of its priceless cut marbles and other art treasures.

These efforts led eventually to the accidental discovery of the Villa dei Papyri, a large seaside villa that had belonged to a patently wealthy and patrician Roman family. During the 1700s, the further excavations of the Villa—which involved digging down to a depth of over sixty feet and then tunnelling horizontally—were conducted under the supervision of Karl Weber, a Swiss engineer. Weber made a detailed plan of the structure, with dimensions, and kept a diary of his discoveries—a novel practice for that time.

The decision to recreate the Villa dei Papyri as the basis for the new Getty Museum was made by Mr. Getty personally in Spring, 1970.

Many difficulties arose in translating Karl Weber's original records into a modern structure. There existed such myriad considerations as the nature of the available site, the practical needs of a museum and its visitors, the necessity of employing modern workmen and equipment, and the requirements of a rigid building code. In addition, it was necessary to supply information for those incomplete or missing portions of Weber's plan: several areas on the ground level and the entire floor above. Fortunately, Dr. Norman Neuerburg agreed to act as consultant for the project. An architectural historian, he combined years of scholarship in antiquities—including research and excavation of Pompeii and Herculaneum—with an acute sense of design and construction problems.

During the year of planning that followed, meticulous care was taken to ensure fidelity to the architectural spirit of the original. When modifications were necessary, the design was drawn from surviving contemporary examples which have been excavated at Herculaneum, Pompeii and Stabiae. This attention to detail even extended to the Museum's gardens and grounds, as extant specimens of plant roots—preserved by volcanic flow—have enabled botanists to identify their types and reconstruct layouts of Roman gardens.

Construction work on the Museum began in December, 1970. The old museum remained open to the public until the final few months when the collection was transferred, assembled (many pieces had been in storage, lent to other institutions or recently acquired) and installed in the new building. The new J. Paul Getty Museum was officially opened to the public on January 15, 1974.

The flouting of conventional wisdom and refusal to conform carry with them many risks. This is nowhere more true than in the Art World, certain quarters of which tend to be very much doctrinaire and elitist. However, I had calculated the risks—and, I say this with an admitted degree of arrogance, I disregarded them. Thus, I was neither shaken nor surprised when some of the early returns showed that certain critics sniffed at the new Museum. The building did not follow the

arbitrary criteria for 'museum construction.' There were those
who thought it should have been more conventional—that is,
I suppose, that it should have been built to look like some of
the museum structures whose architecture can be best described as 'Penitentiary Modern.' In any event, for the first
two months or so, the J. Paul Getty Museum building was
called 'controversial' in many Art World (or should I say
Artsy-Craftsy?) quarters.

I have a fortunate capacity to remain unruffled. I also have
had more than sufficient experience in many areas of life to
know that the shrillest critics are not necessarily the most
authoritative (and seldom the most objective). Beyond this,
the very shrillness of their cries and howls very quickly
exhausts their wind (and the play on words is entirely
intentional).

Therefore, I simply sat back and, for leisure reading, went
over the reports of the Trustees' expenditures—which were
meticulously compiled by my good and unswervingly loyal
friend and Chief Accountant, Norris Bramlett:

Start-up costs	$ 185,568
Land value (est.)	300,000
Building cost	15,819,408
Equipment and furnishing	353,789
TOTAL	$16,658,765

Adding on a few incidental expenses brought the total up
beyond the $17 million mark. All the money spent by the
Trustees originated from donations made to the Museum by
me. But I considered it a fair price, indeed, for a building that
contained a collection—valued by some experts, as I've already noted, at upwards of $200 million—which I had also
donated to the Museum.

I felt that the Museum, its Trustees and I had got our
money's worth. I was certain that critics and public would
soon begin to recognize the real values, too. I didn't have long
to wait.

Henry J. Seldis, making an appraisal of the Museum and its
collection for the Los Angeles *Times*, wrote:

'There is not a handful of museums in this country that can
equal or compete with the best of the (Getty Museum's)

antiquities. Nowhere in America is there a finer collection of Roman sculptural portraits.'

The May, 1974 issue of the *Smithsonian* Magazine had a seven-page article—lavishly illustrated with full-colour photographs—on the Museum. Among other things, the article said:

'The oil billionaire's vast art collection has a luxurious new home in Malibu, copied from an ancient villa in Herculaneum. The controversial J. Paul Getty Museum . . . has emerged as a compelling cultural attraction.'

I suppose I can sum it all up by saying that I've never been one to bet on the weather. It's unpredictable, changing from day to day. I bet on the climate, which follows patterns year after year, decade after decade. While hidebound—and somewhat hysterical—worshippers at the shrines of tradition (or current trends—or should that be fads?) shrieked their protests, less uptight critics spoke in quieter, more reasoned—and thus far more convincing—tones. The Museum and its collection have received rave-notices ever since May, 1974.

Museums do not just happen. Nor are they the work of any one person. Numerous dedicated people contributed thought, time, energy, work—and above all, expertise and talent—to the building and success of the new Getty Museum. Unfortunately, it is impossible to list the names of all who so richly deserve tribute for their part in the project and in the operation of the Museum, but there are several who must be given very special mention.

The project could not have been begun—much less completed—had it not been for the unstinting cooperation and enthusiasm of the Board of Trustees. The building itself could not have been created without the knowledge and the unsparing effort provided by Dr. Norman Neuerburg. Nor can I say enough to express my personal gratitude and appreciation to Stephen Garrett, deputy director of the Museum and its three curators: Jiri Frel (Antiquities); Burton Fredericksen (Paintings); and Ms. Gillian Wilson (Decorative Arts). These are younger people of great knowledge and talent, vital and dedicated. They are of the calibre of such eminently distinguished museum people as Gordon B. Washburn, who until his recent retirement, was the director of John D. Rockefeller

3rd's Asia House; the late Theodore Rousseau of the New York's Metropolitan; and Jack Spinx of the National Gallery in Washington. I doubt if many museums, whether publicly or privately endowed, can boast of an administrative team that surpasses the one formed by Messrs. Garrett, Frel and Fredericksen and Ms. Wilson.

How does one measure the 'success' of a museum?

The J. Paul Getty Museum's sole *raison d'être* is to make fine art freely available for viewing by the greatest possible numbers of people. Therefore, I imagine that public response and acceptance constitute one reasonably valid and accurate yardstick.

The new Getty Museum has been open to the public, free of charge, five days a week (from 10:00 a.m. to 5:00 p.m.) since January 15, 1974. During the fifty weeks that followed, more than 360,000 people visited the Museum. The flow-rate of visitors remained almost the same during 1975. (It would have been much higher were it not for some rather ironic developments which I will relate a bit further on in this chapter.)

I would now like to digress momentarily for a primer-level exercise in arithmetic.

The Museum has a staff of about seventy people. Their salaries and other operating expenses add up to $1.5 million per year. The entire expense is met by the Museum from funds which I—personally and alone—make available. The original cost—$17 million—was also paid by me. Had this amount been invested in, say, nine per cent bonds, it would be yielding me about $1.5 million a year. Thus, it can be said that the total annual cost of the Museum to me is $3 million a year.

Now, taking 300,000 annual visitors as a rounded-off figure for computation, this means that the *gross* cost to me for each visitor to the Museum is about ten dollars. I say gross cost because I am, after all, in the 70% federal income tax bracket. *Thus, my personal, out-of-pocket net cost is around three dollars per visitor.*

I do not submit these figures in order to boast. I present them so that the reader will have some idea of the enormous expense involved in bringing fine art to the public. Even more to the point, I hope the figures are noted and borne in mind by wealthy people who donate art collections to museums but make no provision for the expenses incident to their display, preservation, insurance and other continuing costs. Such donors simply shift the heavy cost-burden to the taxpayer and to the public, which is very often required to pay an admission charge in order to view the 'donated' collections.

By the same token, I hope my words will have some influence on legislators and other politicians who, when faced with a need to make budget cuts, slash first at the allocations for cultural activities. (Naturally, projects designed to rehabilitate switchblade knife-wielders or provide gold-watch longevity awards for those with 25-years of unbroken registry on Welfare Rolls remain untouched. In fact, when a million is carved out of public museum or opera-and-concert allocations, it's almost automatic that ten million be added to some hare-brained socialistic scheme or another.)

Free outings into the country for Welfare clients mean votes. Free admissions to public museums of art for people who are constructively and productively employed do not. At least, that is the apparent belief prevalent among the worthies who control the expenditure (and profligate waste) of our public funds. They are doing their damndest to increase the numbers of cultural barbarians in our midst. I take quiet pride in the knowledge that much of the profit I have personally made through our still-somehow-surviving capitalist system is used in an effort to reduce the numbers of cultural barbarians in our society.

Purblind benefactors who donate art collections and leave others to foot the housing and maintenance bills and barbarian propagating politicians are not alone. They are aided and abetted by goodly (if, perhaps, unwitting) segments of the public. I've said there would—more properly, there *could*—be more visitors to the Getty Museum than there are, were it not for certain ironic developments.

When the decision was made to build the Museum, I donated ten acres of valuable beachfront property to the Trust for use of the Museum. Only a part of it was for the Museum and gardens. The rest was—I specified—to be used as a free parking area for visitors.

According to studies and estimates made by traffic engineers and building planners, the parking facilities that were provided would be more than adequate. But, as it turned out, people came to the Museum at the rate of 1,500, 2,000 and even more per day. Southern California being what it is, most came by automobile. The parking lot, large as it is, couldn't handle all the cars. Whereupon people began parking them along nearby streets—and, immediately the local citizenry was up in arms.

Complaints flooded city, county, state—and, for all I know—federal agencies. The Paul Getty Museum was causing quiet, residential streets to be lined with parked cars. It was attracting crowds of people. The silence was being shattered by the sound of slamming car-doors. The local teen-agers couldn't ride their bicycles—or motor-scooters or dune-buggies or whatever teen-agers ride—along the sidewalks anymore. There were actually *people* walking on them—and they were walking toward (or from) the Getty Museum.

Norris Bramlett, my indefatigable man-on-the-Southern-California scene, brought me news of all this. I blinked disbelieving. Then, I somewhat timidly asked:

'Ah—Norris. Has anyone pointed out to the good burghers that they have a major museum, an important cultural centre near them and that . . .'

'Sure,' Norris nodded—and shrugged. 'But they're claiming that you should have spent your money on something that benefits *them*, and doesn't bring in a lot of what they call outsiders.'

Now visitors to the J. Paul Getty Museum have to obtain a parking-lot reservation in advance. The Museum can only have 1,200 or 1,300 people visiting it daily because of the limited parking facilities—and, believe it or not, the local authorities refuse to permit any expansion of parking facilities on the Museum's property.

(The Trustees—and I—requested permission to build a larger parking-area. It was refused on the grounds that the neighbours were already discommoded because the Museum already attracted too many people and too much traffic.)

So there you are. If the neighbours didn't mind 'outsiders' parking cars along their streets or didn't oppose plans to expand the existing Museum parking facilities, the Museum would doubtless have 2,500 to 3,000 visitors a day—instead of 1,200 or 1,300.

Sometimes—as the ancient wheeze goes—you can't win for losing.

36

MY NEIGHBOURS' REACTION at the presence of the Getty Museum might tend to disappoint and disillusion me were it not that I am much inured and, in some respects, cynical. It's the product of a conditioning process. I would hazard to guess that my motives have been misinterpreted, my meanings misread, my statements misquoted and my movements and actions erroneously reported about as much as those of anyone who is (for whatever reason) in the public eye.

I'm not complaining. I am (and have long been) amused, even bemused by it all. For example, I have found myself to be one of the world's most frequently *mis*placed persons.

Although I have not been in the United States since 1951, I cannot begin to count the number of newspaper items—mainly datelined New York City—that have read something like these:

'J. Paul Getty is in town to help publicize his latest book.' (That, if I recall correctly, appeared in a 1961 Leonard Lyons column.)

Or:

'Seen hand-holding in a dark corner of the cafe at the Hotel Pierre (which he owns): J. Paul Getty, the oil zillionaire. With him: a luscious redhead wearing the plungingest neckline ever seen anywhere.' (I'd rather spare the columnist who cooked up that tidbit the embarrassment of identifying him. However, the squib appeared in a New York City newspaper during 1956—when I was in the Neutral Zone, inspecting drilling rigs and not holding hands or staring down plunging necklines.)

But misplacing me is not a sport confined to newspaper columnists. Ms. Gail Cameron is a distinguished author. Her recent book, *Rose: The Biography of Rose Fitzgerald Kennedy*—gives colourful details of a great ball held in Venice, Italy, in September, 1967. On page 212 of the book, Ms. Cameron lists many of the guests present. My name is sandwiched between the names of Gian-Carlo Menotti and Richard Burton.

I feel greatly honoured. I consider Menotti a brilliant composer. Richard Burton is, in my opinion, one of our finest actors, and he is also a personal friend (as is his gorgeous wife, Elizabeth Taylor, another immensely talented person). There is only one thing wrong with Ms. Cameron's glowing account. I did NOT attend the ball. Indeed, I wasn't even in Italy—much less Venice—at the time it was held.

Then there are the misquotations or the statements taken completely out of context. I once told a prominent writer—not a journalist, an author with the highest of credentials—the following:

'One of the troubles with books, motion pictures, television and advertising today is that everything is sex. I'll be the first to admit that sex is important, but it is being overemphasized, overdone. I think sex, to a certain extent, should be fugitive.'

That is what I *said*.

But the author extracted three words—three only—from my statement. When I read his book, I found myself being quoted as flatly declaring that: 'Everything is sex.'

Was I annoyed? Perhaps—but only momentarily. Feeling in a charitable mood, I told myself the writer doubtless suffered from a widespread aural malady—that of selective hearing.

I must, of course, be charitable on this particular count. I make conscious and premeditated use of the same hearing defect—*plus* another, namely selective reading comprehension. If I did not, I would soon be suffering a major identity crisis from hearing and reading the innumerable myths and fictions about myself.

According to the version you hear or see in print, I am by religious persuasion: Roman Catholic, Presbyterian, Jewish, a

Christian Scientist. One rumour current in 1949–50 even had me converting to the Moslem Faith as a condition for obtaining the Saudi Arabian Neutral Zone concession.

As it happens, I am—and always have been—a Methodist. For the benefit of those whose curiosity compels them to inquire (or probe) into people's religious attitudes, I might state that:

1. I believe in God and in Christian principles.

2. I am a believer in the teachings of the Bible (but I am by no means a Fundamentalist).

3. I have no prejudices against denominations other than my own, be they Christian or otherwise.

My ethnic origins is another matter that has given rise to much speculation and produced some incredibly muddled and inaccurate tales. My father's forebears came from Londonderry County in Northern Ireland, and my mother's family was originally Scottish. But both sides of my family emigrated to the United States—more properly, the American Colonies—in the eighteenth century.

Thus, I am not of French extraction (as some seem to think because my name is *Jean Paul* Getty). Nor are my origins German (as maintained by others, possibly because Adolphine Helme, my third wife, was German).

I am—as I have repeatedly stated in one context or another—a native-born American citizen legally domiciled in the State of California. I carry an ordinary United States passport (not a 'special' or Diplomatic one which some sources claim I possess). Whenever a current passport expires, I go to the nearest United States Consulate and follow precisely the same routines as any other U.S. citizen to have a new one issued.

I also file precisely the same U.S. and California State Income Tax forms as any other American citizen (and Californian) who is resident abroad. I suppose it is safe to say that my income-tax returns are prepared with even greater care and attention to last-penny detail than those of many other individuals. They have to be. (My gross income is such that my returns are automatically subject to meticulous audit by the U.S. Internal Revenue Service.)

The state of my health is yet another subject that appears to arouse much conjecture and comment. Not long ago, *Time*

Magazine breathlessly confided to its readers that I suffer from Parkinson's Disease. Evidently, the Luce Empire's journalists see themselves as being endowed with unique talent as medical diagnosticians. I very humbly and sincerely thank the Good Lord that they are apparently suffering from advanced delusions of Hippocratic grandeur.

Luckily, I can afford the best medical care available. I have frequent medical examinations—remember, I *am* eighty-three years old. So far, the most learned specialists and consultants have been unanimous in their verdicts. I do *not* suffer from Parkinson's Disease, measles, mumps or even migraine headaches (but *I* could have told them about the last). Nor—at least according to the latest reports—do I show any signs of pregnancy.

On the other hand—as I say—I am eighty-three. Cold, damp winters do bring on attacks of bronchitis (I've mentioned this before, too). I can't lift weights or swim for hours or walk five miles at the brisk pace I did ten years ago. However (*Time* Magazine, please copy), as my diary entry for September 20, 1975, shows:

'Played tennis for a while with Marion Anderson.'

Dr. Clive Mackenzie has been my personal physician for more than ten years. For the most part, he merely gives me a periodic checkup (generally complaining that it's a waste of both his time and mine) and my 'flu shot when the 'flu season approaches. A good and close friend, Dr. Mackenzie doesn't mind (or fear) telling me the chilling, depressing truth: I *do* suffer from a touch of chronic hypochondria.

Among other J. Paul Getty myths—there are so many of them—one has it that Howard Hughes and I are close friends and that we have been associated in numerous business ventures. When Hughes (only reputedly, so far as I know) visited London, it was said that I conferred with him secretly in his hotel suite. Some yarn-spinners even have Howard Hughes as my financial backer—while others hold that I'm the man 'behind' Hughes.

Actually, while I knew Howard's father quite well, I have only the barest acquaintance with Howard himself. We have spent only one evening together—and that was in the 1920s.

We did attend a few—a very few—of the same parties during the same period, but I doubt if we ever exchanged more than ten words—'I'm fine—and you?'—at any of them.

Of course, we had—and still have—many mutual friends and acquaintances, but our own direct, personal acquaintance is virtually nil.

Another myth is that I once knocked out Jack Dempsey (in a fight over a girl, according to the most popular version). I only wish I could lay claim to such a remarkable achievement—but I can't. There is a microscopic grain of truth to the story, though.

Jack Dempsey and I became friends in the very early 1920s. I was always a physical culture enthusiast, and I loved to box. In 1923, Jack was in Saratoga Springs, New York, training for his title bout against Luis Firpo.

At this point, I must leap forward in time to 1973. Jack visited me at Sutton Place. It was fifty years later—and half a century does have the effect of blurring memories. When newspaper reporters asked each of us how we recalled the incident, we both agreed that I had gone up to Saratoga Springs to visit Jack—and offered to act as his sparring partner.

From there on, our versions differed. Jack gave me very high praise, indeed, by telling the press:

'Paul could box very well. The only difference was that I could hit harder, although we both weighed about the same. I was using him as a sparring partner in a world-title defence. He told me not to pull my punches and fight as well as I could. And that's what I did.'

Dempsey added that I managed to survive the first round, thereby implying that I really managed to hold my own against him.

My recollection is not, I fear, the same. As I remember it, I climbed into the ring and, a few moments after we began to spar, I realized that Jack was pulling his punches. My *macho* was taking all the punishment, for there were two or three very attractive young women friends watching at ringside.

I wanted not only to test my ability as a boxer but also to prove myself. As I remember my words, I said: 'Damn it, Jack, treat me just as you would any professional sparring partner.'

Dempsey still hesitated. Whereupon—in the second round—I

took the foolhardy step of trying to goad him into action. I swung my lefts and rights as hard as I could. Jack took a few of the blows, parried the others—and moved back a pace or two.

'Okay, Paul,' he said. 'If you insist . . .'

The first punch was hard. Jack swung again—and connected. That was that. Some several seconds later, I picked myself up off the canvas, fully and finally convinced that I would thenceforth stick to the oil business.

Jack Dempsey and I have remained very close friends during the decades that followed. In 1969, when he came to Europe, it was my very great pleasure to give Jack a party celebrating his seventy-fourth birthday. Incidentally, on his visit to Sutton four years later—in 1973—we struck a pose, pretending to square off, for the benefit of newspaper photographers. I'm glad to say that Jack didn't swing. I'm sure that even after fifty years, the Manassa Mauler could have still flattened me with a single well-placed punch.

Some other myths:

It has been bandied about that in the late 1930s I walked into New York City's Hotel Pierre, had lunch in the restaurant, was dissatisfied with the service, and promptly bought the hotel so that I could fire the restaurant staff. This is so patently ridiculous that one wonders how the tale could possibly gain any credence.

One does not buy a luxury-class 42-storey hotel by striding into someone's office and signing a cheque. A purchase of this magnitude takes months to negotiate and requires the services of whole regiments of agents, attorneys, bankers, accountants and other specialists. Yes, I *did* buy the Pierre—but as an investment of the Company and only after very protracted negotiations. Incidentally, I had not eaten in any of the hotel's restaurants for months before the negotiations began. Besides, as anyone but a total financial illiterate would know, businessmen buy properties with a view to making a profit—not out of pique.

Another facet of the Getty mythology concerns my eating habits and tastes in food. It is said (variously) that I am a health-food faddist, a vegetarian, an undiscriminating gourmand, a peevish gourmet who demands that he be served only the most exotic dishes.

If it please the Court, I will take the specifications one by one.

I am a health food 'faddist' to the extent that I have for many, many years believed that wheat germ is a healthy food-supplement. I like it on cereal or atop grapefruit—when I eat at home. I certainly do not ask for it in restaurants or expect to find wheat germ placed before me when I dine out at the homes of friends.

I like fresh fruit and have been known to eat fair-sized quantities of it. I also believe it beneficial to fast for a day every now and then or to eat only fresh fruit during a twenty-four hour period, but I am anything but a vegetarian.

My breakfasts are light, served in my bedroom by Bullimore, and consisting of fresh fruit or fruit juice and cereal with skim milk. For lunch and dinner I eat meat, fowl, vegetables and just about everything else. I eat heartily, but I try to use common sense and not *overeat*. Sometimes, of course, I do—especially when my favourite dishes are on the menu. Among these are roast duck, corn-on-the-cob (yes, I do have almost all my own teeth and can nibble the kernels off the cob neatly) and strawberry shortcake (for which I have a weakness that approaches gluttonous lust). I usually have a drink before lunch and dinner and a glass of port after.

Two fairly representative, everyday Sutton Place menus:

Thursday, November 21, 1975, Dinner:
Lobster bisque
Roast chicken
Fresh vegetables
Maple nut ice cream
Cheese board with fresh celery
Fresh fruits
Coffee (for my guests, I pass on coffee)
Appropriate wines
Port

Friday, November 12, 1975, Lunch:
Avocado pear
Mixed grill
Fresh vegetables
Creamed potatoes
Sachertorte with fresh heavy cream

Cheese board with fresh celery
Fresh fruits
Coffee
Appropriate wines
Port

Of course, I also enjoy slightly more exotic dishes such as caviar and lobster, but on the other hand I remain an inveterate *aficionado* of such prosaic American foods as flapjacks and hamburgers. A small private kitchenette adjoins my bedroom at Sutton Place. I can (and on occasion do) mix up a batch of pancake batter or take a patty of minced beef from the refrigerator and make myself entirely palatable flapjacks (which I douse with maple or black walnut syrup) or hamburgers. This is a secret vice I practise in the small hours of the morning when I have worked—or read—until long after the five permanent resident members of the domestic staff have gone to bed and are sound asleep. (This resident staff, I should add, is augmented by four other employees who come in daily. The total of nine does not include security personnel, gardeners and others who cannot be properly classified as 'inside' domestic staff.)

Withal, I try to follow the prescription one of my cousins gave me long ago: 'Eat one-half as much, drink one-fourth as much, laugh twice as much.'

This brings to mind still another popular Paul Getty myth—that I am perpetually straight (or sour) faced and seldom if ever laugh.

Nonsense.

I love to laugh—and I do, whenever I find something funny or have a reason to laugh (very often, it's at myself and some of the things I do). Admittedly, I laugh much more often and easily when I am in the company of friends than when I am in public. I've never been able to laugh artificially on cue, just to prove to some journalist or photographer that I am capable of cracking a smile.

Experience has made me cautious, wary. I'm hesitant to let my guard down unless I know the people I'm with and feel at home with them. This has frequently caused me to become frozen-faced in front of camera lenses or when confronted by can-opener-wielding journalists. I've learned that I can never be sure what the photo caption will read if I obey the cameraman's injunction to 'Smile, Mr. Getty!' It could be (and has been) that the caption will be on this order:

'Candid portrait of a billionaire cackling over his treasure-troves.'

Or:

'What secret deal has J. Paul Getty just completed to make him gloat with such unabashed glee?'

With friends, I feel free to chuckle, guffaw, burst into belly-laughs (and to admit that I am perhaps the world's greatest Laurel and Hardy fan). Innumerable of my friends are amusing, humourous, witty, capable of sending me into paroxysms of laughter. Columnist Art Buchwald—whom I have known since the days when he worked on the Paris *Herald-Tribune*—is certainly one of them. Art can crack me up completely—whether in conversation or in print.

Closer to my intimate circle of friends (or well inside it) there have always been many individuals whose sense of humour has made me laugh 'twice as much' and more. My cousin, Hal Seymour, left me with my sides aching when he told his uproariously funny stories—and so did Jack Forrester. Nubar Gulbenkian vastly amused me—and all those who knew me well—with his caricature imitations of my speech and mannerisms.

Marion Anderson, a friend since Santa Monica Beach Club days, has always been able to make me laugh loud and long with the hilarious tales of her adventures and misadventures. Another dear friend, Lady Ursula d'Abo, knows exactly how to send me into gales of laughter, even at those times when I may feel grouchy and grumpy. My great friend—and attorney *par excellence*—Lansing Hays has a wry, dry (occasionally sardonic) wit that has left me chortling for hours after even the dullest and dreariest of business conferences. And I could extend the list almost indefinitely, for there is no arcane secret in raising my R.Q.—Risibility Quotient—to side-splitting peaks. There is nothing I enjoy more than a good laugh—even though it may sometimes be at my expense.

There are more than a few other Getty myths, but I'll tackle them from a different angle in the next chapter. Right now, I want only to lay one recent rumour to rest.

I have absolutely NO intention of marrying Jacqueline Kennedy Onassis.

What if—1976 being a Leap Year—she proposes to me, you ask?

Hmm. I'll have to give that question some thought—knowing full well that by saying so, I'll merely start another flood of ridiculous rumours.

37

THERE IS OVERWHELMING evidence that I rate very high, indeed, on the list of the world's most eligible and sought-after bachelors.

How many other five-times divorced octogenarians can make *that* statement?

The answer (and it does not bruise my ego one bit) is that there are many. The roster is hardly exclusive. Inclusion calls for only two prerequisites. One, the octogenarian (or nonagenarian, for that matter) must be reputed to possess wealth (the more he supposedly has, the higher he goes on the list). Two, he should be unmarried.

I have already mentioned the inane, cash-and-carry marriage-proposals I receive in the post. (It would not surprise me in the least if one day I opened an envelope and found a mail-order form inside: 'Simply clip the coupon below, attach cheque or money order and receive a wife by return mail. Sorry, no COD's or credit cards.')

But the alluring individual solicitations from nubile pen-pals are minor-league phenomena compared to the Old School tries made by gossip-columnists and just plain gossips. Peering into crystal balls (or, for all I know, at the entrails of freshly slaughtered hens) they risk serious eye-strain as they try to see a sixth wife in my future. The number of women it has been predicted that I will marry defies an accurate tally (even if I wished to make one, and I don't).

My masculine pride swells though when I think that 'reliable sources' have reported me 'on the verge' of marrying such lovely and wonderful ladies as Margaret, Duchess of Argyll; Mrs. Penelope Kitson; Ms. Zsa Zsa Gabor and—most recently—Lady Ursula d'Abo and Mrs. Rosabella Burch.

All five of these delightful, charming—and eminently desirable—ladies have been my close and dear friends for years, some even for decades. I have been a frequent guest in their homes, as they have in mine. I have attended balls, parties and a wide variety of social functions with each of them. However, without in any way lessening the fondness and admiration I have for them, I must go on record to say that I have done the same things with several other ladies who are also my close and longtime friends.

For the benefit of any and all Paul Getty wedding-waiters—be they members of the press or of the general public—I have absolutely no marriage-plans or intentions. (Not now, at any rate. There is always the possibility that I mentioned in the previous chapter. Jacqueline Kennedy Onassis *might* propose, as it's Leap Year. But even then, I'd be in a quandary. I don't know if I could *afford* to accept. I'm a bit dubious whether my personal resources are sufficient for both the Getty Museum and the half-share costs of maintaining the yacht, *Christina*.)

I repeat. Despite all the rumours, reports and gossip-column items, I certainly have no present intentions of marrying again. As I have stated repeatedly to the press, a man who has experienced five marital crash-landings is not inclined to go for another trial spin.

But even a statement like this has given rise to rumours. Some journalist (or journalists, plural) have seized upon it. From time to time I find myself reading newspaper or magazine articles that declare:

'J. Paul Getty, the oil magnate, will not marry for a sixth time because of a fortune teller's prophecy. Many years ago, the seer told him that he would have six wives, and that his death would follow very soon after the sixth marriage.'

Poppycock (to put it politely)!

I remind the reader that December 15, 1975, marked my eighty-third birthday. I do not consider myself immortal. (Ask my attorneys. They know I made a last will and testament as early as the beginning of the 1920s and have periodically updated it.) Mark Twain observed that the only two sure things in life are death and taxes. I pay my taxes. And I am acutely aware that one day I shall die (or, to use the term I prefer, go on to join the great majority). Whether I am single or married will not make one whit of difference.

So much—I hope—about the recurring myths regarding my plans for (or fears of) marrying for a sixth time. I imagine the hope will prove empty. Based on past press-performances, it would not surprise me to pick up my morning newspaper any day and be the last to learn that I am poised and ready to elope with Gloria Steinem, Phyllis Diller or Ann Landers!

Mrs. Roslyn Targ is the effervescent and super-efficient literary agent who undertook to place this book with publishers in various countries throughout the world. She came to Sutton Place from New York to discuss the project with me.

'Will you write about your relationships with your women friends?' Roslyn asked.

As one seasoned business *person* conversing with another, I recognized that her sharp mind and keen eye were focused on potential sales figures. Nevertheless, I shook my head.

'I'm afraid not,' I replied. 'I've never been one to feed my ego by boasting about my sex life or sexual exploits.'

Then, because Roz Targ is a very attractive lady many years my junior, I felt constrained to elaborate a little.

'You're a nineteen-seventies person,' I said. 'I'm quite old-fashioned. I refuse to capitalize on shared intimacies, even though I know that sort of thing is not only fashionable but practically *de rigueur* nowadays.'

Roslyn tried another tack.

'Don't you intend mentioning any of your women friends?'

I assured her that I most certainly intended mentioning as many of my friends—male or female—as I could in reasonable context and provided that I did not violate anyone's rights to privacy.

'But you must realize that people are always fascinated to read about the women in any successful man's life,' Roz persisted.

I pretended to think deeply for a few seconds.

'Well,' I said at last. 'There was Miss Kincaid, my fifth-grade geography teacher—and Miss Mudge, who tried her best to make me improve my penmanship . . .'

Mrs. Targ laughed. She got the point and agreed that it might, after all, be better for me to do it my way. Which is how I have done it and will continue to do throughout the remainder of this book—naming friends, female and male when and where I consider it fitting, recounting anecdotes and describing my impressions and experiences. However, as I sought—successfully—to convey to Roz Targ, I am no *voyeur* and do not palpitate with desire to peek into other people's bedrooms. Nor do I invite audiences into mine.

(The closest I ever came to hitting a reporter was once when an American newsman—now dead, but then notorious for his gall—asked me: 'Which of your wives was the best in bed?' Luckily I had the self-control to jam my fists into my pockets, spin around on my heel and walk away.)

Still and all, I have to concede there is intensely morbid curiosity about the women in the life of any man who—for whatever reason—is considered 'good copy.' Let a man assassinate a President or scale Mount Everest or be named 'the richest American', and the classic *cherchez la femme*—better still, *les femmes*—principle is invoked and made all-out operative.

My name has been linked romantically—as the common euphemism has it—with the names of a very considerable number of women during the last sixty years. Some of these linkages—if that be the term—have caused me considerable embarrassment and difficulty. I have previously touched upon the problems that arose from my, and later Charles Chaplin's, relationships with Miss Joan Barry. Another young woman—I prefer not to name her—threw herself into my lap at a New York nightclub and kissed me passionately while flashbulbs flared. She later 'planted' the photograph in tabloid newspapers, gave out the story that she was my fiancée and tried to make enormous charge-account purchases on the strength of it. I could go on and on citing incidents—but why bother?

As I've seen it during my lifetime, the female of the species is fundamentally no more mercenary, venal or opportunistic than the male. On the other hand, it is surely an eternal verity that there are some women who are on constant alert to find—and seize—their Main Chance with (or, more accurately, *through*) a man. This is a fact of life that I—like innumerable other males reputed to be wealthy—have learned from experience (and rather dismal and depressing experiences).

More than a few young ladies have indicated that they loved me dearly, even desperately, and wished to marry me for myself alone. Their ardour—and marital urges—cooled instantly to minus-zero when they learned that my attorneys would draw up an ironclad financial and property agreement *before* marriage. Such experiences leave scar-tissue—which does not always provide future protection and may even cause over-reaction.

I vividly recall a period between the great wars—and between marriages—when I decided to tour the Continent under an assumed name and in the guise of a vacationing insurance broker. This, I figured, would prevent anyone from learning that I was a multi-millionaire. 'If a girl is attracted to me', I reasoned to myself, 'I won't have to fear that she's merely after my money.'

Well, it so happened that I met a very lovely young woman—let's call her Lucia Antonelli—in Rome. The attraction was instantaneous and mutual. Lucia—I reiterate, her name is fictitious—possessed just about every quality that I, or any man, could ever hope to find in one woman. She was intelligent, charming, understanding, extremely well-educated, a delightful companion and above all else she was exquisitely beautiful. She had a small, tastefully furnished but unostentatious apartment and she dressed elegantly but simply. She told me she was an orphan living on the proceeds of a modest inheritance. If ever there was a dream-girl it was surely Lucia.

Our relationship progressed and improved at each step. I began to think that in Lucia Antonelli I had at last found the perfect wife, for here was someone who did not desire me for my wealth: she was unaware of it.

Then, one evening, we dined in a restaurant near the sea at Ostia. When we had finished our meal, Lucia gave me a long, knowing look.

'You're not an insurance broker,' she said. 'Your name is Paul Getty, and you are something in the oil business.'

A steel door slammed abruptly somewhere in my brain. So it's happened again I thought as I called for the bill. My hopes were shattered. I took Lucia home, returned to my hotel, and, disillusioned, left Rome for Paris the next morning. Money had killed romance.

Two years later I learned the startling truth. Lucia Antonelli had really been as serious about me as I was about her. The story of being an orphan was a mere subterfuge. She was actually the daughter of one of the richer men in Europe, and when she had told her father about us, he had at once made inquiries about me. He did not want his daughter to marry a fortune hunter, and that's how Lucia learned my name and the truth about my occupation!

Thus my protective stratagem had tragically backfired. Lucia could not have cared less about my wealth, for at that time her family's fortune was probably greater than mine. In short, my fears, doubts and suspicions had caused me to break off what might well have been THE romance—even THE marriage—of my life.

Later, when I finally learned the facts, it was *too* late. By then Lucia Antonelli had married a wealthy Italian nobleman—and is still married to him.

If only . . .

But that incident, too, is in the distant past.

Of many other romantic 'linkages' in which I've been involved some have been hilarious.

I remember one occasion when I took a female cousin to a performance of *Aida* at the Metropolitan Opera House in New York City. Since I had but recently purchased the Hotel Pierre, a few holes had been torn in my comfortable cloak of anonymity. I was recognized by a New York *Mirror* columnist who attended the performance. The next morning, this sizzling item appeared in his column:

'John (sic) Paul Getty, the Texas (again, sic) oilman who is the new owner of the Pierre Hotel has also acquired a new flame. He and she were quite a sight to behold during intermissions, standing off by themselves, heads together, paying attention to no one . . .'

Naturally. My cousin and I hadn't seen each other in several years. We were talking away at a mile a minute, bringing each other up to date.

Even funnier was the incident that occurred during the memorable (for me) 80th birthday party Margaret, Duchess of Argyll, gave me at the Dorchester Hotel. I was greatly touched by Margaret's lavish gesture of friendship and affection. She had invited more than 100 of my friends to attend. Among them was President Richard Nixon's daughter, Tricia, and her husband, Edward Cox.

When an enormous birthday cake with eighty candles blazing on it was wheeled in, I asked Tricia to help me cut it (after I'd blown out the candles—no mean feat, considering their number). Several members of the press and newspaper photographers were present. One of the latter was obviously unaware of Tricia Nixon Cox's identity. As he focused his camera on us, I overheard him say to a colleague:

'That's a luscious bird with Getty—the old boy certainly likes them young, doesn't he?'

Margaret Argyll and Edward Cox—who were standing to one side—also heard the photographer's remark. They—and Tricia and I—were convulsed with laughter.

Having mentioned the party, I must also mention the very special gift Margaret Argyll gave me. She not only hired a large dance band for the occasion, but had a 'birthday song' —based on Cole Porter's 'You're the Top'—composed for me. It was played and sung by the band. The amusing lyrics:

> 'You're the top
> 'You're J. Paul Getty
> 'You're the top
> 'And your cash ain't petty
> 'I have an open cheque
> 'That I would like to pop
> 'So if you'll kindly sign the bottom
> 'You're the top.'

Three sample incidents from 'way back will, I think, illustrate why I consider myself a hardened veteran of rumour, myth and innuendo.

In December, 1959, the London *Evening Standard* published an item that went something like this:

'Expatriate American oil billionaire J. Paul Getty was at the circus with Mrs. Penelope Kitson, Miss Robina Lund, Miss Maggie Nolan—and a dashing blonde with a German accent who wore a white fox-fur wrap. Everybody had a good time, especially Mr. Getty, who laughed a lot . . .'

. . . At least, for once it was admitted by the press that I *could* laugh . . .

'. . . except for the lovely blonde, who seemed glum about something—perhaps the presence of Mr. Getty's other three lovely female companions.'

A titillating—if considerably less than accurate—interpretation. The 'dashing blonde' was Baroness Marianne von Alvensleben, one of my very dear and close friends—and it had been her idea that we all attend the circus in the first place. Marianne was not 'glum' about anything. Unless, of course, the reporter happened to look at her just at the moment when some idiot seated a few rows back flung a blob of sticky ice cream that landed on her fur cape—which was mink, not fox.

So much for some reporters' powers of observation—and accuracy.

In 1963, my old friend, the Earl of Warwick, asked if he could rent Sutton Place for a coming-out party for his adopted daughter, Georgiana, which was to be held on Thursday of Ascot Week. The request was approved by the directors of Sutton Place Property Company Ltd., which owns Sutton Place.

I made this diary notation:

'Sutton Place Property Co. is not in the house-renting business, but I am glad of the decision and hope the party will be a huge success.'

(It was.)

To the press, I stated: 'I am very pleased that the Earl of Warwick will have Sutton Place for the party. We have been friends for a long time. I have stayed at Warwick Castle as his guest. I think that giving my wholehearted and enthusiastic approval to the board's decision is the very least I can do.'

Surely, you've guessed it by now. Within days after the party, it was being rumoured all over London—and points beyond—that the Earl of Warwick's adopted daughter, Georgiana, was my 'new girlfriend.'

A year later, the Duke and Duchess of Bedford gave a bowling party. I was invited.

(My diary entry for November 8, 1964: 'Went bowling for the first time in 23 years. I was never a great player, but it seems I have forgotten everything I ever knew. It's the three-pace run-up that's so hard to get right, but on my third bowl, I made a spare.')

After the bowling, Ian and Nicole Bedford entertained forty Miss World contestants and a number of other guests—myself included—at another party given in their private apartments at Woburn Abbey.

True, the forty young women were very beautiful and charming.

True also that I enjoy being in the company of very beautiful and charming young women (what man of any age doesn't?).

However, it is *not* true (and all the worse for me) that—as variously rumoured or reported—Miss Austria or Miss Belgium or Miss Canada or any other Miss through the alphabetical index of countries represented became my girlfriend.

Having gone this far, I might as well proceed deeper into the nitty-gritty of Getty mythology.

38

ACCORDING TO WHAT appears to be a consensus of newspaper and magazine writers' verdicts, I am a recluse.

And, by the same consensus, I am lonely.

If one were to believe what is published so freely, I live a hermit-like existence at Sutton Place. To quote from a recent magazine article:

'There is an aura of sadness about J. Paul Getty, the American-born oil tycoon who is estimated to be worth more than £500,000,000.

'He lives alone . . . sadness and loneliness dominating his declining years. His wealth has brought him . . . solitude.'

Fascinating.

And howlingly funny.

I make no further comment. Instead, I offer some samplings from my appointment book and my diary for different periods during 1975. They are hardly untypical.

The appointment book first:

June 23:
A.M.—Confer with Norris Bramlett.

P.M.—Conference with Harold Berg, Executive Vice President and Chief Operating Officer and Sidney R. Peterson, Group Vice President, Refining Distribution and Finance (both of Getty Oil Co.).

June 24:
A.M.—Meeting with Jack Denton, President Chemplex Co.

P.M.—Continue with Denton until 4:00 p.m.

6:30 P.M.—to London for Reception at Japanese Embassy.

June 25:

A.M.—Discussion with David Rinne about Getty Museum.

P.M.—London; business.

June 26:

Conference with Fraser McKno re: Getty Oil business.

Conference with Paul Louis Weiller re: business.

8:00 P.M.—Dinner party (at Sutton Place) for The Hon. Elliott Richardson, U.S. Ambassador to the Court of St. James.

June 27 (Saturday):

Tea (at Sutton Place) for Sheikh Fahd Al-Khayyal, Sheikh Khadr Herzallah, Mr. and Mrs. Zayyed and other guests.

July 1:

Meeting of executive committee, Neutral Zone.

Dinner party (at Sutton Place) for H.E., the Saudi Arabian Ambassador, his wife, and the executive committee. Total number of guests: 18.

July 2:

Meeting and tea, members of Journey for Perspective (20 guests). Cocktails for representatives of the World Wildlife Fund.

I might add that these entries tell only part of the story. On each of the days, I also took and made numerous telephone calls—mainly long-distance and overseas. I read and answered telexes and letters. I conferred with my aides who are permanently based at Sutton. And, I managed to have a few chats with personal friends and squeeze in a bit of social life, too.

Now for the diary entries—also from 1975.

'September 10: Ursula d'Abo drove me to the Department of Energy for a Government meeting on North Sea participation. The meeting started at 2:30. Clarence Tuck represented the Government with three assistants and a stenographer. There were about a dozen men in our group. McCabe* and Woodson arrived. McCabe sat next to me. Meeting was very constructive and ended at 4 o'clock, Ursula drove me back to Sutton Place. Too busy to take my walk today and yesterday as McKno and McCabe here, and we talk business far into the night. Teresa, my pet lioness, gave birth to four cubs this morning.**

'September 11: Ursula drove me to Claridges after McCabe had said goodbye to fly TWA to Los Angeles. Arrived at Claridges at 1 p.m.—on time. Was shown to the suite of Prince Bernhardt (of the Netherlands). I had lunch with him. We talked of World Wildlife Fund and other conservation matters: He told me many interesting facts about his life. *Daily Telegraph* reporter and photographer paid us a short visit—with the Prince's permission and mine, of course. The Prince walked with me to the car. I introduced Ursula to him. She drove me back to Sutton. I worked on my mail. Dr. MacKenzie came. He examined me and said I was completely healthy.'

'September 12: Gail Getty (Paul Jr.'s ex-wife) and the three children—Aileen, Ariadne and Mark—here. Always a delight to see my grandchildren. Mary Tessier also visiting.'

'October 8: Driven to London at 8 a.m. to North Sea Operating Meeting at the Carlton Tower Hotel. Jerry Williams brought us up to date on North Sea developments and then we considered the budget, much increased due to inflation. Left at 4 p.m. . . .'

'October 9: To London, arriving at 10:50 for the Government meeting on participation in the North Sea. I was the first to arrive and had barely sat down when Mr. Tuck, the chief Government representative, arrived. We had a conversation about North Sea matters while waiting for the others to arrive. They came at 11. Nine men represented our group. The government had four. Mr. Tuck is a very able negotiator. At the same time, he seemed to be fair. The meeting ended at 12:30,

---

* John P. McCabe, vice president and general manager, international exploration and production division, and W. K. Woodson, Corporate Tax Manager, Getty Oil.
** Mr. Getty has a lion, Nero, and the lioness, Teresa, on the grounds at Sutton Place. They are kept in a huge, fenced enclosure.

and I thought it had gone well. Then to David Carritt's office where Mr. Herzer was waiting. We went to a nearby picture dealer's where a bronze statue was covered with a black cloth.

'He unveiled the statue, and I gazed at it with interest, having heard so much about it . . . it is a fine work of art. Ursula liked the statue. She drove me to the Ritz where we picked up Countess Waldner and drove to Ken. Square for lunch. When I returned to Sutton, I found a confidential message waiting for me from Jack Connor, head of Allied Chemical . . .'

'October 10: Had chat with Tom Smith. Joan St. Leger called at 10 a.m., and I invited her to lunch at Sutton tomorrow. Discussed the company's exploration with McCabe and Al Wallace. McCabe left for Los Angeles. He will be back in about ten days. I told him he should get a pilot's license and travel free. Neil Sellin and another man visited me after lunch. I phoned the Saudi Arabian Ambassador . . . he said Prince Mohammed is in London. Walked with Penelope to see the lions and the Rose Garden and then with Pen, Ursula—and four of the dogs—to the Birches and back.'

'October 11: Lunch with Jackie; Ursula; Aileen; her Italian girlfriend; Miss O'Brien (who came with Jackie); Joan St. Leger; Marion; and Tom Smith. Worked on the mail. Penelope here for tea and dinner. English Speaking Union Meeting in the Great Hall and Long Gallery 7:30–10:00 p.m. There were about 160 people.'

'October 23: Lunched in the house. McCabe came after lunch, straight from the airport, having flown in from L.A. We discussed various business matters. At eight I took Ursula d'Abo and Tom Smith to the Saudi Embassy dinner in honor of Wedgewood Benn. Met Mr. Benn. Talked to McFadzean, head of Shell. He would like to sell some big tankers. I sat between Mrs. Trapps, the French wife of a Conservative M.P. and McFadzean's daughter, a very pretty girl. At 11:30 everybody exited and we returned to Ken Square. A very pleasant evening.'

'October 24: Phoned Frances Scarr. She will be here Tuesday evening for dinner with a girlfriend. Always look forward to seeing Frances; she is a very dear friend. Spoke with Tom about business. Mary Maginnis arrived for lunch. She is a thoroughly nice person and very dedicated. She got along very well with Ursula. Henry d'Abo arrived for a visit.'

'October 25: Mary Maginnis had to leave. She is returning to Malibu. Sorry to see her go. Tom left for London. Worked with reports and mail until late.'

'October 27: Lunch at S.P. with Mexican Ambassador, H.E. Senor and Senora Margain; Mr. Davenport, Mr. Scott, Carleton Smith and his son. We were nine for lunch—only three women. Walked with Rosabella Burch. Frances Scarr and her friend from Canada to dinner. Watched North Sea oil programme on TV.'

'October 30: McCabe and Williams left early for a meeting. Ursula, Rosabella Burch and Norris to lunch. Busy on business mail, so didn't go for a walk today.'

'November 1: Lee (my chauffeur) drove me to the American Embassy Residence in Regent's Park for lunch with Ambassador Richardson, Carleton Smith and a friend of the Ambassador.'

'November 2 (Sunday): Penelope and her daughter Juliet, Henry, Rosabella, Ursula, Norris, Carleton Smith and his son, Aileen and a friend for lunch. C. Y. Tung and a group of 15 came for tea. Watched *Upstairs, Downstairs* at 7:55. The episode was concerned with the General Strike in 1926. Went to bed early—about 9:30—but read until almost one a.m.'

'November 4: Long business discussions with Norris. Dictated another chapter of *As I See It* to Joan Zetka and revised and corrected transcripts she had typed of my dictation on previous chapter. Worked on correspondence with Barbara Wallace and Elaine Mellish. Marianne von Alvensleben arrived from Düsseldorf . . .'

I do not think for a moment that I have to present any case for the defence. However, if I did, I would say that the defence now rests.

Stating it in the bluntest English possible, if I am—as the press would have it—a recluse, then I damned well get out and around one hell of a lot more than any 'recluse' in history. If I am 'lonely,' then I am the luckiest lonely human being on the face of the earth, for I am surrounded by dear friends and loyal business associates. If I 'live alone', then the people who come to Sutton Place, often staying for weeks, must be figments of my imagination—or, more accurately, the suggestion that they are NOT there is the product of some extremely warped imaginations.

But then, the idea that people who are reputedly wealthy must necessarily be miserable seems to gladden countless hearts. I imagine certain writers and editors assume that ten million readers will feel better about the problems they're having with their mortgage payments or with their mothers-in-law if they're told that 'millionaire Paul Getty is a sad, lonely recluse.'

Perhaps it's as New York advertising executive Robert C. Binnig has shrewdly observed:

'Average people may envy the rich, but they really can't bring themselves to hate the rich. The reason is that most average people harbour hopes of becoming wealthy themselves someday. But they have to compensate for their feelings of envy. They like to think that wealthy people are unhappy and that one should feel sorry for them. It's a way of assuring themselves that "if it were *my* fortune, I'd really do better, get more fun and pleasure out of *my* money." '

If adman Binnig is right—and it's more than merely possible that he is—I have no objections at all to helping other people be happier by letting them think that I'm a lonely, *un*happy recluse. But I still consider that particular portrait of myself howlingly funny.

39

Had I succumbed to exhortations to provide chapter-headings for the chapters in this book, I would be sorely tempted to entitle the present one:

VARIATIONS ON THE THEME OF MY VENALITY

God and the reading public alone know how many virtuoso renditions there have been. I, personally, have lost all count and track of most, but some are deeply ingrained in my memory, thanks to those who find them perennial favourites, worthy of eternal repetition.

They are, indeed, classics. I find them highly entertaining—in the sense that I derive no little amusement from the compositions or the constructions placed on them.

Among the more familiar of the tales that pop into mind concerns my ten-shilling city-block circumnavigation. The story has been attributed to at least six of my friends or acquaintances (the attributions in most cases being entirely gratuitous).

Date, place, circumstances and other details differ according to the version (or attribution), but here is the gist:

I had invited a friend to attend—take your choice—a dog show/art exhibition/rare book display/the Chelsea Flower Show. We arrived at the ticket-office at 5:50 p.m. A sign hanging prominently in the ticket-office window announced that admission prices were lowered 50 per cent—or by five shillings a ticket—at 6:00 p.m. In other words, a ten-minute wait would save ten shillings in the admission price for two people (my guest and I).

Accounts of the incident continue with whoever is purportedly narrating the yarn saying something to this effect:

'Paul turned away from the window. He told me we might as well take a walk around the block until the admission price went down. And we did, for ten minutes—just to save ten shillings!'

The intended purpose is, of course, to demonstrate the frugal (or, as some commentators prefer to categorize it, the miserly) side of my nature.

I herewith cheerfully confess that the essence of the anecdote is wholly accurate. I make no apologies for my reasoning in the situation. If I have ample time on my hands, the weather is clement and a ten-minute stroll will save ten shillings—well, why not wait and save the money?

Would YOU not be inclined to think (and do) the same?

Let's examine the operative fundamentals of the proposition from another angle. How many times in your life have you bought—as an example—a household appliance for, say, £50, only to see the identical item featured 'ON SALE' two days later for £29·95?

I'm willing to wager that something of the sort has happened to everyone reading these words. I'm willing to wager further that the experience made every individual feel foolish at very minimum. And, while there is a very considerable difference between ten shillings and £20·05, the principle remains the same. No one in his right mind wants to *over*pay for anything, especially not when clearly forewarned (as I was by the sign in the ticket-seller's window).

Next on my list of all time favourite classics is the Sensational Saga (or Scandal) of the Sutton Place coin-box telephone. My sense of the surreal is tickled whenever I think how much newsprint has been used in the endless re-telling of how 'tightfisted oil tycoon J. Paul Getty had a coin-box telephone installed in his palatial mansion.'

Now *there's* a story to warm the hearts of all who take orgiastic delight in picturing the rich as inhospitable, ungracious penny-pinchers. I can't really bring myself to begrudge them their pleasure. I only (and somewhat wistfully) wish that someone, some time, would get a minimal few of the facts straight and then reshuffle them into reasonably proper order and perspective.

Yes.

A coin-box telephone *was* installed at Sutton Place. It was affixed to the wall of a smallish, but easily accessible, room on the ground floor of the house. A large (and, I'm afraid, garish and unsightly) enamelled metal sign bearing the legend PUBLIC TELEPHONE was even mounted on the outside of the door to the room.

Furthermore (and I don't believe the Press got wind of *this*), special dial-locking devices were placed on each of the half-dozen or more regular telephone instruments located in various parts of the house. Keys to these devices were given only to certain employees and members of the domestic staff (naturally, I had one myself). The locks—and the pay-telephone—were a feature at Sutton Place for a period of less than eighteen months. Then all were permanently removed.

These are the facts. As for the inferences that have been drawn, they are—to be charitable about it—well short of being accurate.

I am the first to grant that the whole pay-telephone tempest is minor and laughable. But it does illustrate in microcosm how quick and ready some sources are to misinterpret the motivations and actions of any and all people who have been labelled 'rich.' Propagators of the telephone tale conveniently avoided asking anyone at Sutton for reasons or explanations. Anyone there—myself included—would have been glad to furnish the factual data. Among them:

1. *I* do not personally own Sutton Place. It is owned by a company which is a wholly-owned subsidiary of the Getty Oil Co. Thus, it really belongs to Getty Oil's shareholders.

2. Now, for months after Sutton Place was purchased, great numbers of people came in and out of the house. Some were visiting businessmen. Others were artisans or workmen engaged in renovation and refurbishing. Still others were tradesmen making deliveries of merchandise.

3. Suddenly, the Sutton Place telephone bills began to soar. The reason was obvious. Each of the regular telephones in the house had direct access to outside lines and thus to long-distance and even overseas operators. All sorts of people were making the best of a rare opportunity. They were picking up

Sutton Place phones and placing calls to girlfriends in Geneva or Georgia and to aunts, uncles and third cousins twice-removed in Caracas and Capetown. The costs of their friendly chats were, of course, charged to the Sutton Place bill. (One such call, for example, ran to £101, and there were large numbers in the £10 to £50 range.)

Albert Thurgood, the estate manager—among whose innumerable tasks it is to keep track of expenses—brought the matter and the staggering bills to my attention. He, the Sutton Property Co. directors and I decided there was only one solution (short of hiring round-the-clock phone-watchers to guard every instrument in the house). Dial-locks were placed on the regular telephones, thereby limiting their use to authorized personnel, and the World's Most Famous Coin-Box Telephone was installed for use by others.

Later, the in-and-out traffic flow at Sutton subsided. Management and operation of the house settled into a reasonable routine. With that, the pay-telephone (and the enamelled metal sign) were removed, and the dial-locks were taken off the telephones in the house.

But the story refuses to die. Sutton Place is open to public viewing several times each year. These events are held under the auspices of charities and similar organizations which charge modest admission prices, the monies collected being used by them for their activities. As a result, thousands of people 'go through' the manor house annually. According to the guides and security men on duty during these occasions, no less than one out of every ten visitors gives only cursory looks at the fine art and antique furniture on display and demands to see 'the coin-box telephone.'

It is a popular superstition that all wealthy people are parsimonious—even niggardly—tippers.

It is sheer conjecture on my part, but I think the roots of this wild and in no way valid generalization go back to the days when publicist Ivy Lee set out to 'improve' John D. Rockefeller Sr.'s public image. Lee hit upon the idea of having John D. Sr. carry rolls of shiny new dimes—ten-cent pieces—with him wherever he went and hand the coins out as souvenirs to all and sundry.

At first, it worked very well. People accepted the dimes and kept them as cherished mementos of their meetings—or merely casual encounters—with John D. Rockefeller Sr. Then, a sort of backlash set in—inspired and encouraged, no doubt, by professional Rockefeller baiters (or haters). Instead of being viewed as a good-natured public relations ploy, John D. Sr.'s wholesale distribution of dimes came under heavy fire as a glaring example of a rich man's miserliness.

'With all his millions, he tries to buy friends with lousy dimes!' caustic critics berated Rockefeller.

According to legend, an ambitious young assistant in Ivy Lee's office brightly suggested that instead of ten-cent coins, John D. Sr. hand out ten-dollar bills. Lee, it is said, thereupon calculated the number of dimes that Rockefeller gave out in an average month.

'Sonny, if he gave away ten bucks instead of ten cents at the same rate, John D. would be flat broke in exactly seventeen months,' Lee told his aide.

In any event, the dimes-giveaway campaign ended—but the myth of the millionaire trying to 'buy friends' for ten cents endured and spread.

During more recent years, it was often rumoured that Aristotle Onassis was a 'lousy tipper.' In actual fact, Ari tipped very generously—unless he received poor service, when he was liable to leave no tip at all and explain—in no uncertain terms—why he had failed to do so.

It was also bandied about that another of my good friends, Nubar Gulbenkian, never left more than a two-shilling tip, no matter how large his bill in a hotel, restaurant or nightclub. Any such claim would be a slander on Nubar's memory, were it not for the fact that he had his own—and great—sense of humour. (Remember, Nubar bought a London taxicab to use while driving around London and always wore a huge, flamboyant orchid in his buttonhole.)

The two-shilling tip was one of Gulbenkian's standing (or running) gags. A magnanimous host, he would invite a large group of friends to dinner or to a nightclub. His bill for the evening often ran into hundreds of pounds. After settling up the bill, he would ostentatiously place two shillings on the table.

'All for you,' Nubar would say to the waiter—or *maître*.

Those not acquainted with Gulbenkian were likely to gape in embarrassment or even horror. His friends would laugh, knowing that Nubar invariably left his real tip later, when no one could see. Of course, the legend lived, and will probably continue to live as long as Nubar Gulbenkian is remembered.

Which brings me to my own tipping habits (about which there have been many tales—and fables). My tipping patterns are what I, at least, consider more or less average. Most restaurants, hotels and nightclubs I have patronized in the last twenty-five years or so automatically add a 'service charge' of between ten and eighteen per cent to the total of their bills.

Generally speaking, I leave an additional amount equal to half or perhaps two-thirds of the service charge. Naturally, if the service has been exceptionally good or my guests or I have made extraordinary demands on waiters or staff-members, I leave more.

All the same, it's as I wrote in a magazine article in 1958:

'A man labelled a "billionaire" lives well and he's very lucky to enjoy innumerable privileges and comforts—but he really can't win. If he spends freely, he's accused of being a wastrel and of trying to make an impression by splashing money around. If he lives quietly and without flashy ostentation, he's castigated for being penurious—a "tightwad."

'Even the simple, everyday matter of tipping can become a major problem. If I tip well, someone is certain to accuse me of showing off. If I don't over-tip, that same someone will be the first to sneer that I am a penny-pincher.

'All this tends to make a man extremely cautious and more than a little sceptical. Money is a wonderful commodity to have, but the more one possesses, the more involved and complicated become his dealings and relationships with people.'

The involvements and complications even rub off to cause problems and annoyances for the people with whom one has relationships.

A number of years ago, an American writer-friend interviewed me over dinner at an exclusive London restaurant. When the bill arrived, he insisted on paying it. This was reported to the press—by, I suspect, the waiter who probably received some gratuity for passing on the story. The incident was considered of sufficient importance for *Newsweek* Magazine to have one of its chief correspondents interview the writer, who was asked if I had 'stuck' him with the bill.

'Hell, no!' my friend replied. 'I snatched it. It gave me a huge kick to grab the tab from a guy who's supposed to be the richest man in the world.'

Newsweek reported his reply accurately, and when I read the item, I chuckled. Then, as the years passed, accounts of the incident were apparently filtered through whole series of distortion lenses and I occasionally read:

'Billionaire J. Paul Getty makes writers who interview him pay for his meals at swank restaurants . . .'

Withal, I am careful about money. I was brought up in an era when thrift was still considered a virtue. The ten per cent down payment, credit card and the buy-now-pay-in-the-hereafter concept were all unknown. People lived within their means, saved for rainy days—and swallowed no tranquilizers and had far fewer ulcers.

I must confess that I did go through a profligate period in my life, spending—to use the popular idiom—as though money was on the verge of going out of fashion. For instance, I allowed myself to be bitten—and deeply—by the yacht-owning bug. I began in the 1920s by buying the 102-foot *Sobre las Olas*. Then I traded up, first to the 160-foot *Jezebel* and then to the 1,500-ton, 260-foot *Warrior*.

My yachts were, I suppose, outstanding status-symbols—to say nothing of serving as fabulously popular social, athletic—and drinking—clubs for the most variegated assortment of people (some friends, more of them professional freeloaders). I certainly never encountered the slightest difficulty in finding guests (invited or otherwise) to join me aboard them.

One day, I woke up. I realized that because business prevented me from going on long, leisurely cruises, the pro-rated cost of spending a single day aboard the *Warrior* worked out to several thousand dollars. (The *Warrior* had a fulltime crew of forty.) As my accountants pointed out, I could charter an ocean-going liner for less money per day. In 1936, I sold the *Warrior* to a French newspaper publisher. There have been no more yachts in my life since.

Automobiles were another of my weaknesses in my younger days. After I made my first million dollars, my automobiles were usually—although not always—luxurious, expensive makes. And there was, I fear, a stage when I believed it a MUST to trade in my car the moment a new model came on the market, no matter how little I had used the one I already owned. That stage, too, passed.

Today, I have two Cadillacs. One is a 1967 model, the other a 1960 model. The latter, purchased new fifteen years ago, has less than 30,000 miles on the speedometer—and is good for at least as many more. Both automobiles look like new and run perfectly. What advantage would I gain by trading in either of them?

I've said earlier that I enjoy (and love) comfort and luxury. But—and let these be my last words on the score—I do not need to overspend or be wildly extravagant in order to bolster my ego or prove anything to the world. I would far rather spend $17 million on a public museum than a like sum on the finest yacht afloat. A new, fully-equipped Cadillac would cost close to $10,000. Allowing for trade-in values, I most certainly would have spent $100,000 over the last fifteen years, buying two new cars annually.

That $100,000 can be put to far better use. It is the same sum as is represented by the two $50,000 prizes I have made available to the World Wildife Fund. The Fund's jury—headed by H.R.H. the Prince of the Netherlands—awards the prizes to individuals who have made outstanding contributions to the cause of wildlife conservation. (In 1974, the $50,000 prize went to Señor Felipe Benavides, President of PRODENA, the World Wildlife Fund of Peru.) Señor Benavides deserves the award infinitely more than I need (or deserve) five new Cadillacs.

Those who wish to call (or consider) me frugal, parsimonious—or even miserly—are welcome to do so. Nothing they can say will alter my personal spending patterns. I long ago outgrew the neon-lighted suit worn by those who believe they should make a great show of wasting money for no other reason than to demonstrate that they can afford to be wastrels.

40

It is 10:30 p.m., Thursday, November 27, 1975.
Thanksgiving Day, 1975.

I am alone in my study, the door closed. Bullimore has built a magnificent log fire in the fireplace for me because he knows I intend spending an hour or two making notes for the chapter I will dictate tomorrow morning.

But I have put my notes aside. It is Thanksgiving Day, and my mood is one of reflection and introspection.

What if I break the thread of my narrative and simply record the free-flow of my thoughts?

Will the reader tolerate it?

I wonder.

It is worth a try.

I turn to my diaries and select the earliest of them—the one I kept in 1904, when I was not yet twelve. Thanksgiving Day is traditionally celebrated on the fourth Thursday in November. In 1904 that was November 24. I find my entry for the day:

'Very fine day for Thanksgiving. I had a dinner, I tell you . . .'

A diary works the magic of transforming the past into the present. Although these are words I wrote seventy-one years ago, I can recall that dinner in Minneapolis as clearly as if I had eaten it only hours ago.

Roast turkey, stuffing, mashed potatoes, creamed onions, cranberry sauce, pumpkin pie . . .

My mouth waters.

I see my mother's face and hear her voice. My father is at the head of the table. He is laughing as I ask for my third helping of turkey. My mother smiles and warns me that I won't be able to do justice to the pumpkin pie later . . .

I read further.

> 'November 25: Fine day. In the morning Mama and I went driving. In the afternoon I played and read. In the evening I played with Mama and read an Abbott book, *Richard I*. It was a good story.'
>
> 'November 26: Fine day. In the morning I went down town with Mama. I got a new suit. In the afternoon Mama and I went to the Metropolitan Theater. The play was: *The Billionaire*.'

Odd, I think, staring into the fire for a moment. The play left no impression on me. Perhaps it is odder still, but the fact that now—more than seven decades later—I am called a billionaire doesn't impress me very much either. For some reason, I reach for my current diary and read the entry I made only yesterday—November 26, 1975:

> 'To Lord Thomson's lunch for the Prime Minister. I said hello to Mr. Harold Wilson, who was seated on Roy Thomson's right. Lord Gibson was on his left, and I was next to Lord Gibson. There were 22 for lunch, and the top management of British Industry were well represented. At the end of the lunch Mr. Wilson remained seated and spoke informally for about twenty minutes explaining his policy and the situation as he saw it. It was all very friendly in spite of the political difference between the views of the guests (which I imagine was strongly Conservative) and Mr. Wilson's political views. I thought Mr. Wilson handled himself very well.'

I have not yet made my diary entry for today, November 27—Thanksgiving Day—1975. What shall I say? It is a very,

very long way—in both time and distance—from Minneapolis, Minnesota, U.S.A. I am in England. The English do not celebrate Thanksgiving. I had forgotten—could it have been by unconscious purpose?—to remind the domestic staff of the holiday. As a result, instead of turkey and trimmings, I had a superb roast beef prepared by Kathy Aipli, the nonpareil Sutton Place cook.

American friends residing in London had invited me to have a 'real' Thanksgiving dinner with them. I was reluctantly forced to refuse their invitation—for the same reason that I have (or have not) done so many things in life. Business required me to stay at Sutton for the day.

There were compensations, though. Dear friends like Beverley Stoop and Jeanette Constable-Maxwell thought to telephone me. Norris Bramlett and I had a chance to talk about old times together for a while in the afternoon—however, this caused me to feel a twinge of conscience. Norris's home is in California. His patient and loving wife, Muriel, is there. How many holidays (and months at a time) has Norris spent away from home on Getty Oil business?

The 1904 diary seems to have an unusual fascination for me this evening. I re-read the November 26 entry which records that my mother and I went to see a play called 'The Billionaire.'

The Billionaire.

I am aware that I lay myself open to snorts of disbelief and derisive jeers when I say that I was never very much interested in making a great deal of money. I harboured no desire to be the world's richest man, not at any time in my life.

Shall I dictate that as the opening statement of the chapter I will have drafted tomorrow?

No, I'll let it stand—as it is—in the free-wheeling notes that I am scrawling on the pad in my lap.

Should I continue making the notes, I ask myself—and an affirmative answer forms in my mind. I have gone this far on this particular bypath. There is no reason why I should not go further and see where it leads. It may well be that I will learn something from it myself.

I made my first million dollars quickly—almost overnight, it seems in retrospect—but I have already related that. I was stunned at the realization that I had so much. I believed it was all the money I could ever use or need, and I stopped working entirely.

I can face myself squarely in the privacy of my study late on a Thanksgiving evening and say that it was not greed or any desire for more money that caused me to come out of retirement at the age of 26 and begin working again. I look back over the years and search my memory—and my conscience—for the reasons that motivated me. I recall the elements as clearly as I recalled the Thanksgiving dinner of 1904. I was bored with doing nothing but having one good time after another. The challenge inherent in the search for oil was another powerful factor. Last—but, as I reflect, I realize far from least—was the sense of responsibility I felt toward my father and the business he had created and built.

What followed was a constant source of astonishment to me. Year after year, no matter how much experience I gained, regardless of how seasoned I became as a businessman, I found it difficult—if not impossible—to believe that my wealth continued to increase. There is only one explanation for the phenomenon that I am able to accept. It is the one Max Aitken, Lord Beaverbrook, gave for his own success. I, too, had a reserved seat in life.

Even so, I hardly 'did' it by myself. It is less than likely that I could have held the reserved seat had it not been for the loyalty and devotion of men like Fero Williams, Harold Rowland, Emil Kluth, H. P. Grimm, David Hecht, David Staples, H. M. Macomber, Tommy Milburn, Steven Cavanaugh and so many others.

If I can claim personal credit for having made the best of my advantages, it is by likening myself to a tennis player. Once into the game, I did my damndest to be competitive. I always sought to return the ball—no matter from which direction or with what velocity it came into my side of the court.

Nostalgia often leads to idle speculation.

It is doubtful if I would have chosen a business career had I not been an only child and only son. Even today, I am firmly convinced that if I'd had a brother—or brothers—I would have stepped aside and let him (or them) enter my father's oil business. Then I would have almost certainly realized one or another of my youthful ambitions—to enter the U.S. Diplomatic Service, become a writer or to attend Annapolis and serve as an officer in the Navy.

Would I have achieved any degree of success in any of the three career-fields?

The question is moot, unanswerable. I suppose it is fair for me to think that I would have devoted as much energy to any other career as I have to business. It is pleasant to flatter myself and believe that hard work, concentration of effort and determination would have enabled me to achieve at least modest success in any of the fields.

I will work from these notes tomorrow. The chapter I had originally intended to dictate can wait until another day, for I find myself going off on a tangent that is not really a tangent at all.

There is no more fitting time than Thanksgiving Day for me to tell myself—and the world at large—how grateful I am for the countless blessings I have received in life.

Yes, of course, wealth is among them—but not as wealth, *per se*.

It is impossible for me ever to forget my father's words: 'It's not how much money a man has, it's what he does with it that counts.'

George F. Getty Sr.'s credo was that money should be used, put to work in business enterprises that produced goods and services, provided gainful employment for others and contributed to the progress and welfare of society. He lived and laboured by that credo. I am into my eighth decade of life. I can only hope that I have lived up to his example. I have tried to do so.

On May 30, 1975, I learned that Standard and Poor had upgraded the Getty Oil Company's credit rating to AAA. The prestigious financial service issued a statement declaring that this was due to Getty Oil's 'overwhelming financial strength, professional management team, strong domestic crude position and conservative philosophy.'

Every Getty Oil Co. executive and employee at every level played an important role to make the company deserving of this high endorsement. It is obviously impossible for me to name every one of the 12,000 men and women on Getty Oil

Co. payrolls who have done—and are doing—their part and more to insure the company's strength and success.

I will, however, on this Thanksgiving Day, express my gratitude to the company's officers and the members of its board of directors. By naming them I am—by extension—paying tribute to all the men and women who work for the Getty Oil Company.

The Executive Officers are:

Harold E. Berg, Executive Vice President and Chief Operating Officer

J. Earle Gray, Group Vice President, Natural Resources

Sidney R. Peterson, Group Vice President, Refining, Distribution and Finance

Paul E. Carlton, Vice President, Exploration and Production, Corporate Natural Resources

Ralph D. Copley Jr., Vice President, Chief Counsel and Corporate Secretary

Stuart W. Evey, Vice President, Corporate Administration

Jack D. Jones, Vice President, Manufacturing and Marketing

John P. McCabe, Vice President and General Manager, International Exploration and Production Division

Edward H. Shuler, Vice President and General Manager, California Exploration and Production Division

George H. Turran, Vice President and General Manager, Mid-Continent Exploration and Production Division

Bill E. Williams, Vice President and General Manager, International Supply and Transportation Division

Duane A. Bland, Controller

Hugh M. Slawson, Treasurer

These are the men about whom *Forbes* Magazine said:

'Getty's executives are a tight, closemouthed band of longtime employees who toil energetically and anonymously . . . there is a strong sense of loyalty and the close team feeling of "it's Getty challenging the big oil giants." '

The Members of the Board of Directors are listed below (I have omitted the titles of those who are also officers of the company):

Harold E. Berg

Willard S. Boothby Jr., Chairman of the Board and Chief Executive Officer, Blyth Eastman Dillon & Co., Incorporated, investment bankers.

J. Earle Gray

C. Lansing Hays Jr., Partner, Hays, Landsman & Head, attorneys at law.

Frederick G. Larkin Jr., Chairman of the Board and Chief Executive Officer, Security Pacific Corporation and Security Pacific National Bank, commercial bank.

Chauncey J. Medberry III, Chairman of the Board, Bankamerica Corporation and Bank of America NT&SA, commercial bank.

Sidney R. Peterson

John M. Schiff, General Partner, Kuhn, Loeb & Co., investment bankers.

Joseph A. Thomas, Managing Director, Lehman Brothers, investment bankers.

Dr. Norman Topping, Chancellor, University of Southern California, educational institution.

I, of course, am the president of Getty Oil and also one of the company's directors. But with executives and board members of such calibre and long proven ability as these, I imagine I could—if I chose—hang up a GONE FISHING sign and never have a moment's worry.

There have been occasions in my life when I wished I could do just that—hang up a sign and wander off on my own, leaving business far behind me.

Why haven't I?

Possibly it was because of a sense of responsibility, or a desire to insure personally that the continuity of what my father began is maintained. Or is it because, as I once noted in my diary, I kept—and still keep—on working out of force of habit?

Whatever the answer, I have no regrets over my choices and decisions. I pride myself on being a realist. If naught else, it is far too late for me to have any regrets.

I cannot help but think that while there is much—very much—that money can buy or make possible, there are not enough millions in the world to make every wish and desire come true.

In no manner do I lessen my gratitude to fate for my good fortune when I realize there are still many things I wish I could have done, was unable to do and may never be able to do.

I have travelled a great deal in my lifetime, yet not enough to satisfy my craving to go, see, observe, experience at firsthand. I am sorry that I have never been able to visit India and see that country's famed temples and plains. I've always wanted to tour Persia—Iran; the only glimpse I have had of that country was from Basra, Iraq, across the mouth of the Euphrates. Another unfulfilled desire has been to go on a *camera*-safari to Africa. (I emphasize the word 'camera' because I could never bring myself to hunt, to kill any animal.)

Although I have always been a voracious reader, there are still hundreds—even thousands—of books that I would love to read, but have not found time to read.

There are innumerable people whose companionship has stimulated me, but I did not have the time to cultivate their friendship—or cultivate it to the extent that I would have wished.

I have long held hopes . . .

No.

The logs in the fireplace have burned down. It is almost midnight on this Thanksgiving Day, 1975. It is not a time to wish that this or that might have been different. Rather, it is a time to be grateful. And I am, for I have an infinite number of things for which to give thanks.

I mix myself a nightcap, a mild Meyer's rum and Coca-Cola, and sip it.

I am alone, but I exclaim aloud in astonishment. The familiar flavour of the dark rum and Coke is somehow momentarily transmuted into one of roast turkey and cranberry sauce. Another sip and all is back to normal. My taste-buds—and I—have overcome nostalgia. When I go upstairs to my bedroom, my thoughts are on the work I will have to do tomorrow.

41

VICE PRESIDENT NELSON A. ROCKEFELLER did me the honour of saying that my entrepreneurial success in the oil business put me on a par with his grandfather, John D. Rockefeller Sr.

My comment was that comparing me to John D. Sr. was like comparing a sparrow to an eagle. My words were not inspired by modesty, but by facts.

John D. Rockefeller began life poor. He began work as a lowly-paid bookkeeper—and worked (and fought) his way up the ladder. I enjoyed the advantage of being born into an already-wealthy family, and when I began my business career I was subsidized by my father. While I did make money—and quite a bit of it—on my own, I doubt if there would be a 'Getty Empire' today if I had not taken over my father's thriving oil business after his death.

Therefore, if there is any comparison to be made between me and any members of the Rockefeller family, I suppose it would be more accurate to use Nelson and his brothers as examples. Although they are the grandsons, rather than the sons, of the Rockefeller Dynasty's founder, they—like me—have built their careers on the solid foundations of established and inherited wealth.

It is, I think, interesting to note the different paths that John D. Sr.'s grandsons have chosen. Nelson entered politics. Although frequently misunderstood and maligned, he is a practical, soundly conservative individual of great ability. At this writing, the political winds in America are shifting and swirling. No one can possibly predict what patterns and directions they will take in November, 1976, but it is not impossible that he might even become America's next Chief Executive.

I have done considerable business with David Rockefeller—as I have mentioned before. Aggressive, imaginative, David has certainly inherited his grandfather's entrepreneurial genius. It is always a pleasure to deal with David—but I would not like to be a person who tried to hoodwink him.

Although I met Winthrop a number of times, I never came to know him very well. However, his wife Bobo and I were—and are—very good friends, and thereby hangs a mildly amusing story. Some years ago, Bobo and I were in Rome, and I invited her to dinner.

A friend of mine came into the Via Veneto restaurant where Bobo and I were dining together with a boy of twelve or thirteen. The friend stopped by our table. He didn't know Bobo or the boy, and I made the introductions: 'Mrs. Rockefeller and Cornelius Vanderbilt Whitney.'

My friend—I omit his name to save him embarrassment—gave me a snide look and acknowledged the introductions. Then he went on his way. I met him accidentally—again on the Via Veneto—a few days later. His attitude was hostile.

'What kind of sucker do you take me for?' he demanded. 'And since when have you started putting on the dog and giving people high-faluting names?'

When I assured him that he had, indeed, met Bobo Rockefeller and young Cornelius Vanderbilt Whitney, my friend's jaw dropped so far I was afraid he might dislocate it.

John D. Rockefeller 3rd and his captivating wife Blanchette are my good friends, and they have been frequent guests at Sutton Place. They are a warm, cordial couple. Yet at times I experience an almost uncomfortable feeling with them because they are so unremittingly dedicated to good works. John D. 3rd is, of course, the oldest of the brothers and has a strong—and in my view, highly commendable—sense of Rockefeller Family tradition. There are many stories that he is 'aloof'. The truth is that he is a somewhat shy man—but the shyness evaporates immediately when he is among people he feels are friends.

Any attempt—by anyone—to compare the Rockefeller 'Empire' with the Getty 'Empire' is ridiculous. John D. Sr. went into the oil business at a time when America's petroleum industry was in chaos. Whatever his detractors may say of him, he brought order out of that chaos. Conventional interpretations of history damn the 'Standard Oil Trust (or Monopoly)' as a kind of Satanic cabal. Whatever its faults—and it had many—John D. Rockefeller Sr.'s 'monopolization' probably saved the U.S. oil industry from total disintegration.

The Rockefeller and Getty 'Empires' cannot be compared, they can only be cited as contrasts. For example, the Exxon Corp. (formerly Standard Oil of New Jersey) is just one part of the Rockefeller-controlled 'Standard Oil Monopoly' that was ordered broken up under Anti-Trust Laws early in this century. Today Exxon Corp. is the second largest U.S. company in terms of sales or revenues, topped only by the General Motors Corp. Its net *profits* in 1973 were almost double Getty Oil Co.'s total sales for the year ($2.4 billion versus $1.4 billion).

Nevertheless, I feel no qualms or reticence about likening the Getty Oil Company to an 'Empire'—and myself to a 'Caesar'.

In fact, I'm willing to go so far as to argue that Getty Oil is more of an 'Empire' than Exxon or a great many other oil companies far larger than Getty Oil. This is because there *is* a 'Getty'. That fact is known to and by every employee of Getty Oil, by every member of the 'Empire'. And every Getty Oil employee knows that he or she can always make a final and direct appeal to Caesar—to an individual named Getty who is not only the president of the company, but who also owns or controls the majority of the company's stock-shares.

What I'm seeking to make clear and underline is that the Getty Oil Company is not a faceless, impersonal corporation. Its ownership is not widely and thinly dispersed. The company is not operated by a self-perpetuating management, no member of which owns more than a tiny fraction of the company's stock.

I assure the writers of management manuals and the erudite professors in Business Schools that this keeps production and morale higher—and labour problems and turnover lower—than all the rousing pep-talks and 'incentive' frills in the world.

I have used the term 'Getty Empire' in order to emphasize my point. In day-to-day operative fact, all that I have said about Getty Oil and there actually being a 'Getty' at the top serves to make the company's executives and employees know they are part of a large, yet closely-knit, family.

And, as far as I am concerned—as *I* think and feel—they are just that.

They are part of the Getty Family.

Unfortunately—even tragically—for not only business but our society as a whole—the era of the company whose employees feel themselves to be participating members of a family is rapidly passing. Indeed, it has all but passed.

We are well into the Age of the Megacorp. This is the super-structured, organization-charted, computerized, committee-controlled corporation in which the individual is not a person but a Social Security Number. In many countries, the picture is bleaker still. Socialization sandwiches (and usually crushes) even the Megacorp between bureaucratic infrastructures and superstructures. The pressures these exert slow production to a hopeless crawl—and, worse, pulp the individual and his or her individuality into an unrecognizable blob.

Vide Italy.

I must make a few prefatory remarks before I proceed with my basic Italian theme, for one cannot simply appear to turn on an old and dearly beloved friend and attack him without some prior explanation.

Italy is a country I have long loved—and still love. I have spent much time and some of the happiest days of my life there—awed and dazzled and bewitched by Rome, Florence, Venice and other of its beautiful cities and by its magnificent countryside. And, as I have noted earlier, the Getty interests owned an oil company and refinery in Italy for several years.

Beyond this, I should add that my love of Italy has been great and deep enough for me personally to buy two houses (which I still own) there. A word or two about the houses to make my case even stronger.

In the mid-1960s, I purchased a largely ruined 55-room villa from Prince Ladislao Odescalchi. Generally known as the *'Posta Vecchia'*, the structure was located on the sea at Ladispoli, not far from Rome. It had a long and colourful history. Records indicated it had been built in the 1500s and that the great master, Raphael, had himself approved the architectural plans.

Renovation of the villa was estimated to take five years (and did). Preliminary work uncovered hidden art treasures, including a 4th-century mosaic floor that was in almost perfect condition. I hardly need say that restoration of the ancient villa, the installation of modern facilities and decoration and furnishing were extremely expensive. But I consider the costs—which I paid personally—justified. It has brought me much gratification to know that I saved and restored one of Italy's ancient and magnificent relics.

(The villa is made available on occasion to captains of the tankers and supertankers owned by the Getty interests and to Getty Oil Co. executives on holiday in Italy. Many of my personal friends also stay there when vacationing in that country.)

At about the same time that I bought it, I also bought a smaller, picturesque house at Gaiola from my friend Gianni Agnelli. Built on an island a short distance from the shore, it is situated near Gaeta, where the Italian refinery then owned by the Getty interests was located.

However, the Italian oil company and refinery were sold—and at a good profit—by the Getty interests before I got around to establishing an Italian residential base for myself at either Palo or Gaiola. (The latter house is unoccupied save when I lend it to friends for their use on Italian visits or vacations.)

Thus, while I have absolutely no business interests in Italy, I do own two houses there. And, I am forced to say that I'm glad I have no Italian business holdings. In fact, it is with immense relief that I think how the Getty interests sold Golfo—their Italian oil company—when they did.

Why?

Because Italy is a chilling, textbook example of what the future might hold for many other Western countries.

The Italian economy and business-system have moved into a murky No Man's Land that lies somewhere between the depersonalization of the Megacorp and the chimerical Utopia of socialism. There is still private enterprise in Italy—but it's fighting a losing battle. Under the Italian economic system, there are also ever-growing national monopolies and Megacorps that are freakish hybrids, *'parastatale'* organizations that are partially State, and partially privately owned.

Today, the Italian economic condition and outlook are the gloomiest and most discouraging of any on the European Continent. With the exception of the United Kingdom, Italy's rate of inflation is the highest among the Western democracies. Its unemployment rate continues to rise. The gap between its potential national production and actual output has widened to more than ten per cent.

'Italy is an economic basket-case,' a prominent—and coldly objective—international banking expert remarked recently. 'It is a question whether the patient will long survive.'

And, in the early 1950s, I rated Italy next after Germany as the best bet for business and investment in Europe!

What happened between then and now?

The causes of the Rise and Fall of the Italian Economy should be studied by businessmen, labour leaders, economists, politicians and ordinary citizens in every country that still retains any vestiges of a free enterprise system.

At first, Italy lived up to its promise. Its industry expanded, boomed. The country and its people became affluent—and affluence gradually produced fat, flab and complacency.

Italian businessmen enjoyed large profits—but did not reinvest enough of them in their businesses.

Italian workers found themselves enjoying greatly improved living standards. Bicycles were traded in on Vespa motor-scooters—and soon thereafter, the Vespas were traded in on Fiat automobiles. Whereupon, Italian unions decided their slice of the pizza-pie wasn't large enough—and began to demand more.

The Italian Government—when it wasn't dithering—sought to buy votes by meeting any and all demands made by workers and by embarking on Erehwonian social welfare schemes, paying for them either by borrowing or by pouring out rivers of printing press money. In the meantime, it increased the restrictive pressure on private enterprise and tightened the vise of the bureaucratic infra- and superstructure on the huge *parastatale* Megacorps.

Government deficits zoomed. Prices of consumer goods and services soared at an even faster rate. Militant unions demanded pay-rises and other concessions that outstripped price rises. When these were not granted instantly and in full, strikes and slowdowns cost the country millions of man-and-woman days of lost production. This led to higher production costs, lower exports—and increasing government deficits, which called for more overtime work by the printers operating the presses that spewed out paper money.

Businessmen were not without fault—not by any means. Thinking only of their own welfare, they not only failed to reinvest profits in their business enterprises but began shifting their money out of Italy. They thereby gave another hard kick at the wobbly props of the Italian economy.

Prices rose still higher.

There was even more bureaucratic meddling—and muddling.

The business bankruptcy rate shot up.

The number of strikes and slowdowns increased even further.

I would not like to be in business in Italy today. The economic landscape there is bleak.

The *parastatale* Megacorps are—to a frightening degree—directed by men who are bureaucrats and politicians, not businessmen. The Italian Government is—to equally frightening degree—managed by men who are businessmen rather than political leaders in the sense that they trade and deal for votes rather than governing with a view to resuscitating their national economy.

Legitimate, enterprising businessmen are hamstrung by often conflicting laws, rules, regulations, decrees and other bureaucratic obstacles.

Legitimate, clear-eyed Labour leaders cannot make their appeals to reason heard above the shouts of the wild-eyed, power-seeking Far Left agitators who are apparently hellbent on total destruction of the economy. (Presumably, they expect to pile the resulting rubble into a socialist paradise in which each and every citizen will be guaranteed an equal right to regimented semi-poverty.)

Legitimate, conscientious politicians are rendered powerless by their colleagues who play one side off against another—or play all sides to benefit their own middle.

All Italy—but especially the average Italian citizen and worker—loses. That citizen and worker is not considered an individual, a person, a human being worthy of consideration as such by bureaucratic executives, politics-playing labour agitators or labour-manipulating politicians (whether of Far Left or Far Right). He—or she—is a cipher or, at optimum, a robot to be programmed to provide gain or advantage for one or another side, group, faction or party.

The Italy I have so long loved—and still love—is an object lesson.

It is my earnest hope that the Decline of the Italian Economy can be arrested before the final Fall.

Yet the gloomy observers and commentators who have been watching the Italian drama cannot be blamed if they listen, braced, for the resounding crash. One can only pray that if the Fall does come, it will not set off a chain-reaction.

42

James Branch Cabell wrote:

'The optimist proclaims that we live in the best of all possible worlds; the pessimist fears this is so.'

Were I a Beethoven or a Hoagy Carmichael, I would set the words to music, and the product would be my theme song.

I enjoy a tremendous—and, actuarial figures being what they are, quite uncommon—advantage.

I can afford to say what I wish.

This rare and precious benefit does not accrue to me because of my wealth. It is the concomitant of having reached an age where it is no longer necessary to worry about other people's reactions to my words and what consequences those reactions might have on me. Four score and three years may not automatically confer wisdom, but they most certainly bestow a sense of independence and freedom.

Time being the acid—the only true—test of friendship, I have had more than ample opportunity to ascertain who my genuine friends are. They know me, my views and opinions—and foibles and failings—far too well for any of them to become even mildly upset or annoyed by any statements I might make.

As for those not already proven friends, it is doubtful if they and I will have the chance to run the twenty-year time-test, not at this late date in my life. If they do not like what I say—well, I'm sorry. They are free to take or leave—and, if they so choose, damn or deride—my remarks.

Such, then, is the spirit in which I vehemently deny that I was born a cynic and a pessimist. As a matter of fact, unimpeachable sources—as they would be described were this a news dispatch from Washington—have sworn that I was the most genial and jovial of babies, a child with a consistently sanguine outlook and a buoyantly chiliastic youth.

(The curtain is now lowered to denote the passage of time. The thermostat is also lowered to symbolize the chilling of the chiliast's fervid belief in a Golden Age of future perfection.)

I lay claim to being the world's greatest George Alfred Henty fan.

G. A. Henty, who lived from 1832 to 1902, wrote more than thirty books for boys. They had such titles as *Redskin and Cowboy, With Frederick the Great* and *With Roberts to Pretoria*. I have what I believe is a complete collection of Henty's books—owning the books ever since I was a boy. I've read them all so many times that I believe I could practically recite each of them from memory.

At Sutton Place, my Henty books are ranged on a bookcase shelf I pass every night when I go upstairs from my study or the drawing room to my bedroom. On occasion—perhaps once or twice a month—I will pause, select a volume and take it with me to read yet again.

An eccentricity? Perhaps. Escapism? If the term is taken in the sense that I seek to travel back in time mentally and relive an era in which values and standards that I admire prevailed, then the answer is an unequivocal YES.

I'd be the last person on earth to contend that G. A. Henty was a literary genius or giant. He painted his characters in black or white. There were bad guys and good guys, heroes and cowards, scrupulously honest men and those who were totally amoral.

Henty's heroes lived by a strict code. They were honourable, loyal, fair, incorruptible. Naturally, they always triumphed over the villains—but never without bravely facing danger, overcoming seemingly insurmountable obstacles and often enduring much hardship and suffering. Henty's good guys often employed ruses and stratagems to outwit the bad.

But no hero in a Henty book was ever capable of doing anything that was mean, small, contemptible or despicable.

Of course the characters were overdrawn and greatly idealized.

Of course the real world of my boyhood was not entirely peopled by Henty heroes.

Of course the good guys did not always emerge victorious over the bad guys (nor did the bad guys always receive their just desserts) seventy-some years ago when I first became a Henty fan.

But there were proportionately far more people who held to a Henty-like code in the early 1900s than there are now. It has been one of my more bitter observations that a sense of honour and decency and an awareness of human dignity have diminished steadily over the decades. Sociologists attribute the decline to the effects and after-effects of wars, revolutions, depressions (or of Prohibition, prosperity, the A-bomb or the Affluent Society).

I don't suppose there is any more use in trying to pinpoint reasons and explanations than there is in mourning over past eras and a discarded ethos. Nevertheless, every now and then after reading the daily newspapers and watching the evening television newscasts, 'escape' into a Henty book is as refreshing as the proverbial glass of cold water on a hot day. More, it is—for me—a tonic that braces me for the next few weeks of newspaper reading and TV news-broadcast watching.

I'm afraid I need such tonics. I maintain this was once (and in my own lifetime) a better world and could have been made better still. But people have renounced or rejected more and more of the good—and as I gloomily foresee it, we have not yet seen the worst.

Lew Lehr used to amuse movie-audiences with his line: 'Monkeys are the craziest people.'

It is often remarked that wealthy individuals appear to be extremely wary and chary in forming acquaintanceships and friendships, and the question is asked: 'Why?'

The answer is a scrambled paraphrasing of Lew Lehr's words.

Far too many people make crazed efforts to make monkeys out of anyone they believe to be rich.

As architect Ms. Jan Brenning-Frankian recently said:

'Governments just soak the rich. Whole breeds of failures and freeloaders spend all their time trying to rape the rich. No wonder the rich suspect that every smile directed at them is a barracuda leer'.

Her metaphors are apt, as I am only too aware. The aspiring rapists run an encyclopaedic gamut of types, and there is no limit to their ingenuity.

From the moment it became generally known that I was collecting art, sharpsters began offering me fake Titians and bogus Rembrandts by the dozen. There was even one chap who got as far as my secretary's office, only to be told I was away on a longish trip. He practically burst into tears.

'But I painted this Renoir just to sell him!' he blurted.

I choose the places where I do my personal shopping of any kind with extreme care, and then I become a steady customer. I've had too many experiences of walking into a shop to buy a suit or a lead pencil only to have some clerk recognize me as 'Paul Getty, the billionaire.' It thereupon became a challenge for the entire staff to sell me everything in the store.

'But I really don't want a solid-gold watering can—or mink-lined bedroom slippers or platinum cigar-cutter,' I have protested in these instances. Invariably, the sales clerks stared at me as though I were not only mad, but had impugned their family honour to boot.

I have had the most casual acquaintances—even people I met for the first time—ask me to lend them large sums of money, or invest even larger sums in 'surefire' business propositions. Then there is the type who wants a job (invariably high-paying) for himself, a son just out of college or for a brother-in-law he's tired of supporting himself. Other species (and these are extremely common) ask for Stock Market 'tips' or for personal introductions to wealthy or prominent people who happen to be my friends.

Another familiar variety buttonholes the successful businessman and requests specific advice on how to achieve Instant Success. It's useless to tell such individuals that there are no dark, secret formulas or arcane incantations that work overnight miracles.

'You millionaires are all alike!' I had one man rage at me. 'You have secret tricks and won't share them with anyone! Just wait—we'll get all of you yet!'

I was truly sorry I could not give him a magic formula. I would have loved to see this particular character make a huge fortune—so that he could be among the first to be 'gotten.'

There is an amusing story about Dr. Armand Hammer, a man whose friendship I value most highly and for whom I have the greatest respect, both as a businessman and as a person. It seems that someone once cornered Armand and asked him the 'tell-me-the-secret-of-making-millions' question.

Armand, I am told, furrowed his brow and said: 'Actually, there's nothing to it. You merely wait for a revolution in Russia. Then you pack all your warm clothes and go there. Once you've arrived, you start making the rounds of the government bureaus that are concerned with trade, with buying and selling. There probably won't be more than two or three hundred of them . . .'

At this point, Dr. Hammer's questioner muttered something in anger and disgust and stomped away.

I assure you it is not a very easy matter to make monkeys out of seasoned, successful businessmen—out of 'the rich.' They have had all the tricks tried on them long ago and have consequently developed highly sensitive antennae to pick up and identify virtually every conceivable opening gambit.

Governments, of course, can—and do—soak the rich. But—to use Ms. Brenning-Frankian's words—the failures and freeloaders who have delusions of committing rape would be well advised to channel their rapacious energies elsewhere. The wealthy—to carry her sexual simile a step further—usually wear armour-plated chastity-belts. They were forced to don them early on, after having been the victims of a few dozen—or hundred—attempts.

After a time, a person who is reputed to be wealthy grows a tough, impervious skin. It's a protective carapace, essential for survival.

The rich are not born sceptical or cynical. They are made that way by events, circumstances—and most especially by the countless people who have barracuda leers (and barracuda instincts and intentions) hidden behind their broad and beatific smiles.

L'envoi

MY STATED PURPOSE in writing this book has been to share some of what I have observed, experienced and learned in eighty-three years of living and more than sixty years as an active businessman. I have looked back over the past, sought to communicate how the present appears when examined through my eyes and made a few (I hope educated) guesses about the future.

As you have doubtless gathered, I am not overly optimistic about the future. I fear that unless there are many and drastic changes in both basic philosophies and actual practices in every sector of human existence our society—our whole civilization—will deteriorate and decline. It may well be wracked by upheavals far greater than any recorded in previous history. It could—and I do not take the possibility lightly—be totally destroyed.

I say I am pessimistic, but that by no means implies that I have lost all hope. Notwithstanding my age, I intend to continue as I've done, looking ahead to whatever years are left to me and ignoring my pessimisms as I direct my business interests and strive to strengthen and expand them.

I repeat the words ascribed to Abraham Lincoln, which I quoted at the beginning of the first chapter.

You cannot bring about prosperity by discouraging thrift. You cannot help the wage-earner by pulling down the wage-payer. You cannot further the Brotherhood of Man by encouraging class hatred. You cannot help the poor by destroying the rich. You cannot keep out of trouble by spending more than you earn. You cannot build character and courage by taking away a man's initiative. You cannot help men permanently by doing for them what they could and should do for themselves.

This is as Abraham Lincoln saw it.

This is as I see it.

This is as I hope a very great number of people will come to see it again. If they do, our society's chances of surviving and seeing a peaceful, prosperous future will be vastly increased.

But it is up to each and every one of you to make the decisions and take the actions. Whatever you may decide, whatever you may do, I wish you—and yours—luck, health and happiness.

J. PAUL GETTY

Index

THE BEST BUSINESS GUIDES AVAILABLE TODAY FROM JOVE PAPERBACKS

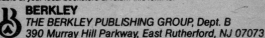